Springer Proceedings in Business and Economics

More information about this series at http://www.springer.com/series/11960

Silvia L. Fotea • Ioan Ş. Fotea
Sebastian Văduva
Editors

Navigating Through the Crisis: Business, Technological and Ethical Considerations

The 2020 Annual Griffiths School of Management and IT Conference (GSMAC) Vol 2

Springer

Editors
Silvia L. Fotea
Griffiths School of Management
Emanuel University of Oradea
Oradea, Romania

Ioan Ş. Fotea
Griffiths School of Management
Emanuel University of Oradea
Oradea, Romania

Sebastian Văduva
Griffiths School of Management
Emanuel University of Oradea
Oradea, Romania

ISSN 2198-7246 ISSN 2198-7254 (electronic)
Springer Proceedings in Business and Economics
ISBN 978-3-030-82750-2 ISBN 978-3-030-82751-9 (eBook)
https://doi.org/10.1007/978-3-030-82751-9

This Springer imprint is published by the registered company Springer Nature Switzerland AG
The registered company address is: Gewerbestrasse 11, 6330 Cham, Switzerland

Contents

Chapter 1
The Significance of Wellness and Its Presence in the Life of the Romanian Young Generation

Elisabeta Ilona Molnar and Greta Gulyas

Abstract Identifying the significance of wellness for young people in Romania has been both a challenge for the present chapter and a source of inspiration. The increasingly popular alternative medicine combined with various other healing activities leads to the prevention of illnesses, and this triggers the growing popularity of wellness, a concept already acknowledged on an international level. This trend prevails all over the world on various levels and in various forms – and intertwined with tourism, they form a new dynamic and fast-developing branch of the industry, i.e. wellness tourism. Naturally, in different parts of the world, this entails various forms which depend on the mentality, culture and living standards of the given region.

The present study features the literature review and a quantitative research conducted based on a questionnaire completed by young people, Millennials and Z Generations. The results of the research reflect young people's motivation to travel for wellness, destination as wellness travellers, and their willingness to spend money when travelling.

Keywords Wellness · Wellness tourism · Young generation · Tourism destination

1.1 Introduction

The term wellness is difficult to pinpoint being the outcome of a complex process which varies according to the context it is used in. As a concept, its origins can be traced to the United States of America in the nineteenth century; at that time, it was associated with ideas concerning change of lifestyle as well as promotion and advocacy of health. The development of the concept of wellness can be attributed to

E. I. Molnar (✉) · G. Gulyas
University of Szeged, Szeged, Hungary
e-mail: molnar.elisabeta@eco.u-szeged.hu

S. L. Fotea et al. (eds.), *Navigating Through the Crisis: Business, Technological and Ethical Considerations*, Springer Proceedings in Business and Economics,
https://doi.org/10.1007/978-3-030-82751-9_1

well-known individuals of that time, like Kellogg, Quimby, Eddy, and Fletcher; however, the term was introduced by Dr Halbert Louis Dunn (Miller, 2005). In one of his studies, Dr Dunn claimed, "It is quite possible that much of chronic disease could be eliminated if physicians knew how to recognize various levels of wellness" (Dunn, 1957, pp 229–230). The social dimension is very important for which reason he defines, "High-level wellness for the individual is defined as an integrated method of functioning which is oriented toward maximizing the potential of which the individual is capable. It requires that the individual maintain a continuum of balance and purposeful direction within the environment where he is functioning" (Dunn, 1961, pp 4–5). Travis continues to develop the ideas presented, and through Wellness Resource Center founded in 1975 – the world's first wellness centre, he concentrates on the idea of helping people be responsible for their own health (Miller, 2005). In WHO Regional Committee for Europe magazine, M. Chan emphasizes, "promoting health and well-being is the key to the future" (Chan, 2013, pp 8).

Well-being is a phenomenon that is realized through the combination of physical condition and a state of mind as a result of certain processes which entails individuals satisfying their daily needs. Travelling and the need for a change, to relax and to get to know something new are decisive factors in establishing well-being.

On the level of concept, wellness tourism may encompass staying outside of the home, the motive being to achieve a state of well-being, an optimal health status and prevention of diseases (Printz-Markó et al., 2017).

Health tourism encompasses both medical and wellness tourism, in which case the motivation of tourists is maintaining their health, in some cases, to improve it. The path to the final aim, which could be recovery or even prevention, is via the services provided by health tourism (Sziva, 2010).

1.2 Literature Review

Wellness is one of the most decisive travel trends; its fundamental principle is harmony between body and soul. The central idea is that physical beauty must be associated with inner beauty and spiritual balance. (Törőcsik, 2006.)

Global Wellness Institute (GWI) defines wellness as the active pursuit of activities, choices and lifestyles that lead to a state of holistic health. (Global Wellness Institute, 2020). In the Oxford English Dictionary, the term is defined in the following way: behavioural scientists define it as physical, mental, social and spiritual well-being (Clothier, 2007).

The aims of wellness participants are to look as well as possible, improve well-being, lose some weight if need be, slow down the ageing process, avoid or reduce pain and relieve discomfort, manage stress, or improve health outcomes with natural support and supplements, like vitamins and minerals (Stănciulescu et al., 2015).

Institutions that provide wellness services are characteristic first of all of Europe, in particular of the German-speaking countries and of the countries in the Mediterranean basin, South-East Asia and North America (Csirmaz & Pető, 2015).

Two new concepts must be introduced according to which wellness tourism travellers can be grouped. One group is that of primary-purpose wellness travellers whose main motivation is both choice of destination and that wellness be part of provided services, while the other group is that of secondary-purpose wellness travellers who avail themselves of wellness services as well while travelling (Stará & Peterson, 2017). Thus, a secondary-purpose wellness traveller group include a business traveller, and they can have several roles in promoting the destination. Marin-Pantelescu mentions they can also become unpaid 'ambassadors' for a destination by communicating to colleagues and others their positive impressions and favourable experiences (Marin-Pantelescu, 2011).

"Education represents a potentially powerful, but not yet well-harnessed, force for advancing wellness" (Cowen, 1991). We should take as a concrete example for the development of wellness as an occupation the parameters that we need to pay attention to in schools when the youth must choose a career path.

In the past decades, international organizations and the European Union have campaigned for the implementation of social policies that will help both companies and public authorities to find solutions aimed at promoting the health and well-being of the population. Within these social measures, the scheme of vouchers with specific destinations in different countries was born: meal vouchers, services vouchers, childcare vouchers, transport vouchers, "green "vouchers, holiday vouchers, and wellness vouchers. It is important to mention the wellness vouchers used in Sweden and Finland "constitute important tools to build mentally and healthy workplaces" (Renaudin, 2014, pp 130). This system was also implemented in Romania; the purpose and the use of holiday vouchers or holiday cards are regulated by legislative decisions. (OUG 8/2009; HG 215/2009; HG 940/2017). The holiday voucher/holiday card system has contributed significantly to the development of domestic tourism in Romania.

A great part of wellness tourism is generated by spa and wellness services offered by the great hotel groups (Kadieva, 2015). One of the best-known forms of the beneficial effects of water, both in health tourism and wellness tourism, is spa facilities, spas and hydrotherapy and their application in the field of stress management. (Printz-Markó & Molnar, 2019). It is necessary to distinguish between a relatively passive form of physical and mental relaxation and an active form of relaxation. (Voigt et al., 2011)

On an international level, it is already well-known that there is a close relationship between the business tourism product and that of wellness. Hotel owners/managers have identified among business travellers that the latter 's' need to prevent diseases and maintain health; therefore, in most four- and five-star hotels, wellness services have come to be considered basic criteria. As far as travel time is concerned, business tourism complements wellness tourism very well, and conferences are usually held during the week, whereas wellness tourists arrive for the weekend (Happ, 2008).

However, one must have in mind that wellness services are usually offered by four- and five-star hotels. This segment has experienced strong growth in the entire country in the past few years (Table 1.1).

Table 1.1 4–5-Star hotel capacity in Romania

	Rooms				Beds			
Stars	2017	2018	2019	2020	2017	2018	2019	2020
4	24,483	27,328	29,189	33,960	47,746	53,339	57,137	57,717
5	3867	4061	4092	4332	7610	7733	7808	8434

Source: Tourist reception structures with classified accommodation functions http://turism.gov.ro/web/autorizare-turism/, author's editing

In wellness tourism, we may distinguish between two factors of attraction in terms of destination: one of them is the services that are offered, the desire to relax and to network in the local environment of the destination, while the other one is the natural and cultural attraction of the chosen destination which generates a longer stay and a high level of satisfaction. (Težak Damijanić & Šergo, 2013)

The analysis of destinations is quite complex; however, the most important characteristic one must have in mind is the nature of the tourism product at the analysed destination (Magliulo, 2014)

Destination marketing aims to create and maintain the population's interest, but one must bear in mind that destinations have a cycle of life similar to tourism products. (Iosub et al., 2017)

When promoting destinations, even wellness tourism ones, online communication plays an important role; thus, the so-called intelligent platforms were created to promote products, destinations or images. Online platforms and phone applications are already consolidated tools to promote sites/venues and tourism products. (Privitera, 2019). A wellness app can be exciting for the born e-travellers regarding blogs related to the hotel area or travel informations. Additional applications help formulate the diet or workout plan (Ivancsóné Horváth & Printz-Markó, 2017).

Decision to travel is influenced by several factors; however, with the advent of globalisation, this aspect has simplified, certain impediments that were present when crossing borders or during longer distances, having been eliminated. Due to the development of air travel and crossing borders having been facilitated, development in tourism had been increasingly dynamic.

1.3 Wellness on Global Level

Wellness is one of the most dynamically developing sectors of tourism. Based on the data published by the Global Wellness Institute (GWI), this branch of tourism yielded around $4.2 trillion in 2017, which it surpassed in 2018 with a little yielding a $4.5-trillion income in the sector. The sum contains income from the various fields of wellness tourism such as traditional and complementary medicine, preventive and personalized treatments, healthy diet and weight loss, physical activity, spa, workplace wellness, beauty and anti-ageing.

The wellness economy stands for service providers that enable customers to integrate wellness activities and lifestyles into their everyday lives (GWI, 2020).

GWI distinguishes between 10 wellness economy sectors:

- Wellness real estate
- Workplace wellness
- Wellness tourism
- Spa economy
- Thermal and mineral springs
- Fitness and mind-body
- Healthy eating, nutrition, and weight loss
- Personal care, beauty, and anti-ageing
- Traditional and complementary medicine

The map below shows the wellness services that a geographical area can provide on a global level to those who do wellness tourism. It is to be noted that in the case of Europe, these can be saunas, climatic health resorts, wellness retreats and camps for weekends, mountain wellness, hotels and thalassotherapy. However, on a global scale, it is clear that there is a wide range of services from the various types of yoga, to hammam and to detoxifying treatments (Fig. 1.1).

Since an increasing part of our society believes wellness to be the solution to many of its problems, for this branch of tourism, the period between 2015 and 2020 has been predicted to be one in which it experiences substantial and great increase.

Fig. 1.1 Wellness services on a global level. (Source: Global Wellness Institute, Global Wellness Tourism Economy, November 2018)

Table 1.2 Planned growth of wellness sector

Wellness sectors	Projected market size (US $ billions) 2015	2020	Projected average annual growth rate 2015–2020
Spa facilities	$77.60	$103.90	6%
Thermal/mineral springs	$51.00	$64.60	4.80%
Wellness tourism	$563.20	$808.00	7.50%
Workplace wellness	$43.30	$55.10	5.00%
Wellness lifestyle	$118.60	$152.80	5.20%

Source: Global Wellness Institute, based upon economic and industry sector projections from the IMF, ILO, Euromonitor and GWI's data and projection model, in Global Wellness Economy Monitor, January 2017, author's editing

Based on its own data, Global Wellness Institute (GWI) came to the conclusion that there is great economic development in this five-year period – as the projection below shows, the planned growth for 2015–2020 is to develop the following way (annual means): in case of spa establishments, a 6% growth is to be expected, while thermal baths will yield a 4.80% growth. The expected growth in wellness tourism is 7.50% and that of workplace wellness is 5%, whereas in that of wellness real estate, it will be 5.2% (Global Wellness Economy Monitor, January 2017) (Table 1.2).

1.4 Wellness Trends

As far as wellness trends are concerned, the overall picture is quite varied if the trends in the past year are to be compared with those in the forthcoming period. The list offered by the Global Wellness Institute illustrates this perfectly (Table 1.3).

Research shows that wellness cluster brands are not subject to great public awareness. However, what is known to characterize a brand is the quality of the service they provide, and this prevails especially among the population below the age of 40 (Bertsch & Ostermann, 2011).

An important aim of the European Spa Association (ESPA) must be mentioned, along with synchronization of the European resorts on the health market – the promotion of health spas, in particular the natural medicinal properties offered by these, rehabilitation techniques, teaching healthy lifestyle and acquainting customers with activities that aim prevention. This sector must be on good terms with policy-makers as well as leading representatives of the academia and business, which may result in great business relationship – innovative product development, promotion, exchange of experiences, practices, offering up-to-date information, establish standards, training programs, as well as synchronizing marketing activities (ESPA, 2020).

As far as Romania is concerned, it highlights major treatment sectors such as cardiovascular conditions, dermatological disorders, gastrointestinal disorders, gynaecological diseases, urinary tract diseases, musculoskeletal diseases, metabolic

Table 1.3 Changes in wellness trends from 2017 to 2020

2017	2018	2019	2020
Sauna Reinvented	Mushrooms Emerge from Underground	Well Fashion – Way Beyond Athleisure	Circadian Health
Wellness Architecture	A New Era of Transformative Wellness Travel	Wellness Takes on Overtourism	Aging Rebranded: Positively Cool
Silence – from silent spas to wellness monasteries and downtime abbeys – to silent eating	Reframing the First 1.000 Days	Meditation Goes Plural	J-Wellness
Art and Creativity Take Center Stage	The Wellness Kitchen	Prescribing Nature – Nature as Medicine	Mental Wellness and Technology: Rethinking the Relationship
Wellness Remakes Beauty	Getting our "Clean Air Act" Together	MediScent: Fragrance Gets a Wellness Makeover – Aromatherapy	Energy Medicine
The Future is Mental Wellness	Extreme Wellness	China – Uncovering the Wealth in Wellness	Religion and Wellness – Organized Religion Jumps Into Wellness
Embracing the C-Word	Wellness Meets Happiness	Nutrition Gets Very Personalized	The Wellness Sabbatical
Beyond the Elite 'Ghettos' of Wellness	A New Feminist Wellness	Dying Well – A "Better Death" Is Becoming Integral to the Idea of a "Well Life"	Fertility boom

Source: GWI – Wellness trends 2017, 2018, 2019, 2020, author's editing

disorders, disorders of the nervous system, overweight, respiratory disease and rheumatism (ESPA 2020).

Attractive culinary experiences in wellness resorts are becoming increasingly important. The food customers have, along with the taste and quality, must also qualify in terms of nutritional value, calories and energy standards in order to contribute to holistic well-being of the wellness tourist. These experiences have an impact on their future decisions on their healthy diet (Dillette et al., 2020).

Besides the trends formulated by the Global Wellness Institute, there are the ones projected by Euromonitor for 2020 as well that encompass areas such as flexible and customized transport, the increased application and use of robots, increased value of staying at home, the personalized experiences, authenticity, promotion of customs and culture, movements for clear air, satisfying mental needs and making the best use of one's own resources more effectively (Westbrook, 2020).

In terms of wellness, credibility, well-being and inclusion are important factors. At this point, persons with disabilities are to be highlighted – based on data published by WHO, over 1 milliard people live with some sort of disability in the world – and their needs be taken into account; also it is important to have in mind their needs and include those in the offer. Originality/authenticity, well-being and inclusion are the keywords according to which the meaning of well-being and beauty must be < I feel good about myself. > (Uduslivaia, 2020 pp. 28–29). In addition to these, there are multifunctional homes in which with the help of one application (Heal App), patients can get in touch with physicians and can ask for their help, while the latter pay them a visit if need be (Sirimanne, 2020). "Accessibility is of paramount importance, which may seem a special area of accessible tourism despite it being a natural requisite" (Gondos, 2019, pp 66).

However, it must be noted that the restrictions imposed in the spring of 2020 due to the virus that has spread on the globe rendered travelling impossible; transport and hospitality industry are the branches of industry to suffer the most because of the outbreak of the pandemic.

On a global level, 45% of the destinations have closed down their borders either partially or totally. Air travel towards 30% of the possible target places has been suspended. Under these circumstances, fewer tourists arrived in Q1 of 2020 as the following data shows (Table 1.4):

From an economic point of view, the estimated loss in the area of tourism export is somewhere between \$910 billion and \$1.2 trillion, while on the international level, the jobs that are at risk vary between \$100–120 million. Depending on the course of the pandemic, the case scenarios that can be set up for 2020 indicate excessive drop, up to 58% if restrictions are removed at the beginning of July, whereas the decline can reach 78% if restrictions are removed in December (UNWTO World Tourism Barometer May 2020). Tourism is estimated to recover in 2021, especially in the area of leisure tourism, rather than business travel.

Due to the situation created by the effects of COVID-19 on the international level, the travel and tourism sector was fundamentally affected in Romania as well. In this context, the tourist accommodation establishments (hotels, motels, pensions, villas) recorded substantial financial losses; the index of the net use of accommodation places in the period between January 1, 2020, and June 30, 2020, was 19.4%, registering a decrease of 9 percentage points compared to the same period of 2019 (Press Communication nr.199 INSSE 2020).

Analysing the data below, we find that the number of overnight stays has decreased drastically, as well as that of the arrivals of tourists in the accommodation establishments (Tables 1.5 and 1.6).

Table 1.4 International tourist arrivals by region in Q1 2020

Regions	Arrivals
Europe	19 %
America	15 %
Africa	12 %
Middle East	11 %
Asia and Pacific	35 %

Source: UNWTO World Tourism Barometer May 2020, author's editing

Table 1.5 Night spent at tourist accommodation establishments, period 1 January–30 June in Romania

Tourist	2019	2020	difference
Residents	9.034.500	3.635.300	−59.77 %
Non-residents	2.374.600	644.700	−72.86 %
Total	**11.409.100**	**4.280.000**	**−62.49 %**

Source: Press Communication nr.199 – INSSE -National Institute of Statistics, 2020, author's editing

Table 1.6 Arrivals of residents/non-residents at tourist accommodation establishments, period 1 January–30 June in Romania

Tourist	2019	2020	difference
Residents	4.409.700	1.849.900	−58.05
Non- residents	1.206.600	298.300	−75.28
Total	**5.616.300**	**2.148.200**	**−61.75**

Source: Press Communication nr.199 – INSSE -National Institute of Statistics, 2020, author's editing

Between January 1, 2020, and June 30, 2020, border checkpoints registered 5,121,000 departures of Romanian citizens to destinations abroad, the rate decreasing by 46.6%; whereas the number of arrivals of visitors to Romania was 2,724,800, which is a 50.80% drop as compared to the same period in 2019. The effects of the pandemic had the situation aggravate in June 2020; thus as compared to June 2019, there was a 68.1% drop in the rate of departures of Romanian citizens, while that of foreign visitors arriving in Romania dwindled by 68.7% (Press Communication nr.199 INSSE, 2020).

1.5 Research Methodology

The research investigates the importance of wellness and its presence in the lives of the youngsters, Millennials and Z Generations, as well as the way they relate to wellness tourism, having in mind that the young generation not only desire to travel and have the motivation to do so, they are able to travel to a greater extent than previous generations were.

Similarly, to other age groups, the youth is also characterised by a particular lifestyle in which they experience particular situations. The youth is a heterogeneous age group the members of which have not yet found their own true buyer persona; therefore, for specialists in the field, it is of great importance to approach this group in a segmented manner (Prónay, 2011).

It is worth mentioning that the young generations have various reasons to travel: curiosity encourages them to have adventures, they want to learn about other cultures, they would like to have fun and expand their social relations, or they would like to gain unforgettable experiences (Bulin et al., 2019).

It is important to become acquainted with the decreasing tendency of the Romanian population; in January 2017, the population was 19,613,949, whereas in January 2019, it was 19,414,458. What is relevant to the present research is that the number of people aged between 16 and 30 in 2017 is 5,545,306, whereas in 2019, it was 5,116,288 (Resident population on 1 January 2019, INSSE, 2020), since the present research investigates the travelling habits of the youth in the country, in particular, their attitude toward wellness and health tourism and the choices they make in this area. A significant development of the domestic economy in developing tourism is the introduction of holiday tickets or holiday cards for the employees in the public sector.

Health tourism and wellness tourism is a sector in which fees are higher; therefore, material well-being is essential for the population to afford this product (Puczkó & Smith, 2012).

The aim of the research is to have an image about wellness travellers among the young population, if there is the motivation of the trip in terms of wellness, which would be the destination, domestic or international travel, which is the intention to spend in wellness tourism, respectively for wellness services during the travel. In order to achieve that, we have conducted a survey with the help of a questionnaire. The method used to assess the questionnaire was partial the Pearson correlation and Regression analysis created through IBM SPSS 25.

The hypotheses of the present research are the following:

H1. In the wellness sector, the young generation is found in the category of secondary wellness travellers.
H2. Willingness to travel and the destination areas youngsters choose points to areas outside the country.
H3. Low willingness to specific wellness tourism spending compared to their income.

1.6 Results and Discussion

Regarding the travel motivation of the young generation in the wellness tourism sector, after analysing the results, we can conclude that is a big difference between primary wellness travellers (N=15) and secondary wellness travellers (N = 105), from total of 120 respondents, so we can affirm that the Romanian youngers are part of secondary wellness travellers, they travel for reasons other than wellness, but during the trips if they have the opportunity, they use the wellness services as well (Fig. 1.2).

Analysing the processed data can be found a significant deviation of the trend regarding the travel destination from previous years presented in different statistical data. Certainly, the COVID-19 pandemic effect played a significant role in this regard, so the results in this research show that destinations in the country are preferred over destinations outside the country. It turned out that out of 120 respondents, 69 people would go on a journey in the country, rather than abroad, 23 people

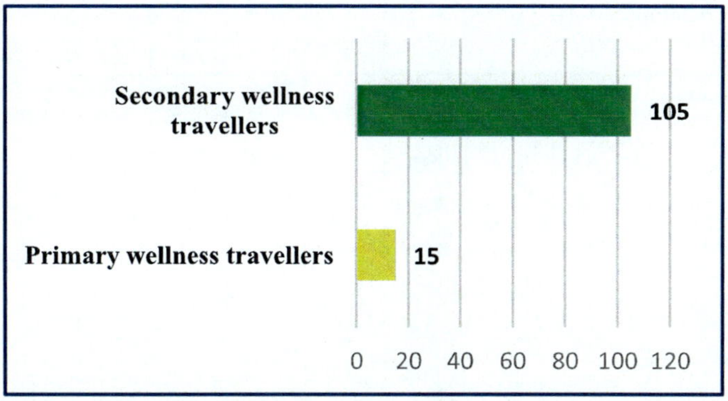

Fig. 1.2 Type of wellness travellers. (Source: Authors' computation based on data collected, own research)

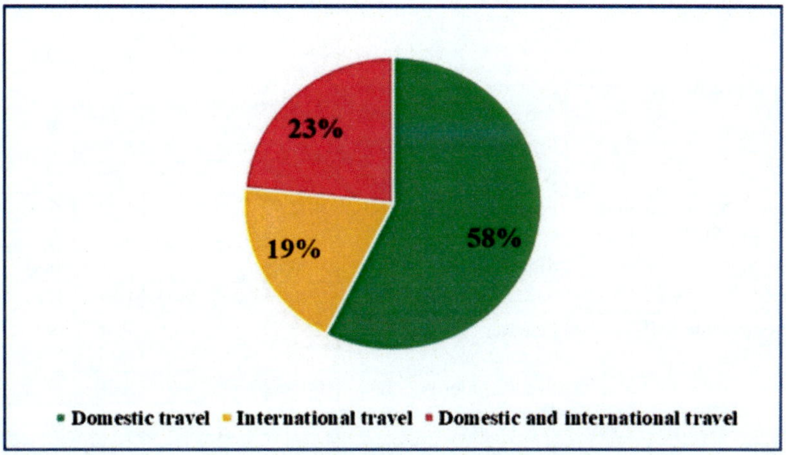

Fig. 1.3 Wellness travel destination. (Source: Authors' computation based on data collected, own research)

are willing to choose an international travel destination, and 28 people marked as response both domestic and international travel destinations (Fig. 1.3).

A part of the collected data was analysed with the Pearson`s correlation model, presented in the table below (Table 1.7), which shows us the relevance and significance of all entered variables.

The correlation between the motive to travel in wellness tourism (MT) and travel time (TT) variable has been observed, in the case of which the correlation coefficient is −.013 and its P-value is .361; however, this result is not significant because the value is not lower than .050, and hence, there is no significant relationship between the two (thus, $r = -.013$ $p > .050$ its value: 0.361).

However, it is notable that the Pearson correlation coefficient between the amount of money intended for travel (AT) and the duration of the journey, travel time (TT),

Table 1.7 Correlation

		MT	TT	DT	IT	DI	AT	MI	AG
Motive to travel in wellness tourism (MT)	Pearson correlation	1	−.083	.[a]	.[a]	.[a]	.145	.059	.040
	Sig. (2-tailed)		.368	.	.	.	.113	.524	.662
	N	120	120	69	23	28	120	120	120
Travel time (TT)	Pearson correlation	−.083	1	.[a]	.[a]	.[a]	.402**	.252**	.070
	Sig. (2-tailed)	.368		.	.	.	.000	.005	.450
	N	120	120	69	23	28	120	120	120
Domestic travel (DT)	Pearson correlation	.[a]	.[a]	.[a]	.[a]	.[a]	.[a]	.[a]	.[a]
	Sig. (2-tailed)	.	.		.	.	.	.	.
	N	69	69	69	0	0	69	69	69
International travel (IT)	Pearson correlation	.a	.a	.a	.a	.a	.a	.a	.a
	Sig. (2-tailed)	.	.	.		.	.	.	.
	N	23	23	0	23	0	23	23	23
Domestic and international travel (DI)	Pearson correlation	.[a]	.[a]	.[a]	.[a]	.[a]	.[a]	.[a]	.[a]
	Sig. (2-tailed)	.	.	.	.		.	.	.
	N	28	28	0	0	28	28	28	28
Amount of money intended for travel (AT)	Pearson correlation	.145	.402**	.[a]	.[a]	.[a]	1	.638**	.226*
	Sig. (2-tailed)	.113	.000	.	.	.		.000	.013
	N	120	120	69	23	28	120	120	120
Monthly income (MI)	Pearson correlation	.059	.252**	.[a]	.[a]	.[a]	.638**	1	.286**
	Sig. (2-tailed)	.524	.005	.	.	.	.000		.002
	N	120	120	69	23	28	120	120	120
Age (AG)	Pearson correlation	.040	.070	.[a]	.[a]	.[a]	.226*	.286**	1
	Sig. (2-tailed)	.662	.450	.	.	.	.013	.002	
	N	120	120	69	23	28	120	120	120

**Correlation is significant at the 0.01 level (2-tailed)
*Correlation is significant at the 0.05 level (2-tailed)
[a]Cannot be computed because at least one of the variables is constant
Source: Authors' computation based on data collected, own research

is .402, which is higher than the average, and it is positive and significant due to a significance level of .000 (i.e. r =.402 p<.010, value: .000). Therefore, there is a 99.99% probability of correlation between the amount of money intended for travel and the duration of travel, i.e. if the amount of money increases, so does the time dedicate for travel.

Another connection to be noted is that between monthly income (MI) and the travel time (TT); in this case, the Pearson correlation coefficient is .252, and its significance value is .005, (r=.252 p<.010, value: .005). This proves that the probability of a correspondence between the monthly income and travel time is 99.5%; therefore, a higher income level means longer travel time as well.

The Pearson correlation coefficient between monthly income (MI) and the amount of money intended for travel (AT) was .638, which is the highest value in the present research. In addition to this, it shows a positive-oriented relationship stronger than the average, while the significance level is .000, (r =.638 p<.010, value: .000). The correlation between monthly income and the amount of money intended for wellness travel is 99.9%. Therefore, the increase of monthly income may trigger a greater willingness to spend money. But as a result of the research, it can conclude that the respondents are willing to spend a higher amount of money during trips than their average monthly net income.

Another correspondence to be noticed is that between age (AG) and the amount of money intended for wellness travel (AT), in which case the Pearson correlation coefficient is .226 and the significance level is .013 (r =.226 p<.050, value: .013). Age and the amount of money intended for wellness travel also correlate, which shows a positive relationship weaker than the average, i.e. the chance is 98.7%.

Another Pearson correlation level to be noted is that between the two variables – age (AG) and monthly income (MI), the value of which is .286, and its significance is .002 (r =.286 p =.002). In this case as well, there is a correspondence between age and monthly income, the correlation between the two factors is 99.8%.

Having in mind this data, the following may be concluded: the strongest correspondence is the one between income and the amount of money intended for travel, which is followed by the connection between the amount of money intended for wellness travel and travel time, next is the relation between age and income and, last but not least, the correspondence between monthly income and travel time – all these may have a positive influence on the traveller's choices and willingness to spend.

1.7 Regression Analysis

To understand the relation and significance between the amount of money intended for travel (AT) and monthly income (MI), regression analysis was used. The Pearson`s correlation shows the significance of the variable included in the research, in our case the monthly income (MI). It can be seen, however, that p < .010, so the significance is relevant (Tables 1.8, 1.9 and 1.10).

Table 1.8 Descriptive statistics

	Mean	Std. deviation	N
Amount of money intended for travel (AT)	2.00	.870	120
Monthly income (MI)	1.82	.970	120

Source: Authors' computation based on data collected, own research

Table 1.9 Correlation

		AT	MI
Pearson correlation	Amount of money intended for travel (AT)	1.000	.638
	Monthly income (MI)	.638	1.000
Sig. (1-tailed)	Amount of money intended for travel (AT)	.	.000
	Monthly income (MI)	.000	.
N	Amount of money intended for travel (AT)	120	120
	Monthly income (MI)	120	120

Source: Authors' computation based on data collected, own research

Table 1.10 Variables entered/removed[a]

Model	Variables Entered	Variables Removed	Method
1	Monthly income[b]	.	Enter

[a]Dependent variable: Amount of money intended for travel
[b]All requested variables entered
Source: Authors' computation based on data collected, own research

Their value shows the value of the correlation coefficient (.638), while R square shows the value of the coefficient of determination (0,406), which represents the percentage explanation of the total standard deviation (40,1%). In this case, the possibility of standard error of the estimate is (0,673); from the low level of this, it can be concluded that the performed research proves to be effective (Table 1.11).

The analysis of variance is actually used to examine the relationship between two variables. The elements in Table 1.12 highlight the relation between the amount spent on wellness travel and the monthly income. We can also find out the significance of the F test, which is less than .010, so there is a relation. It can be seen that the significance of the F value is .000, so the amount intended for travel and the monthly income is significant, and there is a 99.99% correlation between them. So according to this, the regression model is significant. Overall, therefore, the data obtained during the Pearson correlation which shows the connection between the amount spent for wellness travel and the monthly income seems to be strengthening.

The significance level of the t-test is also less than .010, so the monthly income has an impact on the amount intended for travel. The Standardized coefficients data give the regression line formula (Table 1.13).

The results of this research are summarized as follows:

H1. In the wellness sector, the young generation is found in the category of secondary wellness travellers.	
Primary wellness travellers Secondary wellness travellers Findings	N = 15 N = 105 Validated
H2. Willingness to travel and the destination areas youngsters choose points to areas outside the country.	

Table 1.11 Model summary

Model	R	R square	Adjusted R square	Std. error of the estimate
1	.638[a]	0,406	0,401	0,673

[a]Predictors: (Constant), Monthly income
Source: Authors' computation based on data collected, own research

Table 1.12 ANOVA[a]

Model		Sum of squares	df	Mean square	F	Sig.
1	Regression	36.582	1	36.582	80.811	.000[b]
	residual	53.418	118	0.453		
	Total	90.000	119			

[a]Dependent variable: Amount of money intended for travel
[b]Predictors: (Constant), monthly income
Source: Authors' computation based on data collected, own research

Domestic travel International travel Domestic and international Findings	69 23 28 Rejected
H3. Low willingness to specific wellness tourism spending compared to their income.	
Variable Coefficient Findings	Amount of money intended for travel .638 p< .010 Rejected

Table 1.13 Coefficients[a]

		Unstandardized coefficients		Standardized coefficients	t	Sig.
Model		B	Std. error	Beta		
1	(Constant)	.962	.131		7.350	.000
	Monthly income	.572	.064	.638	8.989	.000

[a]Dependent variable: Amount of money intended for travel
Source: Authors' computation based on data collected, own research

1.8 Conclusions

Wellness tourism requires an adequate infrastructure, also a culture for this type of tourism, and in Romania, both phenomena have a not very distant past. The wellness infrastructure, often intersected with the Spa, is constantly evolving in all regions of the country, so in trips with a purpose other than special for wellness, tourists can benefit from the opportunities of wellness services. The culture for health prevention and care has many gaps, the reasons being multiple-, more or less objective. Thus, as a result of the current research, young people, millennials and Generation Zs are part of the secondary wellness traveller category, but given their willingness to spend for wellness confirmed in current research, we consider that there are forecasts for future increases in the number of primary wellness travellers.

Regarding the obtained result of the present research and the published statistical data concerning the selection of travel destinations, it can be concluded that the popularity of domestic tourism has grown lately. A large number of respondents indicated domestic travel as their next travel destination; this aspect is also confirmed by the recent statistical data previously mentioned in the chapter. As we mentioned before, the current restriction created by the pandemic COVID-19 can have a significant influence in this regard. The hypothesis according to which among the youth, there is a strong demand for destinations abroad has not been proven, since research shows that travel choice is characterized by demand for destinations in the country.

The result of the research regarding the willingness to spend money for wellness travel was a surprise because compared to their income, respondents are willing to spend more than their average net wage on this kind of travel on a yearly level. Based on Pearson`s correlation calculations, we may conclude that there is correspondence between the amount of money intended for wellness travel and income – this is supported by the regression model results as well – also between travel time and the amount of money intended for wellness travel, between the amount of money intended for wellness travel and age, and between income and age – these are the factors that have great influence on each other. The weakest correspondence is to be found between age and travel time – these factors correlate the least.

A further point to be considered is to acquaint the youth with a philosophy of life that focuses on a preventive lifestyle that would not compel or urge individuals to demand medical treatments in the end. Thus, a sustainable level of demand could be established that points towards wellness.

The present research has a somewhat limited scope; it studies the needs of the youth highlighting some of the aspects; however, it could be continued by studying other phenomena related to wellness, e.g. the dimensions of wellness in the country, which is the topic of the following research.

References

Bertsch, G., & Ostermann, H. (2011). The effect of wellness brand awareness on expected and perceived service quality. *Tourismos, 6*(2).

Bulin, D., Marin-Pantelescu, A., Molnar, E. I., Şchiopu, A. F., & Ţigu, G. (2019). Ethical issues in hospitality: Management implications for Youth Tourism in Romania. In S. Fotea, I. Fotea, & S. Văduva (Eds.), *Challenges and opportunities to develop organizations through creativity* (Technology and ethics). Springer. https://doi.org/10.1007/978-3-030-43449-6_5

Chan, M. (2013). Health 2020: A European policy framework supporting action across government and society for health and well-being. *Health 2020 A European policy framework and strategy for the 21st century*, WHO Regional Office for Europe, pp. 8.

Clothier, P. J., 2007. Oxford dictionary of sport science and medicine, Michael Kent (Ed.), Oxford University Press, Oxford (2006), ISBN: 0-19-921089-6.

Csirmaz, É., & Pető, K. (2015). International trends in recreational and wellness tourism. *Procedia Economics and Finance, 32*, 755–762. https://doi.org/10.1016/S2212-5671(15)01458-6

Cowen, E. L. (1991). In pursuit of wellness. *American Psychologist, 46*(4), 404–408. https://doi.org/10.1037/0003-066X.46.4.404

Dillette, A., Douglas, A., & Andrzejewski, C. (2020). Dimensions of holistic wellness as a result of international wellness tourism experiences. *Current Issues in Tourism*, pp. 1–17. https://doi.org/10.1080/13683500.2020.1746247

Dunn, H. L. (1957). Points of attack for raising the levels of wellness. *Journal of the National Medical Association, 49*(4), 229–230.

Dunn, H. L. (1961). *High level wellness* (pp. 4–5). R. W. BEATTY, LTD. ISBN 0-87948-030-0.

European Spa Association ESPA. (2020). https://www.europeanspas.eu/en/. Accessed 14 July 2020.

Global Wellness Institute. (2020). What wellness is, Wellness definitions. https://globalwellnessinstitute.org/what-is-wellness/wellness-economy-definitions/. Accessed 15 May 2020.

Global Wellness Economy Monitor. (2017). The Spa Economy, Global Wellness Institute, January 2017, pp. 7–15. https://globalwellnessinstitute.org/wpcontent/uploads/2018/06/GWI_WellnessEconomyMonitor2017_FINALweb.pdf. Accessed 17 June 2020.

Global Wellness Economy Monitor. (2018). Global wellness economy for 2018, Global Wellness Institut. https://globalwellnessinstitute.org/wpcontent/uploads/2018/10/Research2018_v5FINALExecutiveSummary_webREVISED.pdf. Accessed 15 May 2020.

Gondos, B. (2019). The possibilities to create equal opportunities in tourism for people with disabilities. *Knowledge Horizons Economics, 11*(4), 54–69.

Happ, É. (2008). Wellnesshotel vagy konferenciaszálloda? *Értékőrzés és értékteremtés*. XI. Apáczai Napok.2007, Győr, pp. 500–509.

Hotărâre, HG Nr.215/2009 pentru aprobarea Normelor metodologice privind acordarea tichetelor de vacanţă, Monitorul Oficial nr. 145 din 9 mai 2009

Hotărâre, HG Nr.940/2017 pentru modificarea şi completarea Normelor metodologice privind acordarea voucherelor de vacanţă, aprobate prin Hotărârea Guvernului nr. 215/2009, Monitorul Oficial nr. 1026 din 27 decembrie 2017.

Ivancsóné Horváth, Z., & Printz-Markó, E. (2017). Generation investigations in the wellness tourism in Hungary. In *DIEM: Dubrovnik International Economic Meeting*. Sveučilište u Dubrovniku, 3(1), 793–809.

Iosub, I., Platon, O. E., Neacşu, M. N., & Fruth, A. (2017). Contributions to the sustainable development of romania's tourism brand, *Basiq International Conference Proceedings New Trends in Sustainable Business and Consumption*, pp. 337–345.

Kadieva, S. (2015). Contemporary changes in the hotel product for spa and wellness tourism and their distribution. BizInfo (Blace) *Journal of Economics, Management and Informatics*, 6(1), 1-10. https://doi.org/10.5937/BIZINFO1501001K

Magliulo, A. (2014). Sustainable and competitive tourism: targets, determinants and measurement systems, in Tourism *Research in a Changing World*, Tourism Research Group of Polytechnic Institute of Leiria, pp. 15–23.

Marin-Pantelescu, A. (2011). The business travellers' motivation and behaviour. *Cactus Tourism Journal*, pp. 73–79.

Miller, J. W. (2005). *Wellness: The history and development of a concept*. Spektrum Freizeit 27(1).

Ordonanţa de urgenţă a Guvernului, OUG Nr.8/2009 privind acordarea tichetelor de vacanţă, Monitorul Oficial nr. 110 din 24 februarie 2009

Press Comunication nr.199/3 aug 2020, Institutul National de Statistica – INSSE (2020). https://insse.ro/cms/sites/default/files/com_presa/com_pdf/turism06r20.pdf. Accessed 7 Aug 2020.

Printz-Markó, E., & Molnar, E. I. (2019). Health tourism—A new system-model based on the four basic elements. In S. Fotea, I. Fotea, & S. Văduva (Eds.), *Challenges and opportunities to develop organizations through creativity, Technology and Ethics* (pp. 253–267). Springer. https://doi.org/10.1007/978-3-030-43449-6_14

Printz-Markó, E., Darabos, F., & Ivancsone Horvath, Z. S. (2017). Dimensions of wellness tourism in Hungary. *Knowledge Horizons Economics, 9*(1), 24–35.

Privitera, D. (2019). Smart wellness. *Esplorando le innovazioni digitali, AGEI – Geotema, 60*, 190–198.

Prónay, S. (2011). Fiatalok fogyasztásának vizsgálata: szegmentáció. *Marketing & Menedzsment, 45*(1), 26–37.

Puczkó, L., & Smith, M. (2012). An analysis of tourism QOL domains from the demand side. In *Handbook of tourism and quality-of-life research* (pp. 263–277). https://doi.org/10.1007/978-94-007-2288-0_15

Renaudin, N. (2014). Service vouchers: Tools to prevent stress and enhance well-being. In C. Biron, R. J. Burke, & C. L. Cooper (Eds.), *Creating healthy workplaces: Stress reduction, improved well-being, and organizational effectiveness* (pp. 129–146). Routlege Taylor & Francis Group.

Resident population on 1 January 2019 by age groups and ages, sexes, areas of residence, macroregions, development regions and counties / Populația rezidenta la 1 ianuarie pe grupe de vârstă si vârste, sexe, medii de rezidență, macroregiuni, regiuni de dezvoltare și județe, POP 105A Institutul Național de Statistică – INSSE, http://statistici.insse.ro:8077/tempo-online/#/pages/tables/insse-table. Accessed 14 July 2020.

Sirimanne, E. (2020). Multifunctional homes – A broadband connected safe space. In A. Angus & G. Westbrook (Eds.), *Top 10 Global Consumer Trends 2020* (pp. 38–39). Euromonitor International.

Stará, J., & Peterson, C. (2017). Understanding the concept of wellness for the future of the tourism industry: A literature review. *Journal of Tourism & Services, 8*(14), 18–29.

Stănciulescu, G. C., Diaconescu, G. N., & Diaconescu, D. M. (2015). Health, spa, wellness tourism. What is the difference. *Knowledge Horizons, 7*(3), 158–161.

Sziva, I. (2010). Öntsünk tiszta vizet… Az egészségturizmus fogalmi lehatárolása és trendjeinek válogatott bibliográfiája. *Turizmus Bulletin, 14*(4), 73–76.

Težak Damijanić, A., & Šergo, Z. (2013). Determining travel motivations of wellness tourism. *Ekonomska misao i praksa, 1*, 3–20.

Törőcsik, M. (2006). Fogyasztói magatartás-trendek. *Új fogyasztói csoportok, Akadémia Kiadió Zrt.*, Budapest.

Tourist reception structures with classified accommodation functions. http://turism.gov.ro/web/autorizare-turism/. Accessed 25 July 2020.

Uduslivaia, S. (2020). Inclusive for all – Disabilities in the spotlight. In A. Angus & G. Westbrook (Eds.), *Top 10 global consumer trends 2020* (pp. 28–29). Euromonitor International.

UNWTO World Tourism Barometer May 2020 Special focus on the Impact of COVID-19, https://webunwto.s3.eu-west-1.amazonaws.com/s3fs-public/2020-05/Barometer%20-%20May%202020%20-%20Short.pdf. Accessed 02 June 2020.

Voigt, C., Brown, G., & Howat, G. (2011). Wellness tourists: in search of transformation. *Tourism Review, 66*(1/2), 16–30. https://doi.org/10.1108/16605371111127206

Westbrook, G. (2020). What are we in 2020? In A. Angus & G. Westbrook (Eds.), *Top 10 global consumer trends 2020* (pp. 2–6). Euromonitor International.

Chapter 2
Systemic Risk Causality Among Economic Sectors: An Analysis of the Banking and Real Estate Sectors

Cristina Georgiana Zeldea

Abstract The real estate sector has usually gathered high common exposures of financial institutions, thus driving background risk buildup in the financial systems. Although not traditionally recognized as a primary source of risk, tantamount to the banking sector, the global financial crisis of 2008 has pinpointed real estate's systemic importance. This chapter is centered on two conditional capital shortfall methods. We compute the systemic risk for the banking and real estate sectors in the United States and the European Union and then investigate the causal relationships between them and their direction. Strong evidence of causality between the two sectors is provided.

Keywords Systemic risk · Banking sector · Real estate · Conditional capital shortfall · Causality

2.1 Introduction

The ever-changing nature of the financial system has been the strongest incentive for risk measurement techniques to develop in line with the waves of financial innovation. Existing work demonstrates that alternative measurement methods produce different estimates of systemic risk, which may lead to conflicting risk assessments of some institutions or groups of institutions. Therefore, systemic risk assessment using a single method must be approached with caution (Kleinow et al., 2017). For this reason, much of the existing literature applies more than one method for assessing systemic risk, and we are following in these footsteps.

C. G. Zeldea (✉)
Bucharest University of Economic Studies, Bucharest, Romania
e-mail: cristinazeldea@iem.ro

S. L. Fotea et al. (eds.), *Navigating Through the Crisis: Business, Technological and Ethical Considerations*, Springer Proceedings in Business and Economics,
https://doi.org/10.1007/978-3-030-82751-9_2

We approach the issue of systemic risk empirically, from a multidimensional perspective. We use two methodologies, namely, marginal expected shortfall (Acharya et al., 2010) and systemic risk index (Brownlees & Engle, 2016) to measure systemic risk in the banking and real estate sectors, both in the United States and in the European Union. The results we obtain provide us a tool for a retrospective analysis of the dynamics of systemic risk on the sample financial markets. Our main assumption is that banks are traditionally, and according to most of the reference studies in this field, the primary sources of systemic instability.

We compare, based on the dynamics patterns, the systemic risk in the banking system with the systemic risk in the real estate sector. We then test for Granger causality in terms of systemic risk between the banking system and the real estate sector in the two markets. We find differences in terms of dynamics both between the sectors analyzed and between the measurement methods used. The Granger causality tests performed indicate the existence of interdependencies between the banking and real estate sectors both in the United States and the European Union. Our findings do have relevant implications for banks and financial market regulation. The systemic importance revealed by the real estate sector and the causality relations in terms of risk of the banking-real estate pair confirm the need for heightened prudential regulation of banks exposures. For instance, establishing limits on banks' common exposures to the housing sector may represent a useful systemic risk management tool, all the more so in the light of the real estate origin of the 2008 crisis.

The remainder of the chapter is organized as follows: Sect. 2.2 is the literature review, Sect. 2.3 presents the data used and the methodologies, and Sect. 2.4 discusses the obtained results. Conclusions are drawn in Sect. 2.5.

2.2 Literature Review

Brownlees and Engle (2012) have developed a new empirical tool, the systemic risk index (also known as SRISK). In their framework, systemic risk is the average expected loss of an institution, caused by a severe market decline. They calculate SRISK for 94 US financial institutions, divided into banks, brokers, dealers, insurers, and others, between 2000 and 2010. Their method requires data on market capitalization, debt, and marginal expected shortfall. Marginal expected shortfall – hereinafter MES – is a function of debt, the size of the institution, and the loss that occurs in the event of a market decline. MES is calculated by means of dynamic conditional correlation models (Engle, 2009) in order to obtain long-term and short-term dynamic volatility and dynamic correlations of returns. The sum of the individual firms' SRISK values approximates the aggregate systemic risk of the entire financial system. Engle et al. (2015) apply the systemic risk index, to a range of large European financial institutions, and draw the conclusion that in some cases rescue costs become too high for the authorities to bail these institutions out in case of default.

Coleman et al. (2018) apply SRISK for the banking and insurance system, on the Canadian market. Their changes brought to the method consist, on the one hand, in excluding actuarial debts from the total debts of insurance companies and on the other hand in changing the prudential capital threshold by considering financial reporting standards. Chang et al. (2018) apply CoVaR – of Adrian and Brunnermeier, 2016 – and SRISK to assess the systemic importance of the Taiwanese insurance sector and conclude that the indebtedness of insurers and their share in the financial system determine a great portion of the systemic risk that this industry propagates. Gehrig and Iannino (2018) test the Granger causal relationships between banking and insurance risk in the European Union and prove that causal relationships are generally one-way, from the banking system to the insurance system, and also that they grow stronger during periods of financial instability. Pagano and Sedunov (2016) address the co-movements between the systemic risk of the financial market, calculated using MES, and the yield on government bonds and show that they are strongly correlated especially in turbulent times. Acharya et al. (2017) use asset price data and credit-default swaps to calculate systemic expected shortfall for a financial institution's contribution to systemic risk. They provide the renowned definition of systemic risk as "an institution's tendency to be undercapitalized when the system as a whole is undercapitalized. The systemic expected shortfall proposed by Acharya et al. (2017) is relatively similar to SRISK. The systemic expected shortfall is calculated as a linear combination of the degree of indebtedness and MES with a lag. MES can be, in fact, an independent method of measuring systemic risk. For example, Cipra and Heyndrich (2017) or Battaglia and Gallo (2013) use MES to calculate systemic risk in the financial markets of the Czech Republic and Italy, respectively. Ben Ameur et al. (2018) use high-frequency data to test for risk transmission between the United States and the European Union. Their MES-based approach revealed that risk has a bidirectional flow, both from the United States to the European Union and reversely.

Lin et al. (2016) and Stolbov and Shchepeleva (2017) have a relatively similar approach to ours from a methodological point of view. The first calculates CoVaR, ΔCoVaR, SRISK, and MES for the banking system, the insurance sector, and other financial companies. They rank the institutions of systemic importance according to the estimates by the four methods. They test the Granger causal relationship between SRISK estimates and two real economy variables – the industrial production index and the unemployment rate – and show that the link is one-way from SRISK to the industrial production index. Stolbov and Shchepeleva (2017) test Granger causal relationships between several risk measures, including SRISK, and the industrial production index, for 22 European countries. Their results deny the existence of causal relationships between systemic risk and the industrial production index.

2.3 Data and Methodology

The daily frequency data covers banks and companies operating in the real estate sector, between January 2004 and March 2019. The Bloomberg platform has been used to retrieve the daily prices, capitalization, and debt levels. We mention that the selection of assets from SP 500, respectively from Stoxx 600 to be analyzed, was made according to Industrial Classification Benchmark-ICB (FTSE Russell), which is a reference global classification of companies by activity sectors. Companies that either did not have data available or did not have a sufficiently extensive data history to cover events of global impact – minimum 3650 daily data, specifically – have been removed. Returns have been processed by taking the first difference of the natural log.

Appendix 2.1 shows the list of companies and the descriptive statistics for each series of returns.

We follow Acharya et al. (2010) and consider MES to be the average expected loss beyond a Value-at-Risk threshold i. If R is the firm stock return and M the market return, we can first define the expected shortfall as:

$$ES_j = E\left[R \mid R < C\right]$$

where C defines market tail risk. It follows that MES is given by:

$$MES_{i,j} = E_j(R_{i,j+1)}M_{i,j+1} < q_{\alpha,j}\left(R_{j+1}\right) = C$$

Following Brownlees and Engle (2016), we further compute SRISK:

$$SRISK = E_t(CS_{i,j}R_{i,j} < C = \delta E_j\left(D_{i,j} \mid R_{i,j}\right) < C - (1-k)E_t\left(W_{i,j} \mid R_{i,j}\right) < C$$

where CS is the capital shortfall defined as the difference between the value of the prudential capital reserve required and the market capitalization of the firm, expressed as:

$$CS_{i.j} = \delta A_{i,j} - W_{i,j} = k\left(D_{i.j} + W_{i.j}\right) - W_{i,j}$$

where W stands market capitalization, D is the debt, and δ is the required prudential capital reserve. It follows that SRISK can be derived as:

$$SRISK = \delta D_{i,j} - 1(1-\delta)W_{i.j}\left(1 - MES_{i.j}\right) = W_{i.j}\left[\delta L_{i.j} + (1-\delta)MES_{i.j} - 1\right]$$

where L is the leverage and MES is the long-run marginal expected shortfall.

In both cases, we compute the MES components using the dynamic conditional correlation approach of Engle and Sheppard (2008).

We investigate causal relationships using the method proposed by Granger (1969), in order to observe whether the values of a series y have predictive power for the present and future values of another series x. The regression equations on which the test is based are the following:

$$y_t = \beta_0 + \sum_{i=1}^{n} \beta_i y_{t-i} + \sum_{j=1}^{n} \alpha_j x_{t-j} + e$$

$$x_t = \gamma_0 + \sum_{i=1}^{n} \delta_i y_{t-i} + \sum_{j=1}^{n} \alpha_j x_{t-j} + \varepsilon$$

where e and ε are the errors and n is the number of lags. The null hypothesis accounts that $\alpha = 0$; $\delta = 0$ for any lag. The alternative hypothesis is that $\alpha \neq 0$; $\delta \neq 0$ for at least one lag. Where appropriate, the results may reveal unidirectional, bidirectional, or the lack of causality. The Akaike and Schwarz criteria used indicated two lags to be consistent with our data.

2.4 Results and Discussion

Figures 2.1 and 2.2 show the daily frequency estimates of systemic risk between January 2, 2004, and March 14, 2019, according to the two methods, for both the United States and the European Union. We mention that the sectoral risk is

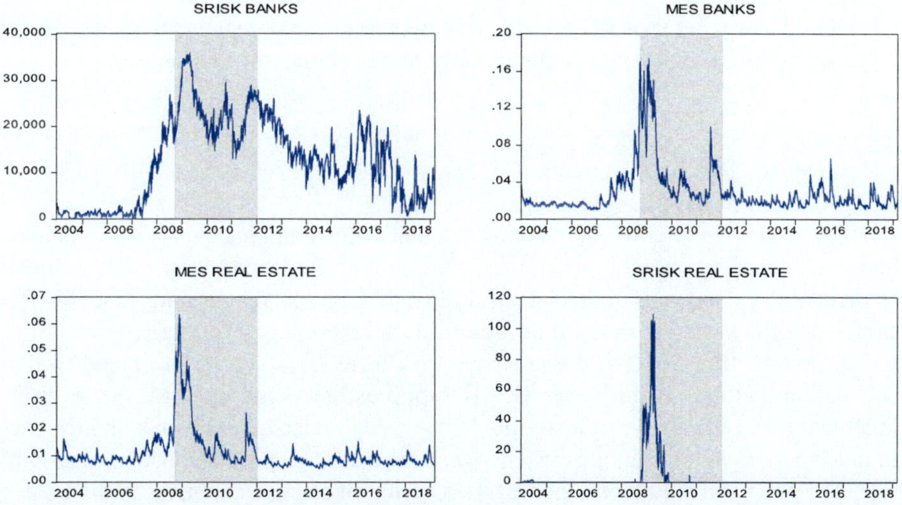

Fig. 2.1 Systemic risk in the banking and real estate sectors of the United States. (Source: Author's own processing. The shaded area represents the 2008–2012 global financial crisis)

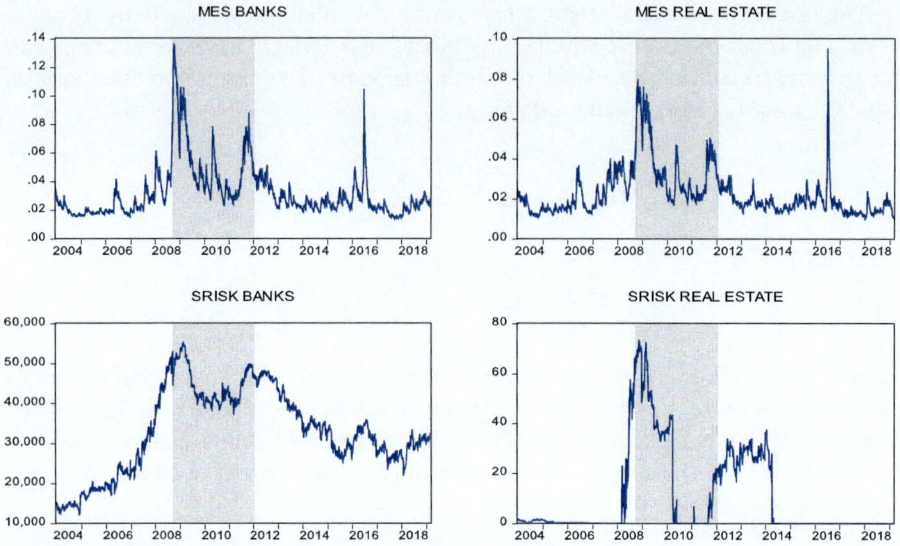

Fig. 2.2 Systemic risk in the banking and real estate sectors of the European Union. (Source: Author's own processing. The shaded area represents the 2008–2012 global financial crisis)

calculated as the average of the estimates for the individual institutions (see Appendix 2.1 for sample composition).

The preliminary analysis of the results reveals a series of aspects:

- The generalized impact, but of different amplitudes, of the global financial crisis on systemic risk
- Different dynamics patterns between the estimation methods used
- Heterogeneity in terms of systemic risk dynamics in the real estate sector, compared to the banking system, particularly in what concerns SRISK estimates

We observe relatively similar dynamics between the United States and EU banking systems from the point of view of MES, with a notable difference in the EU, in the case of the Brexit referendum. Generally speaking, markets reacted simultaneously to the turmoil of the global financial crisis.

With regard to SRISK in banking systems, the graphical analysis indicates increased volatility, with higher jumps in the case of the United States, which hints at persistent episodes of financial instability. It is worth mentioning that SRISK shows that the systemic risk did not return to the pre-crisis level, unlike the MES, which returns after 2016 to the pre-crisis risk level. This can be attributed to the calculation method. In this case, SRISK supposes the weighting with the level of indebtedness of the analyzed institutions. It is fairly understandable that an increase in indebtedness in the banking system over time leads to a proportionate increase in risk. The MES, on the other hand, marks a period of relative calmness in the financial markets after 2016.

The dynamics of systemic risk in the European Union show some common patterns with the United States, but with a number of specific elements. The global financial and the sovereign debt crisis of the Eurozone are leading to a synchronized increase in risk in both sectors. MES and SRISK reach their peak at the height of the crisis, with the bankruptcy of Lehman Brothers and government intervention to rescue Citigroup. MES estimates indicate a reduction in systemic risk immediately after the rescue of Citigroup, marking the beginning of a period of financial stabilization.

Episodes of lower financial instability are also occurring in the United States during the Eurozone sovereign debt crisis. After 2012, MES estimates vary in a narrow range, between 1% and 5%, indicating a resumption of economic activity in normal parameters in the banking and real estate sector.

Following SRISK, the risk in the banking system starts to increase earlier, right after BNP Paribas suspends the three investment funds and remains at high levels until 2012. We observe a period of increased volatility during 2015–2016, which overlaps with the US presidential election. The volatility of the estimates, although in narrower intervals, is maintained towards the end of the analyzed period, hinting at a latent financial instability.

The SRISK dynamics in the real estate sector reveal a lower systemic importance than the banking system, in the sense that the only episode of instability of the sample period takes place in 2008, during the financial crisis. Moreover, estimates in the real estate sector reach a maximum of possible losses of just over $ 100 million, in contrast to the banking system where estimated losses exceed $ 30,000 million in the peak of the crisis. This is natural and easy to explain by the difference in capitalization between the two sectors.

We emphasize that the real estate sector has, according to our estimates, systemic importance but significantly less than the banking system.

In the EU, the global financial crisis and the sovereign debt crisis determine an increase in risk in both sectors. Generally, events related to the economic and financial evolution of Greece have a strong influence on financial instability in European markets. The preparation of austerity programs corresponds to risk spikes, while positive news about Greece temper risk: for example, the news of Greece returning to financing on the capital markets. As was expected, the sovereign debt crisis determines the continuous high-risk pattern after 2012, when the global crisis conventionally ended already for the United States. However, in the EU, the volatility is generally lower than in the United States.

The graphical analysis of the dynamics showed that the episodes of instability were synchronized in the two sectors. However, this does not necessarily imply simultaneity, causality, or contagion. The relationship between systemic risk and financial contagion between financial institutions, respectively between systems, is widely recognized in the literature. There are numerous studies addressing this topic, of which we mention, among others, Allen and Gale (2000), Kaminsky and Reinhart (2000), and Claessens and Forbes (2001).

Therefore, we investigated further the Granger causal relationship between the banking and real estate sectors in the United States and the European Union. We

Table 2.1 ADF test

Sample averages	US banks	US real estate	EU banks	EU real estate
MES	0.0033	0.0073	0.0205	0.001
SRISK	0.0646[a]	0.0034	0.3286[a]	0.2642[a]

Source: author's computation
[a]Integrated of 1st order

Table 2.2 Granger causality results

Bidirectional causality		
MES United States – banks	↔	MES United States – real estate
MES European Union – banks	↔	MES European Union – real estate
MES United States – banks	↔	MES European Union – banks
SRISK United States – banks	↔	SRISK European Union – banks
Unidirectional causality		
SRISK United States – banks	→	SRISK United States -real estate

Source: Author's computation

also test the causal relationship between the US and European Union banking systems.

The stationarity of the time series has been tested beforehand. Table 2.1 shows the probabilities of the Augmented Dickey-Fuller test, with the null hypothesis that the tested series is not stationary). The series marked in the table with an asterisk were subsequently processed by taking the first difference.

Table 2.2 shows the probabilities obtained after testing the causal relationships between the sectors. We test the first pair, between the MES of the banking system and the MES of the US real estate sector, and in both cases, we reject the null hypothesis of non-causality. Causality is therefore bidirectional, both from the banking system to the real estate sector and vice versa. Causal relationships are in line with the dynamics patterns discussed in the previous section. As we have seen, from the point of view of the MES, the risk in the US banking and real estate sector has shown similar episodes of financial instability during the relevant events on international markets.

The second pair tested is SRISK of the banking system and SRISK of the US real estate sector. The results show this time a one-way causal relationship, running from the risk of the banking system to the risk of the real estate sector. This finding is consistent with the results of other works that identify the banking system as a primary source of systemic risk, of which we mention Billio et al. (2012); López-Espinosa et al. (2012); and Engle et al. (2015).

The third pair concerns the causal links between the MES of the banking system and the MES of the real estate sector in the European Union. In this case too, the causality is bidirectional, both from the banking sector to the real estate sector and from the real estate sector to the banking sector. However, things are different from the SRISK point of view: the hypothesis of non-causality could not be rejected.

Systemic risk estimates in the banking system have no predictive power for current or future real estate risk.

Non-causality from the SRISK point of view can also be attributed to the significant difference in capitalization between the two sectors. We can deduce that the echo that the global financial crisis had on the dynamics of risk in the real estate sector occurred through channels other than banking in the European Union.

Next, we have investigated the causal relationship between the US and European Union banking systems. Both the MES – based and SRISK – based pairs of estimates show bidirectional causal relationships between the banking systems analyzed. We understand, therefore, that the existing interdependencies between the banking systems in question represent channels for the spread of systemic risk, both from the United States to the European Union and vice versa. Ben Ameur, Jawadi, Louhichi and Cheffou (2018) also identify the bidirectionality of systemic risk in the US-EU relationship.

2.5 Conclusion

We approach the issue of systemic risk empirically, from a multidimensional perspective. We use two methodologies, namely, marginal expected shortfall (Acharya et al., 2010) and systemic risk index (Brownlees and Engle, 2016) to measure systemic risk in the banking and real estate sectors, both in the United States and in the European Union. We compare, based on the dynamics patterns, the systemic risk in the banking system with the systemic risk in the real estate sector

The graphical analysis of the dynamics showed that the episodes of instability were synchronized in the banking and real estate sectors. However, this does not necessarily imply simultaneity, causality, or contagion. Therefore, we investigated Granger causal relationships between the banking and real estate sectors in the United States and the European Union. The results obtained confirm the existence of causality. In the United States, it is bidirectional according to MES, respectively unidirectional, from the banking sector to the real estate one according to SRISK. Similarly, in the European Union, the causal links between the systems are bidirectional according to the MES but are rejected according to SRISK This suggests that the echo that the global financial crisis had on the dynamics of risk in the real estate sector would have occurred through channels other than banking in the European Union. Main findings are consistent with the results of other works that identify the banking system as a primary source of systemic risk, of which we mention Billio et al. (2012); López-Espinosa et al. (2012); and Engle et al. (2015).

Last but not least, we tested the causality between the US and EU banking systems. Both the MES-based and SRISK-based pairs of estimates show bidirectional causal relationships between the banking systems analyzed. We understand, therefore, that the existing interdependencies between the banking systems in this case represent channels for the spread of systemic risk, both from the United States to the

European Union and vice versa. Ben Ameur, Jawadi, Louhichi and Cheffou (2018) also identify the bidirectionality of systemic risk in the US-EU relationship.

We have noticed certain heterogeneities in terms of systemic risk in the banking and real estate sectors. The differences between the sectors show that the risk in the banking system was, from the perspective of both methods, constantly higher than in the real estate sector. Our findings do have relevant implications for banks and financial market regulation. The systemic importance revealed by the real estate sector and the causality relations in terms of risk of the banking-real estate pair confirm the need for heightened prudential regulation of banks exposures. For instance, establishing limits on banks' common exposures to the housing sector may represent a useful systemic risk management tool, all the more so in the light of the real estate origin of the 2008 crisis.

Appendix 2.1

	Mean	Median	Maximum	Minimum	Std. dev.	Skewness	Kurtosis
SP500	0.000234	0.000362	0.109572	−0.0947	0.011327	−0.36734	15.53434
US Banks							
Zions Bancorp	−5.62E-05	0	0.243392	−0.26396	0.029177	0.087735	19.83842
Wells Fargo & Co 7	0.000135	0	0.283407	−0.2721	0.02458	0.944709	32.66163
US Bancorp	0.000143	0	0.205722	−0.20047	0.020166	−0.04181	24.21712
SunTrust Banks Inc	−2.76E-05	0	0.266688	−0.31705	0.027809	−0.42431	25.24186
SVB Financial Group	0.000484	0	0.171795	−0.26668	0.023564	−0.47894	15.4097
Regions Financial Corp	−0.00016	0	0.394808	−0.52884	0.033099	−0.5568	41.86378
PNC Financial Services	0.000217	0	0.315474	−0.53437	0.023567	−1.74308	88.22914
PBCT Financial Services S U	0.000234	0	0.164507	−0.16998	0.015814	0.007404	16.27899
M&T Bank Corp	0.000143	0	0.191098	−0.16972	0.019519	0.133585	15.74765
KeyCorp	−0.00013	0	0.433421	−0.40547	0.029625	−0.50847	41.96095
JP Morgan Chase & Co	0.000266	0	0.223917	−0.23228	0.022936	0.35038	22.82886
Huntington Bancshares	−0.00012	0	0.365315	−0.36508	0.034638	0.331341	33.00375
Fifth Third Bancorp	−0.00019	0	0.472288	−0.57317	0.034111	−0.38551	61.39024

	Mean	Median	Maximum	Minimum	Std. dev.	Skewness	Kurtosis
Comerica Inc	9.64E-05	0	0.188052	−0.2072	0.024213	−0.1084	14.83332
Citigroup Inc	−0.00051	0	0.456316	−0.4947	0.031656	−0.57507	48.4837
Truist Financial Corp	6.57E-05	0	0.211982	−0.26608	0.021447	−0.01472	23.48689
Bank of America	−7.85E-05	0	0.302096	−0.34206	0.030216	−0.35867	31.39779
US Real estate							
Welltower Inc	0.000195	0.000644	0.141688	−0.15637	0.017591	−0.36384	12.57184
Ventas Inc	0.000301	0.000461	0.176224	−0.22391	0.021226	−0.3149	18.76545
Vornado Realty Trust	0.000145	0.000172	0.200332	−0.21592	0.021949	−0.04536	19.37383
UDR Inc	0.000236	0.000281	0.160968	−0.21115	0.021759	−0.28464	18.70443
Apartment Invt & Mgmt	0.000176	0.000258	0.243378	−0.31667	0.025376	−0.643	24.66404
American Tower Corp	0.00072	0.000384	0.184152	−0.11035	0.016746	0.382326	12.19714
Alexandria Real Estate	0.000226	0.0003	0.16605	−0.27631	0.020546	−0.81465	21.55359
AvalonBay Communities	0.00037	0.000326	0.166147	−0.18785	0.020491	−0.0812	15.17943
Boston Properties Inc	0.00026	0	0.21456	−0.18255	0.021194	−0.11209	19.05964
Duke Realty Corp	−2.37E-06	0	0.322494	−0.38037	0.0281	−0.98662	40.03925
Equinix Inc	0.000693	0	0.16879	−0.40148	0.023076	−0.89498	31.47305
Equity Residential	0.000235	0	0.211477	−0.24365	0.022481	0.01823	23.9968
Essex Property Trust	0.000381	0.00033	0.138639	−0.21948	0.018829	−0.45574	16.83427
Federal Realty Invt Trust	0.000314	9.76E-05	0.196025	−0.25391	0.019313	−0.21772	24.69016
Healthpeak Properties Inc	7.64E-05	0.000288	0.205232	−0.18215	0.022197	0.227078	17.85481
Host Hotels & Resorts	0.000118	0	0.238871	−0.23922	0.026949	0.059738	19.43702
Iron Mountain Inc	0.000211	0	0.182771	−0.17249	0.017841	0.032029	17.21204
Kimco Realty Corp	−5.64E-05	0	0.290338	−0.28258	0.025231	0.132334	24.01983
Mid-America Apt	0.000295	0.000214	0.207401	−0.25937	0.020313	−0.16078	23.64525
Macerich Co	1.30E-05	0	0.275917	−0.31225	0.027395	−0.523	27.41899
Realty Income Corp	0.000323	0.000336	0.200101	−0.22018	0.019422	0.38602	21.546
Public Storage	0.000408	0.000429	0.184683	−0.20668	0.019702	0.142077	18.47387
SBA Corp	0.000987	0.000551	0.243341	−0.18743	0.022249	−0.05345	15.3049

	Mean	Median	Maximum	Minimum	Std. dev.	Skewness	Kurtosis
SL Green Realty Corp	0.000202	0.000266	0.34249	−0.32503	0.028615	−0.42238	32.81212
Simon Property Group	0.000369	0.000504	0.22596	−0.22316	0.022591	0.26563	20.90644
STOXX600	9.96E-05	0.000222	0.108364	−0.09906	0.013197	−0.18941	11.84002
EU Banks							
Unicredit	−0.0006	0	0.201474	−0.28827	0.029718	−0.2088	11.03684
UBS Group AG	−0.00023	0	0.260983	−0.19079	0.023305	0.198326	16.69166
Swedbank *AB*	4.00E-05	0.00011	0.199356	−0.22603	0.025529	−0.3587	13.68583
Standard Chartered PLC	−0.00012	0	0.314792	−0.18568	0.024719	0.329283	18.35024
Santander Bank Polska	0.000405	0	0.151246	−0.14611	0.024288	−0.04049	6.661492
Barclays PLC	−0.00033	0	0.565815	−0.28044	0.030848	0.997377	44.06421
Banco Bilbao	−0.0002	0	0.207304	−0.1931	0.022023	0.064619	10.99846
Banco Comercial Portugues	−0.0009	−0.00073	0.238434	−0.16337	0.028608	0.19903	8.691612
Bank of Ireland Group	−0.00093	0	0.402591	−0.79818	0.044518	−1.24319	42.32995
Bankinter SA	0.000118	0	0.142731	−0.11186	0.022031	0.350314	6.879947
Close Brothers Group	0.000107	0	0.189948	−0.20307	0.019512	−0.42869	21.49299
Commerzbank AG	−0.00068	0	0.206834	−0.28906	0.029883	−0.20684	11.96634
Credit Suisse Group	−0.00026	0	0.236077	−0.17498	0.02325	0.203835	13.77327
Danske Bank A/S	−1.87E-05	0	0.135645	−0.19158	0.021038	−0.19999	9.802614
Deutsche Bank AG	−0.0005	0	0.239743	−0.18776	0.026296	0.22134	12.51628
DNB ASA	0.000278	0	0.214043	−0.22819	0.025376	−0.20829	14.19829
Erste Group Bank AG	5.22E-05	0	0.168311	−0.21477	0.028517	−0.2608	10.65312
ING Groep NV	−9.27E-05	0.000112	0.262309	−0.31764	0.02956	−0.08324	19.41407
Intesa SanPaolo	−0.0001	0	0.195033	−0.27721	0.026454	−0.45981	12.63882
KBC Group NV	0.000101	0.000351	0.412661	−0.28649	0.032261	−0.07667	22.54907
Nordea AB	0.000106	0	0.198328	−0.1471	0.022275	0.379314	11.73315
People Corp	−6.11E-07	0	0.163018	−0.23464	0.02506	−0.18015	8.84059
Banco de Sabadell SA	−0.00028	0	0.165837	−0.23095	0.020611	0.028397	10.97982
Banco Santander SA	−0.0002	0	0.217003	−0.23833	0.022478	−0.14056	13.38307

	Mean	Median	Maximum	Minimum	Std. dev.	Skewness	Kurtosis
SEB-Skand Enskilda Banken	7.18E-05	0	0.258119	−0.25294	0.02607	−0.00788	17.87895
Svenska Handelsbanken	0.000126	0	0.172158	−0.141	0.020752	0.052933	11.88577
AIB Group PLC	−0.00171	0	0.361506	−0.88944	0.049472	−1.63681	37.94672
EU Real estate							
Unite Group PLC	0.000343	0.000228	0.262104	−0.20843	0.02453	0.004391	16.87783
TAG Immobilien AG	0.000307	0	0.31056	−0.16598	0.020534	0.723015	21.89614
Swiss Prime Site AG	0.000225	7.42E-05	0.118891	−0.08229	0.011874	0.171214	10.05746
Segro PLC	−0.00013	0	0.173524	−0.29726	0.021523	−1.34667	25.6146
Lundberg-foretagen	0.000338	0.000218	0.171336	−0.11502	0.017192	0.026449	9.852099
Klepierre SA	0.000148	0.00029	0.123282	−0.17334	0.019676	−0.69156	9.928043
Land Securities Group PLC	−8.94E-05	0	0.150389	−0.24265	0.019181	−0.69049	16.58668
Hammerson PLC	−0.00011	0	0.223631	−0.21353	0.020416	−0.33635	14.17401
Great Portland Estates	0.000247	0	0.13999	−0.32463	0.020374	−1.22366	24.09493
Gecina SA	0.000184	0.000343	0.150805	−0.14352	0.019848	−0.26738	10.83867
Fabege AB	0.000429	0.000139	0.20224	−0.13443	0.022364	0.0601	9.523574
Derwent London	0.000297	5.26E-05	0.12302	−0.35574	0.020407	−1.47822	32.4349
Inmobiliaria Colonial Socimi	−0.00073	−0.0007	0.413664	−0.33279	0.036506	0.414613	16.97178
Cofinimmo	−6.55E-06	0.000175	0.097031	−0.09115	0.013047	−0.45418	9.155307
Castellum	0.000332	0	0.128254	−0.10449	0.020182	−0.11327	7.048358
British Land Co	−2.04E-05	0	0.123851	−0.29111	0.020218	−1.05599	19.46397

References

Acharya, V., Pedersen, L., Philippon, T., & Richardson, M. 2010: *Measuring systemic risk*. Federal Reserve Bank of Cleveland Working Paper.

Acharya, V. V., Pedersen, L. H., Philippon, T., & Richardson, M. (2017). Measuring systemic risk. *The review of financial studies, 30*(1), 2–47.

Adrian, T., & Brunnermeier, M. K. (2016). CoVaR. *American Economic Review, 106*(7), 1705–1741.
Allen, F., & Gale, D. (2000). Financial contagion. *Journal of Political Economy, 108*(1), 1–33.
Battaglia, F., & Gallo, A. (2013). Securitization and systemic risk: An empirical investigation on Italian banks over the financial crisis. *International Review of Financial Analysis, 30*, 274–286.
Ameur, H. B., Jawadi, F., Louhichi, W., & Cheffou, A. I. (2018). Modeling International Stock Price Comovements with High-Frequency Data. Macroeconomic Dynamics, 22(7), 1875-1903.
Billio, M., Getmansky, M., Lo, A. W., & Pelizzon, L. (2012). Econometric measures of connectedness and systemic risk in the finance and insurance sectors. *Journal of Financial Economics, 104*(3), 535–559.
Brownlees, C. T., & Engle, R. F. (2012). *Volatility, correlation and tails for systemic risk measurement*. In *Working Paper*. Available at https://bfi.uchicago.edu/sites/default/files/research/SSRN-id1611229.pdf
Brownlees, C., & Engle, R. F. (2016). SRISK: A conditional capital shortfall measure of systemic risk. *The Review of Financial Studies, 30*(1), 48–79.
Chang, C. W., Li, X., Lin, E. M., & Yu, M. (2018). Systemic risk, interconnectedness, and non-core activities in Taiwan insurance industry. *International Review of Economics & Finance, 55*, 273–284.
Cipra, T., & Heyndrich, R. (2017). Systemic risk in financial risk regulation. *Czech Journal of Economics and Finance, 67*(1), 15–38.
Claessens, S., & Forbes, K. J. (2001). *International Financial Contagion*. Springer.
Coleman, T., LaPlante, A., & Rubtsov, A. (2018). Analysis of the SRISK measure and its application to the Canadian banking and insurance industries. *Annals of Finance, 14*(4), 547–570.
Engle, R. (2009). Anticipating correlations: a new paradigm for risk management. Princeton University Press.
Engle, R., Jondeau, E., & Rockinger, M. (2015). Systemic risk in Europe. *Review of Finance, 19*(1), 145–190.
Engle, R., & Sheppard, K. (2008). *Evaluating the specification of covariance models for large portfolios*. In *Working paper*. Available at: https://www.researchgate.net/publication/228596699_Evaluating_the_specification_of_covariance_models_for_large_portfolios
Gehrig, T., & Iannino, M. C. (2018). Capital regulation and systemic risk in the insurance sector. *Journal of Financial Economic Policy, 10*(2), 237–263.
Granger, C. W. (1969). Investigating causal relations by econometric models and cross-spectral methods. *Econometrica: Journal of the Econometric Society*, 424–438.
Kaminsky, G. L., & Reinhart, C. M. (2000). On crises, contagion, and confusion. *Journal of International Economics, 51*(1), 145–168.
Kleinow, J., Moreira, F., Strobl, S., & Vähämaa, S. (2017). Measuring systemic risk: A comparison of alternative market-based approaches. *Finance Research Letters, 21*, 40–46.
Lin, E. M. H., Sun, E. W., & Yu, M. T. (2016). Systemic risk, financial markets, and performance of financial institutions. *Annals of Operations Research, 262*(2), 579–603.
López-Espinosa, G., Moreno, A., Rubia, A., & Valderrama, L. (2012). Short-term wholesale funding and systemic risk: A global CoVaR approach. *Journal of Banking & Finance, 36*(12), 3150–3162.
Pagano, M. S. & Sedunov, J. (2016). A comprehensive approach to measuring the relation between systemic risk exposure and sovereign debt. *Journal of Financial Stability, 23*, 62–78.
Stolbov, M., & Shchepeleva, M. (2017). Systemic risk in Europe: Deciphering leading measures, common patterns and real effects. *Annals of Finance, 14*(1), 49–91.

Chapter 3
Destination Management as Determinant of Tourist Attractiveness

Faur Monica and Ban Olimpia

Abstract The attractiveness of a tourist destination sums up a combination of subjective factors (needs, opinions, expectations, impressions, personal experiences) and objective factors (the existence of natural and man-made tourist attractions, the range of tourist services) which influence the tourist's option for leisure. Establishing the elements which determine the attractiveness of a tourist activity represents the constant interest of the involved parties (stakeholders) in carrying out tourist activities. This chapter proposes a study meant to illustrate the contribution of tourist destination management to the growth of tourism attractiveness in the case of the city of Oradea (Romania). The objectives of this research are establishing the factors which influence the tourist attractiveness for the studied tourist destination and analysing the role of the tourist destination management in the growth of the attractiveness of the city of Oradea. The research methodology consisted of data processing and analysis (from 2007 until November 2019) provided by the National Institute of Statistics from Romania regarding tourist movement in the city of Oradea. The selected quantitative indicators for measuring tourist attractiveness indicate the high degree of attractiveness of the city of Oradea as a result of the tourism development activities undertaken by the local authorities.

Keywords Tourist attractiveness · Tourist destination · Tourist destination management · Indicators · Tourist attractiveness evaluation

F. Monica (✉) · B. Olimpia
University of Oradea, Oradea, Romania

S. L. Fotea et al. (eds.), *Navigating Through the Crisis: Business, Technological and Ethical Considerations*, Springer Proceedings in Business and Economics,
https://doi.org/10.1007/978-3-030-82751-9_3

3.1 Introduction

A constant interest of the World Tourism Organization (UNWTO) is that of offering support for the strategic development of the tourist destination through a competitive and efficient management. Therefore, an efficient management of tourist destinations implicitly leads to an increase in their attractiveness and competitiveness. The current challenge for the management of any tourist destination is being able to offer attractive alternatives for leisure activities.

The interest in studying the factors that determine the attractiveness of a tourist destination as well as the indicators measuring the attractiveness lead to a series of research that reflect the relative character of this factor of tourist demand. (Gearing et al., 1974; Ritchie & Zins, 1978; Hu & Ritchie, 1993; Vengesayi, 2003; Formica & Uysal, 2006; Kim & Perdue, 2011).

The attractiveness of a tourist destination sums up all natural and anthropic tourist resources, general and specific infrastructure, conditions for marketing products and tourist services, and the efficient management of the tourist destinations through strategic development programs of the tourist activities in the area.

This chapter attempts to illustrate the way in which efficient management of a tourist destination can lead to an increase in its attractiveness.

The first part of the chapter offers a theoretical approach to the attractiveness of tourist destination, the factors that determine the attractiveness of a destination, and the second part of the chapter focuses on a study on destination management regarded as a crucial element of tourist attractiveness.

For the case study, the city of Oradea was chosen (the residence of Bihor County, which is located only 10 km from the border with Hungary and 12 km from Băile Felix resort – the largest spa resort in Romania). Also, Oradea is famous for its monument buildings, built in different architectural styles: renaissance, baroque, romantic, secession, classical, and eclectic.

In June 2019, the city of Oradea also known as the "Capital of Art-Nouveau" received the "Golden Appeal" distinction for tourist attractiveness from FIJET (World Federation of Journalists and Travel Writers).

3.2 Literature Review

In order to understand and define destination attractiveness, it is important to distinguish between the notions of tourism attraction and destination attractiveness. As stated before, tourism attractions can be defined as specific destination features (such as climate, landscape features, activities in destinations) which have the ability to attract visitors. On the other hand, destination attractiveness has a more cognitive connotation as it is a mental construct that exists only in the minds of potential visitors. (Kresic & Prebezac, 2011)

The definition of the concept of tourist attractiveness in various specialized studies reflects its importance as a motivating factor of tourist demand.

The approach, formulated by Mayo and Jarvis (1981) allows the direct association of tourist attractiveness with the ability of a destination to meet the needs of tourists.

Another definition of this concept reflects the concern for satisfying the personal needs having as a starting point the subjective perception of tourists regarding the tourist destination. "The attractiveness of a travel destination reflects the feelings, beliefs, and opinions that an individual has about a destination's perceived ability to provide satisfaction in relation to his or her special vacation needs". (Hu & Ritchie, 1993, p. 25)

The definition formulated by Vengesayi indicates the relative character of the attributes of tourist attractiveness. "The attractiveness of a destination reflects the feelings and opinions of its visitors about the destination's perceived ability to satisfy their needs". (Vengesayi, 2003, p. 638).

Formica and Uysal (2006) define the concept of tourist attractiveness as the relationship between the demand and supply of tourist attractions.

Analysing the different points of view expressed above, tourist attractiveness of a destination can be defined as a set of factors that generates tourist motivation to choose a certain region/country, having at the same time the ability to offer multiple possibilities to spend free time.

The first research papers on identifying the elements that determine the attractiveness of tourist destinations date from the 1960s and 1970s.

Gearing (1974) sets the following 17 criteria for evaluating tourist attractiveness: "natural beauty"; "climate"; "artistic and architectural features"; "festivals"; "distinctive local features"; "fairs and exhibits"; "attitudes toward tourists"; "ancient ruins"; "religious significance"; "historical prominence"; "sports facilities"; "educational facilities"; "facilities conducive to health, rest, and tranquillity"; "nighttime recreation"; "shopping facilities"; "infrastructure above minimal touristic quality"; and "food and lodging facilities above minimal touristic quality". (Gearing et al., 1974, p. 3)

These criteria show the complexity of tourist activities as well as the determinant factors of tourist competitiveness.

Hu and Ritchie (1993) indicate two groups of attributes to evaluate the attractiveness of a destination: the universal attributes (landscape, climate) and the particular elements of tourist destinations.

Also, Laws (1995) indicates two categories of indicators of tourist attractiveness. The first category is comprised of natural, anthropic resources, and the second is comprised of tourist services.

Brida (2012) identifies the following elements that determine the tourist attractiveness of a town: "primary elements are cultural facilities (i.e. museums and art galleries), amusement and sport amenities, as well as physical and socioeconomic characteristics, which represent the main purpose for tourists to visit a city. Secondary elements (i.e. accommodation and shopping) and additional elements (i.e. transportation and tourist information)". (Brida et al., 2012, p.731).

The research studies on measuring/evaluating tourist attractiveness (Fotheringham et al., 2000; Calvo-Mora et al., 2011; Brida et al., 2012; Cugno et al., 2012; Bui, 2012; D'Hauteserre, 2015; Ariya et al., 2017) emphasise the difficulty of formulating universally accepted determining indicators for tourist activities.

In evaluating the attractiveness of a tourist destination, there are a number of subjective elements (needs, opinions, expectations, impressions, personal experience, age, education, social status of the tourist) as well as a number of objective elements (natural environment, natural and anthropic tourist objectives, tourist services supply, ways of free time, ease of access, political situation).

3.3 Methodology of the Research

The objectives of this research are:

- Identifying the factors that influence the tourist attractiveness of Oradea
- Selecting quantitative indicators measuring the tourist attractiveness for the studied tourist destination
- Analysing the role that management of tourist destinations has in increasing the attractiveness of Oradea

Research period: December 2019–July 2020

Steps taken in carrying out the research:

- Study of specialised literature
- Research on the chosen tourist destination-Oradea
- Formulating research hypotheses
- Studying sources in order to select necessary data for the research
- Processing the data provided by the National Institute of Statistics (Romania)
- Issuing conclusions

The city of Oradea is a destination that has some advantages as follow as:

- Proximity to 1 Mai Spa, Băile Felix (the most important balneoclimateric resort in Romania, tourists coming for treatment, relaxation in Băile Felix, also choose to visit the city)
- Proximity to the Hungarian border (a large number of foreign tourists visiting the city come from Hungary, the journey between Oradea-Budapest takes 3 hours by car)
- Cultural heritage of the city: "Baroque Palace, Roman Catholic Basilica, Canonical Row, Palace of Finance, State Theater, State Philharmonic, Capuchin Monastery, Astoria Hotel, Arcadia Children's and Youth Theater, Black Eagle Palace, Moskovits Miksa Palace, Residence of the Romanian Orthodox Episcopate, Ullmann Palace, Apollo Palace, Palace of Justice, Zion Neolog Synagogue, Oradea City Hall Palace, Greek Catholic Episcopal Palace in Oradea, St. Ladislaus Church, Moon Church, Oradea Fortress, City Hall Tower, The

Darvas House" (Integrated Urban Development Strategy of Oradea 2017–2023, pp. 115–120)

- Business tourism: due to the proximity to the Hungarian border, the city is transited by people travelling for business purposes and choosing to book accommodation in town. Also, local authorities run four industrial parks (located 4 km away from the border with Hungary), where 90 companies operate, mostly with foreign capital. During the week (Monday–Thursday), the available accommodation in Oradea is mostly booked by people coming to town for business purposes.

After having researched a number of papers that evaluate/measure the attractiveness of a tourist destination through different research methods (Ritchie & Zins, 1978→mail questionnaire; Hu & Ritchie, 1993→survey; Formica & Uysal, 2006→qualitative and quantitative statistical analysis; Cracolici & Nijkamp, 2008→survey; Chen et al., 2010→survey; Lee et al., 2010→expert panel; Iatu & Bulai, 2011→regional analysis by Smith; Calvo-Mora et al., 2011→concept mapping; Brida et al., 2012→survey; Cugno et al., 2012→data from Italian National Institute of Statistics; Kim & Perdue, 2011→Internet survey; D'Hauteserre, 2015→qualitative analysis and observation; Ariya et al., 2017→questionnaire) the next chosen step was analysing the statistic data regarding the studies tourist destination available at the National Statistics Institute of Romania.

The objective of the data analysis was to identify a different method to measure the attractiveness of a tourist destination (the majority of studies had used the questionnaire).

A total of 6 quantitative indicators had been chosen (5 out of a total of 40 indicators had been taken over from the National Institute of Statistics): tourist reception structures with tourist accommodation facilities function by types of structures and counties (number of units of accommodation), existing tourist accommodation by types of tourist reception structures, counties (number of places in accommodation), tourist accommodation availability by types of tourist reception structures and counties (number of availabilities/days), arrivals of tourists in tourist accommodation by types of structures and counties (number of people/tourists), overnight stays in tourist accommodation by types of structures and counties (number of overnight stays). In addition to the indicators analysed from the National Institute of Statistics, average length of stay indicator was also analysed.

These indicators have been chosen because they are frequently used (in research studies, statistical yearbooks) to indicate data on tourism activity in a certain destination/region. The National Institute of Statistics, Romania, collects every year statistical data from tourist accommodation structures with an existing accommodation capacity of at least five beds.

The existing (installed) tourist accommodation capacity represents the number of tourist accommodations registered most recently in reception documents, homologation, and classification of tourist accommodation, excluding the extra beds that can be installed at request. The National Institute of Statistics used the following method for collecting data: self-registration and questionnaires completed online by tourist accommodation enterprises (National Institute of Statistics Romania, February, 2020).

The local authorities from of Oradea have elaborated in 2008 the Tourism Marketing Strategy for the Oradea Historic Centre in which the vision of tourist development of the city was formulated: "revival of the Historic Centre of Oradea and Oradea Fortress, European cultural tourist complex, in order to introduce in the tourist circuit a responsible exploitation of natural tourist resources of Oradea". (Oradea Historic Centre tourist marketing strategy, 2008, p .50).

In order to achieve the vision of tourist development of the city, the local authorities have formulated a series of strategic objectives:

- Achieving the partnership between tourism and patrimony management
- Improving the quality of tourist experience
- Improving the spatial and financial accessibility of visitors
- Promoting the city as a cultural tourist destination

In order to fulfil the above formulated objectives, the local authorities carried out a series of concrete activities: establishing an interdepartmental coordination office for the programs and projects in the historical centre; making the inventory of buildings and owners in the historic centre, technical expertise of monument buildings and rehabilitation of historic buildings; revitalization of Oradea Fortress – design and execution of restoration works in the Fortress; rules and regulations on terraces and outdoor sales spaces in the area of the historic centre; developing and implementing a public lighting concept for the historic centre; redevelopment of the historic centre of the city; inventory of tourist interest points by categories of routes, design, and creation of information panels for each tourist destination; setting up a tourist information centre in the historic centre; developing the "Visit Oradea" Campaign (Tourism Marketing Strategy for the Oradea Historic Center); setting up the Association for the Promotion of Tourism in Oradea and Region – with the role of promoting and developing tourism in Oradea and in the region; and designing a brand of the city "Art Nouveau, Life Nouveau".

3.3.1 Analysis of Data Provided by the National Institute of Statistics

The period chosen for the case study is 2007–2019. 2007 was chosen as the first year of the research in order to show the contribution of the management of tourist destination/management performed by authorities in increasing the attractiveness of the city, considering the setting up of the marketing strategy of the city in 2008 by local authorities and the implementing of the first projects for the development of tourist activities in the historic centre of the city (Table 3.1 and Figs. 3.1, 3.2, 3.3, 3.4, 3.5, 3.6).

Table 3.1 Data containing the quantitative indicators selected for the tourist destination Oradea

Year	Number of accommodation facilities	Accommodation capacity	Number of availabilities-/days	Number of tourists	Number of Overnight stays
2007	11	777	282693	67467	110415
2008	14	959	322648	66630	114203
2009	18	1061	390764	63920	106782
2010	22	1254	444673	71388	119362
2011	29	1727	524309	88520	141416
2012	30	1869	616108	110900	153502
2013	27	1850	631862	106187	156396
2014	28	2687	862474	128746	277706
2015	37	2514	1019768	163416	360432
2016	37	2525	1131831	190022	421062
2017	38	2608	1136373	223362	407225
2018	43	2709	1087021	250395	459210
2019	43	2733	915730	236793	394784

Source: National Institute of Statistics, Romania, http://statistici.insse.ro:8077/tempo-online/#/pages/tables/insse-table accessed on 30 July 2020

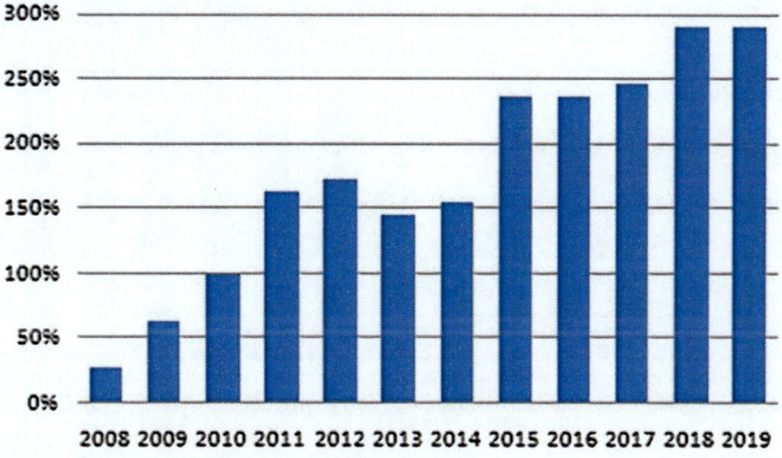

Fig. 3.1 The accommodation facilities since 2007

3.4 Conclusion

This chapter attempts to illustrate the contribution of local authorities in increasing the tourist attractiveness of a destination tourist destination. In order to support these hypotheses, the chapter provides an analysis of the statistical data on tourist frequency for the studied destination.

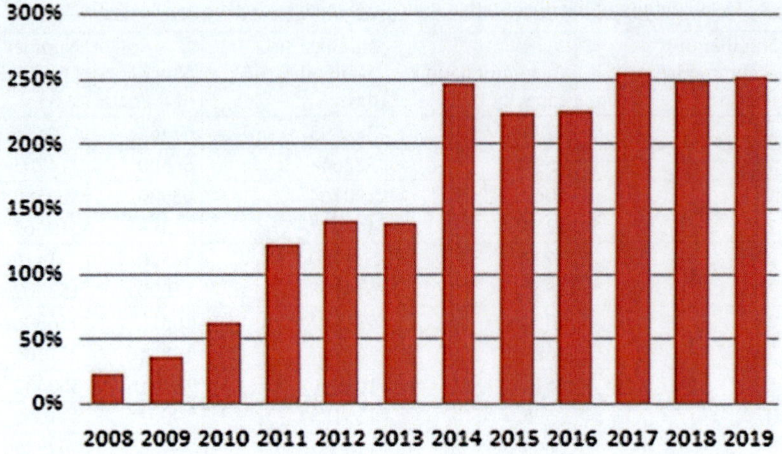

Fig. 3.2 The percentage growth rate of accommodation facilities since 2007

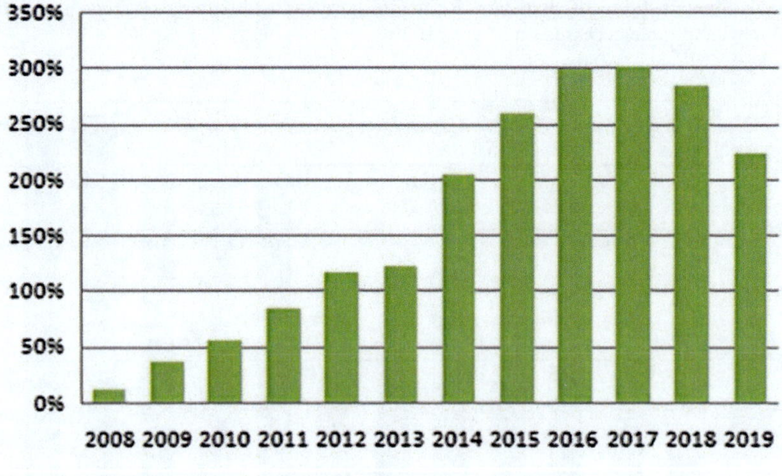

Fig. 3.3 The procentual evolution of availabilities/days since 2007

The following results had been obtained as a result of data analysis from the National Institute of Statistics, Romania: analysing the indicator "Tourist accommodation by types of structures for the city of Oradea from 2007 to 2019", we can acknowledge an increase in the number of tourist accommodations by 290.90% in 2019 compared to the reference year 2007; As far as the indicator "Existent tourist accommodation capacity by types of tourist accommodation structures for Oradea", we can acknowledge an increase in the number of places in tourist accommodation units by 251.73% in 2019 compared to 2007.

For the indicator "Tourist accommodation capacity by types of tourist accommodation structures (number of availabilities/days), there is an increase by 223.93% in 2019 compared to 2007. Analysing the evolution of the number of tourists during

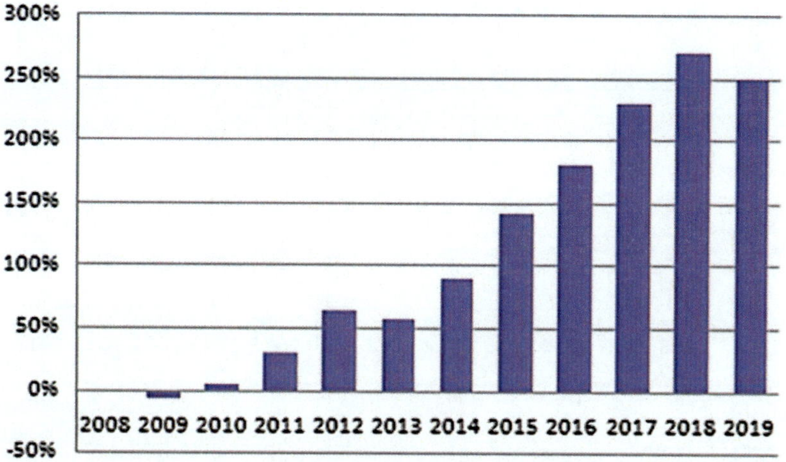

Fig. 3.4 The procentual evolution of the number of tourists since 2007

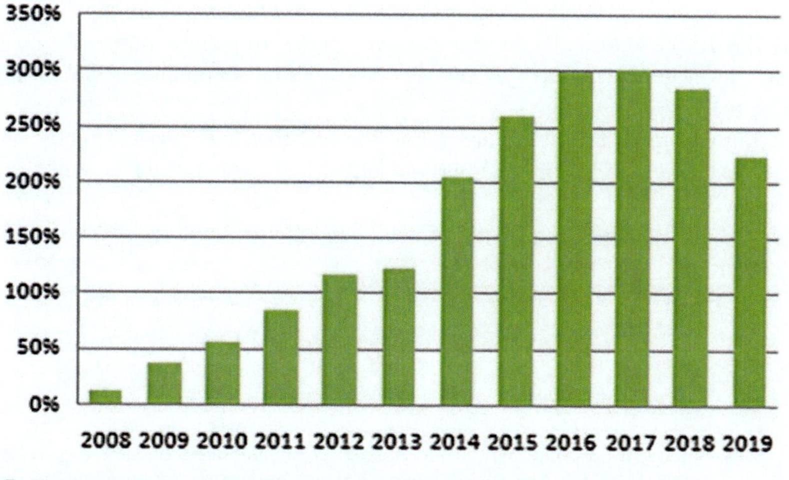

Fig. 3.5 The procentual evolution of the number of overnight stays since 2007

the period 2007–2019, we can notice an increase in the number of tourists by 250.97% in 2019 compared to 2007. For the indicator "Overnight stays in tourist accommodation by type of structures" in Oradea, there is an increase in the number of overnight stays by 257.54% in 2019 compared to 2007.

As far as the indicator "Average length of stay" for the period 2007–2019 is concerned, the average length of stay increased by only 1.84% compared to 2007, although there were significant increases such as 31.90% in 2014 and 35.58% in 2015–2016.

The indicators selected to measure the tourist attractiveness of Oradea show an increase in the interest of tourists to visit the studied destination. This increase is

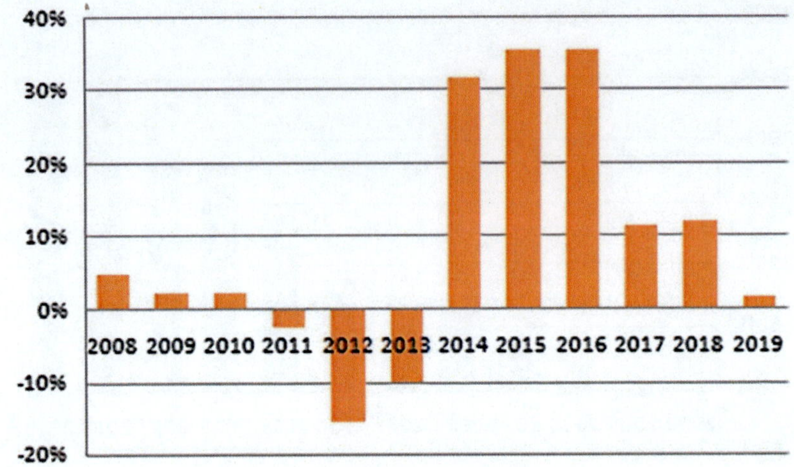

Fig. 3.6 The procentual evolution of the average length of stay in tourist accommodation since 2007

largely due to the actions taken by local authorities (implementation of a coherent tourism development strategy, intense promotional campaigns, public-private partnership).

The limitations of this study are due to the fact that the tourist attractiveness of Oradea was analysed using quantitative indicators. For further research, direct methods will be used for perception analysis (e.g. the questionnaire), in order to identify the profile of tourists visiting the city and the personal reasons for choosing this destination.

References

Ariya, G., Wishitemi, B., & Sitati, N. (2017). Tourism destination attractiveness as perceived by tourists. Visiting Lake Nakuru National Park, Kenya. *International Journal of Research in Tourism and Hospitality, 3*(4), 1–13. https://doi.org/10.1515/ejthr-2017-0014

Brida, J. G., Meleddu, M., & Pulina, M. (2012). Understanding urban tourism attractiveness: The case of the Archaeological Ötzi Museum in Bolzano. *Journal of Travel Research, 51*(6), 730–741. pp 731–741. https://doi.org/10.1177%2F0047287512437858.

Bui, T. T. (2012). Application of contextual approach for measuring tourism destination attractiveness. *Journal of Science., 70*(1), 217–226. https://doi.org/10.1177%2F004728759303200204.

Calvo-Mora, A., Berbel-Pineda, J. M., Perianez R., & Suarez, E. M. (2011). Determining factors of a city's tourism attractiveness. *Tourism & Management Studies* No 7, International English Edition, ISSN:1646-2408, pp 9–23.

Chen, C., Chen, S. H., & Lee, H. T. (2010). The destination competitiveness of Kinmen's tourism industry: Exploring the interrelationship between tourist perceptions, service performance, customer satisfaction and sustainable tourism. *Journal of Sustainable Tourism, 19*(2), 247–264. https://doi.org/10.1080/09669582.2010.517315

Cracolici, M. F., & Nijkamp, P. (2008). The attractiveness and competitiveness of tourist destinations: A study of Southern Italian regions. *Tourism Management, 30*, 336–344. https://doi.org/10.1016/j.tourman.2008.07.006

Cugno, M., Grimmer, M., & Viassone, M. (2012). Measuring local tourism attractiveness: The Case of Italy. ANZAM, ISBN: 9780987415806. pp. 1–22.

D'Hauteserre, A. (2015). Affect theory and the attractivity of destinations. *Annals of Tourism Research, 55*(C), 77–89. https://doi.org/10.1016/j.annals.2015.09.001

Formica, S., & Uysal, M. (2006). Destination attractiveness based on supply and demand evaluations: An analytical Framework. *Journal of Travel Research, 44*, 418–430. 10.1177%2F0047287506286714.

Fotheringham, A. S., Champion, T., Wymer, C., & Coombes, M. (2000). Measuring destination attractivity: A migration example. *International Journal of Population Geography, 6*, 391–421. https://doi.org/10.1002/1099-1220(200011/12)6:6%3C391::AID-IJPG200%3E3.0.CO;2-5.

Gearing, C. E., Swart, W. W., & Var, T. (1974). Establishing a measure of touristic attractiveness. *Journal of Travel Research., 12*(4), 1–8. https://doi.org/10.1177/004728757401200401.

http://www.insse.ro/. Accessed 30.07.2020.

http://www.oradea.ro/fisiere/module_fisiere/26163/SIDU%20Oradea.pdf. Accessed 16.02.2020.

http://www.oradea.ro/fisiere/userfiles/orasul_turistic/strategia%20marketing%20turistic.pdf. (03.02.2020)

https://www.adlo.ro/. Accessed 09.03.2020.

Hu, Y., & Ritchie, J. R. B. (1993). Measuring destination attractiveness: A contextual approach. *Journal of Travel Research, 5*, 25–34. https://doi.org/10.1177%2F004728759303200204.

Iatu, C., & Bulai, M. (2011). New approach in evaluating tourism attractiveness in the region of Moldavia (Romania). *International Journal of Energy and Environment, 5*(2), 165–174.

Kim, D., & Perdue, R. R. (2011). The influence of image on destination attractiveness. *Journal of Travel & Tourism Marketing, 28*(3), 225–239. https://doi.org/10.1080/10548408.2011.562850

Kresic, D., & Prebezac, D. (2011). Index of destination attractiveness as a tool for destination attractiveness assessment. *Tourism Original Scientific Paper, 59*(4), 497–517.

Laws, E. (1995). Tourist destination management: Issues, analysis and policies, routledge, New York, NY in Kozak, M., Rimmington, M. (1998). Benchmarking: destination attractiveness and small hospitality business performance. *International Journal of Contemporary Hospitality Management, 10*(5), pp.184–188. http://doi.org/10.1108/09596119810227767

Lee, C., Huang, H., & Yeh, H. (2010). Developing an evaluation model for destination attractiveness: Sustainable forest recreation tourism in Taiwan. *Journal of Sustainable Tourism., 18*(6), 811–828. https://doi.org/10.1080/09669581003690478

Mayo, E. J., & Jarvis, L. P. (1981). *The psychology of leisure travel. Effective marketing and selling of travel services*. CBI Publishing Company.

Ritchie, J. R. B., & Zins, M. (1978). Culture as determinant of the attractiveness of a tourism region. *Annals of Tourism Research, V*(2), 252–267. https://doi.org/10.1016/0160-7383(78)90223-2

Vengesayi, S. (2003). A conceptual model of tourism destination competitiveness and attractiveness. ANZMAC, ISBN: 0868039837, pp. 637–647.

Chapter 4
Mapping the Performance of Smart Cities in the European Union

Adriana AnaMaria Davidescu, Catalin Corneliu Ghinararu, and Eduard Mihai Manta

Abstract Smart city defines an urban area which incorporates the needed communication and information technologies to boost the performance and quality of urban services, such as transportation, utilities, and energy to decrease resource consumption, waste, and total costs and to increase also the quality of life for its citizens by using intelligent technologies. A circular city incorporates the assumptions of the circular economy in all its functional areas, establishing a renewable and accessible urban system, abundant in design. These cities desire to defeat the concept of waste, carry them active at their biggest value at any time, and are activated by technology. A circular city aims to generate accomplishment, increase habitability, and enhance the flexibility of the city and its people, seeking to decouple the value creation from the consumption of finite resources. Cities will play a considerable role in a worldwide transition to a circular economy. A lot of factors are merely position cities to drive the worldwide transition to the circular economy. They will have many benefits: proximity of materials and people in the urban space, efficient markets, the ability of governments to model urban planning and policy, and the digital revolution. In this context, the aim of the chapter is to determine the main determinants of smart cities and also to measure the smart city performance building a composite index for smart cities of 28 European countries and Schengen area using principal component analysis combined with cluster analysis based on 22 variables at the level of 2018. The empirical results revealed that green spaces, finding a job, schools, citizens' safety, and the integration of expats are the main determinants of

A. A. Davidescu (✉)
National Scientific Research Institute for Labour and Social Protection, Bucharest University of Economic Studies, Bucharest, Romania
e-mail: adriana.alexandru@csie.ase.ro

C. C. Ghinararu
National Scientific Research Institute for Labour and Social Protection, Bucharest, Romania

E. M. Manta
Doctoral School of Cybernetics and Statistics, Bucharest University of Economic Studies, Bucharest, Romania

S. L. Fotea et al. (eds.), *Navigating Through the Crisis: Business, Technological and Ethical Considerations*, Springer Proceedings in Business and Economics,
https://doi.org/10.1007/978-3-030-82751-9_4

European smart cities. The classification of cities, according to these components, revealed that Zurich and Oslo are the smartest cities in Europe, while Athens and Rome were situated on the opposite side. Switzerland and Norway are the countries with the best overall performance in terms of smart city performance, all cities of these two countries belonging to the first category. In addition, most cities from the Nordic countries, along with some from Austria and Germany, got the best performance. On the opposite side, there are the cities of Italy, Greece, Bulgaria, and Cyprus. An interesting finding is the fact that Italy as a whole performs poorly; four of the cities from the last positions in the ranking are Italian cities, namely, Rome, Venice, Genoa, and Palermo. In the case of Romanian cities, the results were divided. On the one hand, there is Bucharest and Craiova, with the modest performance, and on the other hand, there is Cluj-Napoca, Timişoara, and Oradea with an acceptable level of performance and Iaşi, Constanţa and Braşov registering average values. The Romanian leader in terms of smart city performance is considered to be Cluj-Napoca. Cluj has reached Western standards in terms of smart cities.

Keywords Smart city · Circular economy · Principal component analysis · Panel data · EU countries

4.1 Introduction

A smart city defines an urban area which incorporates the needed communication and information technologies to raise the performance and the quality of urban services like energy, utilities, and transportation; to decrease resource consumption, waste, and total costs; and to increase also the quality of life for its citizens by using intelligent technologies. A circular city incorporates the idea of the circular economy in its functional areas, establishing a renewable and accessible urban system, abundant in design. These cities aim to remove the concept of waste, support them active at their highest usefulness at any time, and are activated by digital technology. A circular city aims to create prosperity, increase habitability, and upgrade the flexibility of the city and of the citizens, while seeking to decouple the merit creation from the consumption of finite resources.

The present chapter aims to evaluate the performance of smart cities in the EU countries and those which are part of the Schengen area. Nevertheless, a secondary purpose of the chapter is to analyze the Romanian cities considered to be smart cities in the agreed ranking. In order to do that, multidimensional techniques have been applied, using a dataset mainly from Urban Audit database 2018. Thus, the main components of smart city performance have been identified using the principal component analysis, and furthermore, the cities have been classified based on these synthetic indicators using the cluster method. Also, a composite index has been determined in order to evaluate the performance of European cities.

The chapter is organized as follows. The second section is dedicated to the presentation of theoretical considerations presenting the concept of smart city, circular economy, as well as circular smart city, highlighting also Romania's perspective in the European context of circular economy and smart city. The third section was dedicated to the presentation of data and methodology pointing out the main sources of data and the main techniques used within the research.

The fourth section presents the main empirical results highlighting the main European poles of smart cities, while the last section revealed the main conclusions and future recommendations.

4.2 Theoretical Considerations

4.2.1 Circular Economy in Smart Cities

As major drivers of economic growth, cities use their tools, knowledge, and skills that lead the circular economy agenda and deliver the economic, environmental, and social benefits of the cities. Our cities are struggling with the effects of our waste collection economy. By the year 2050, three-quarters of the population will be living in cities, where we already consume 75% of our natural resources, we generate 60–80% of the greenhouse gases, and we produce over 50% of global waste. Therefore, we need to find solutions for the current environmental challenges in order to support cities to become thriving, viable, and resilient. The implementation of the circular economy will help the city leaders to meet their priorities, strategic and climate goals, allowing them to establish long-term prosperity. The circular economy offers the opportunity to respond to these challenges by rethinking how people use materials, leading to new ways of creating values.

A city is the place where most materials are used and wasted, where buildings, vehicles, and products are constantly subordinated. The implementation of a circular economic vision into the cities can bring a major, social, and environmental economic progress. This may favor the emergence of three main dimensions:

- A thriving city where economic productivity growth is driven by reducing congestion, eliminating waste, and reducing costs; the economic growth and business opportunities can support skills development and job creation.
- A living city with improved air quality and urban health, reducing carbon dioxide emissions and pollution and increasing social interactions.
- A rugged city which includes the preservation of the materials that are in use and the reduction of the virgin material; this works with both local and distributed production capacity.

These benefits can be achieved by modifying the projects, changing the use of the financial resources and the way urban systems are planned. This vision brings its contribution into addressing the major priorities regarding the country's housing, mobility, and economic development. The development goals including the reduction of the greenhouse gas emissions and the ways of adapting to these effects can bring an important climate change and would also support the 2030 Sustainability and Development model.

In the transition process to a circular economy, city administrations are uniquely positioned and allow the stakeholders and the private sector to lead and engage in the process, using a wide range of policy levers and measures at their level. Ultimately, this is a collaborative transition to a prosperous future in which cities are being viable and resilient, using materials in accordance with the principles of the circular economy.

In the cities that incorporate the principles of circular economy, there is greater proximity between where people live, where they work, and where they spend their time. The air becomes drier if switched to zero-emission engines and congestion is reduced as common transit growth. There will be more people walking to the office, stimulating their health and interacting with local businesses and communities. Valuable lands, previously dedicated to roads and cars, should be cleared for green spaces, commerce, offices, houses, and recreation. The city layout and its design change the way materials and products move around them. Instead of "throwing away" materials at the landfill or incinerate them, a new system distributed by the resource management, nutrient flows and vice versa, logistics, return sorting, and reuse of possible products can keep materials in use.

In parallel with the urban plan, the circular economy principles transform the planning process into cities. Infrastructure, vehicles, buildings, and products are designed to be durable, adaptable, modular, and easy to maintain. The materials are not harmful; they come from renewable sources of raw materials as they can be composted, recycled, and reused. We can claim that renewable energy has great power over cities and nature inspires the design. Buildings, vehicles, and products are assembled using waste design techniques. Local ingenuity and skill levels increase as the emphasis is on production decentralization and distribution in cities. With the support of the digital material banks and the composition of buildings, vehicles, and products already in place, it is allowed to reuse them. People gain access to the things they need – be it space, products, or transportation in any way they want. This can be done by sharing, rather than holding, to which people and neighbors can connect, but also their communities, or even through product-to-service contracts. The products are not for single use, people repair and refurbish their products, and these activities start with the individual and continue with the community contribution and at the commercial levels. Vehicles and infrastructure are operated and maintained from roads to street lights so that materials, energy, and water are used efficiently. The buildings are renovated, a fact which would improve the way they are used and operated. By applying these methods, new opportunities and jobs may emerge, and cities that follow the principles of the circular economy may become more prosperous.

The Ellen MacArthur Foundation recognizes cities as a main point for moving to a circular economy. This has influenced cities and the circular economy through leaders, people with the belief that cities based on the circular economy explore the role of digital technology. The efforts are based on evidence and understanding the level of cities based on the national governments that have developed "a set of tools for decision-makers" through research (Banks et al., 2018). Moreover, regionally focused work, such as the circular economy, is an opportunity for urban and industrial innovation for a competitive Europe, providing evidence based on the benefits applicable to principles such as mobility, the built environment, products, and food (Mac Arthur et al., 2018).

Working with companies, governments, cities, and NGOs, systemic initiatives increase unprecedented levels, cooperating across sectors. The value chain to unlock innovation and the new system of solutions is becoming more and more unified. Where creativity, innovation, and growth intersect, cities represent the driving force of the global economy, and this happens because about 54% of the people worldwide live in core areas and cities represent 85% of worldwide GDP. Cities are also materials and nutrients accumulation accounting for 75% of natural resource consumption. In the next decades, cities will become more and more important, and so far, higher significant infrastructure rates of urbanization are expected.

An overview of the most relevant studies in the literature is presented in Table 4.1.

4.2.2 The Vision of a Circular Smart City

A circular city incorporates the assumptions of the circular economy in the entire functional areas, building a renewable and accessible urban system, abundant in design. The aspiration of the cities is to eliminate the theory of waste, carry them active at their maximum value at any time, and are activated by digitalism – a circular city intent to generate expansion, boost the habitability, and develop the flexibility of the city and its citizens while searching to decouple the consumption of finite resources.

A built environment that is modular and flexible designed together with the supply of healthful materials boost the nature of inhabitants' life and curtail the use of virgin materials. It will be completed by adopting adequate techniques and will be able to use office space and housing in a common and flexible way. The building components will be retained and revived when necessary, while the constructions will be used to achieve, rather than consume, food and power by providing water, nutrients, materials, and energy.

An accessible and efficient urban mobility system structures the mobility, which will include public transport by car in order as a flexible result. The transport will be electrically mechanized, automated, and shared. Traffic jam and air pollution will be a story from the past, and disproportionate infrastructure will be transformed to provide another of the citizen's needs. The focal point of automobile design will be efficiency, durability, remanufacturing, and easy maintenance. A metropolitan bioeconomy in which food will be rebounded to the ground, in a convenient way, minimizes waste and generates value. Over urban agriculture, the city will be apt to backlog its own food, restate food, and deplete and reuse wasted water in the local

Table 4.1 The most important specialized literature studies on smart cities topic

Study	Location	Content	Methodology	Results	Limitations
Ellen Mac Arthur (2019)	United Kingdom	Data available for 29 countries (source: The World Bank)	Descriptive statistics Composite indicator	As major drivers of economic growth, cities have the tools, knowledge, and skills to manage the economic agenda and unlock the social, environmental, and economic aspects.	The choice of indicators depends not only on the desired purpose – on the goals that a nation is trying to achieve – but also on the public.
Ellen Mac Arthur (2019)	United Kingdom	Data available for 29 countries (source: The World Bank)	Descriptive statistics Correlation analysis Regression analysis	Initial exploration of the intersection of two emerging megatrends: artificial intelligence and circular economy. Built on insights from over 40 surveys, the work of experts, the study is a collaboration between the Ellen MacArthur Foundation and Google, with the support of research and analysis provided by McKinsey & Company.	The surveys targeted only people who already knew the concept of Artificial Intelligence.
Laura Roman (2018)	Romania	The World Bank and Eurostat data	Descriptive statistics Composite indicator	The paper proposes a synthesis of eco-innovation within the European Union.	
Vanessa Prieto-Sandoval (2017)	Spain	Own data	Descriptive statistics	This study carried out a systematic review of the literature that led to four main results: a map of the knowledge of the circular economy, an analysis of the main notions of the concept, principles, and determinants of a circular economy. Finally, this study reveals some remarkable examples of ecological innovations developed to be implemented in the circular economy.	Data extracted from surveys and researches.

Study	Location	Content	Methodology	Results	Limitations
Andre Luis Guesed (2018)	Brazil	Own data	Descriptive statistics Main component analysis	In this study, there was conducted a comprehensive and detailed literary review, in which 20 potential smart city drivers were identified. The drivers were priorities from the results of a survey conducted with 807 professionals working in the field in question.	Data extracted from surveys and researches.
Vinod Kumar (2017)	India	Smart cities indicators	Descriptive statistics	Emerging models of the urbanization world show different scenarios on different continents, requiring different approaches, policies, and strategies. Smart economic development of the city, suitable for different cities, countries, and continents.	
Joanna Williams (2019)	United Kingdom	Circular economy indicators (2017)	Descriptive statistics	A circular approach to the way we manage resources consumed and produced in cities – materials, energy, water, and land.	
Anders Wijkman (2018)	Netherlands	Climate indicators	Descriptive statistics	The cities of Europe are now joining in a project that focuses on a common circular economy, which seeks to identify best practices and to act as examples to be followed in the rapid pace of circularity.	
Robert G. Hollands (2008)	United Kingdom	Smart city indicators	Descriptive statistics	Conducting the profit motive of global high-tech companies, in collusion with the city's tendency to be governed by a competitive form of „urban entrepreneurship", left little room for ordinary people to participate in the smart city.	Data extracted from surveys and researches.

(continued)

Table 4.1 (continued)

Study	Location	Content	Methodology	Results	Limitations
Patrice Novo (2017)	France	Natural resource indicators in the European Union	Descriptive statistics	How can cities, businesses, and industries increase growth despite the resource deficit? First, they can begin by measuring consumption to manage them more efficiently. Then each of us can move away from a linear pattern of consumption. We can accelerate this transition today, thanks to IoT*, to the digital revolution.	
Ferrovial (2019)	Spain	Educational indicators in the European Union (2016)	Descriptive statistics	Rail services join the main forces with other large companies in "Smarter Cities 2025: Building a Business Plan and Sustainable Financing," a program run by ESI Thought Lab, a think tank of the consulting firm Econsult Solutions. This initiative will analyze more than 100 cities and their models of urban innovation to select current best practices of the smart cities field.	Data extracted from surveys and researches.
Jon Walker (2019)	United States of America	AI indicators	Descriptive statistics	Helping officials learn more about how people use cities. Improving the infrastructure and optimizing the use of these resources. Improving public safety in cities.	Data extracted from surveys and researches.

and locked coil to produce fish, fruits, and vegetables. Such a system could offer even higher resistance, diversity, and profit, by generating electricity from wasted water and biofuels. These will provide further revenues in the city, leveraging the use of nutrients and materials that are already in use. Production organizations encourage the formation of "local value bubbles." This could mean higher local production and higher exchanges of profit in local economies. Factories (encouraged to produce locally will distribute and adjust), shared resource banks (for supply and demand of materials), and applications (at the broker exchange of materials, services, and goods) represent local systems of circular production.

According to Ellen MacArthur Foundation, the principles of the circular economy applied in the city could support decision-makers in achieving the objectives in different ways: "releasing pressure on municipal services and budgets, increasing disposable income, encouraging innovation to enrich the urban economy, reducing carbon emissions, increasing conditions for living in the city, the potential to determine a positive impact on employment opportunities in the city" (MacArthur et al., 2015). The development path of the circular economy in Europe could lead to a 32% growth of the economy by reducing the consumption of raw materials by 2030 and to 53% by 2050, as compared to today. The reduced consumption of raw materials and the intensity of the material used in the economy imply expense reduction and waste management. In addition, public spending on products that could be reduced by the purchase of services or products given through innovative new business models, like performance-based trade models, would again result in lower spending from the stateside (World Bank, 2016).

The ambition to change straight products with products that are "circular designed" can build overturn logistics networks, supporting the circular economy through a strong incentive for contemporary ideas, and could thus provide new sources of innovation in cities. Finding new ways to keep components and materials to their biggest value will boost the development of new business models and will create an urban environment in which communities focus on decision-makers (repair and renovation, exchange of platforms, etc.).

The Mac Arthur Foundation has demonstrated for European countries, a circular economy through their evolution direction in order to bisect carbon dioxide emissions by the end of 2030, compared to today's level. The activities of the circular economy can also influence some aspects of the city's habitability. This would include reducing time wasted in traffic; In Europe, a circular economic path for transportation could decrease time by about 60% by the end of 2050. In addition, a circular economy could have a good impact on air quality (using suitable materials in building construction) and could decrease the pollution of air (through efficient mobility systems).

Cities will show a substantial part in a worldwide transition to a circular economy. Multiple factors that hardly position cities to drive the worldwide changeover to the circular economy. They will have many benefits: closeness of materials and people in the urban surroundings, the digital revolution, and the ability of governments to build urban policy and planning, efficient markets (Novo and Da Silva, 2017). The large concentration of data, resources, capital, and talents on a smaller geographical territory is one of the main characteristics of the cities. Concentration of people allows the exchange and reuse of models (if they are produced or active) being proposed by different users, usually in a neighborhood or in a smaller geographical unit.

The new circular economic business of the models is more susceptible in appearance, at present, and by supplying large, varied materials, the demand being of great potential on the market for the goods and services derived from them. Local administrations have influence on urban planning and a broad infrastructure, local business development, transportation system design, urban, the local job market, and municipal taxes. Hence, local mayors can play an active role in consolidating the assumptions of the circular economy into all policies and urban functions (William, 2017). Since investments must be highly applied to cities, they represent a huge opportunity for local authorities to apply and use them using the assumptions of the circular economy from the beginning. This contributes to the "linear blocking" that exists in the already developed markets (it is necessary to develop the infrastructure and maximize the reduction of traffic congestion). Local governments can use pilot projects locally as showcases to involve national business pillars in this process. In case of lack of leadership at the regional or national level, governments must involve. In addition, research suggests that at the root of local leadership is the trust of citizens, suggesting a better level of influence.

The digital era has allowed a crucial change in how the economy works and has the power to transition to a circular economy, by developing dematerialization, virtualization on the products used, and flows of information and materials based on criticism. Technologies such as asset labeling, data management, and geospatial information have been identified as accelerators of circular economic activity in cities.

4.2.3 Romania's Perspective in the European Context of Circular Economy and Smart City

According to the Eco-Innovational Scoreboard Country Profile, Romania ranks 23rd in the Eco-Innovation Scoreboard for all 28 countries in the European Union. Although Romania is a relatively large country, with a population of 19 million inhabitants, the country's economy is among the least developed in the European Union but experiencing a relatively stable GDP growth, over 4.5% since the year 2016. The Romanian government has consistently placed low-priority environmental policies at the national level and has made small steps towards legislation that could stimulate the circular economy. Romania is a long way from reaching an ambitious level for a sustainable environment.

As circular economy initiatives have begun to develop, more government support is needed to increase them and make them more efficient. While a major step was taken regarding the adoption of the General Waste Management Plan in 2017, one of the waste management objectives was thus achieved, one of the main conditions set by the European Union to receive funds, to eliminate the tax on cars and so on. At the moment, there is no integrated strategy for the circular economy in Romania, and the regulatory framework represents the most important barrier that companies perceive in adopting efficient measures of resource use and, in general, in business development investments. Romania is facing problems in the environment and waste management field. The application of environmental problems is represented by high air pollution, difficult access to clean water, poor treatment of wastewater, and unsustainable resource management practices, including difficulties in the field of waste management and inadequate infrastructure. Only 5% of all types of waste are recycled in Romania, the rest of the waste being dumped or, in a few cases, incinerated. Only 85% of Romanian households are connected to waste collection services. There is a combination of cultural, social, and economic factors that impede progress on these dimensions, accompanied by low environmental awareness and reduced willingness to cooperate between the public and private sectors. The European Commission's analysis regarding the performance of eco-innovation is based on the 28 countries of the European Union in 2017. The eco-innovation index shows the achievement of a country's ecological innovation compared to the average of the European Union. The index was calculated on the basis of 16 indicators that were aggregated into five components: eco-innovation activity, eco-innovation input, environmental result, ecological results, and socio-economic result.

Romania ranks 23rd in the analysis, obtaining a score of 65. It indicates that it is well below the average level of the European Union. The best performers are Sweden, Finland, Germany, and Luxembourg, with scores between 139 and 144 (Fig. 4.1).

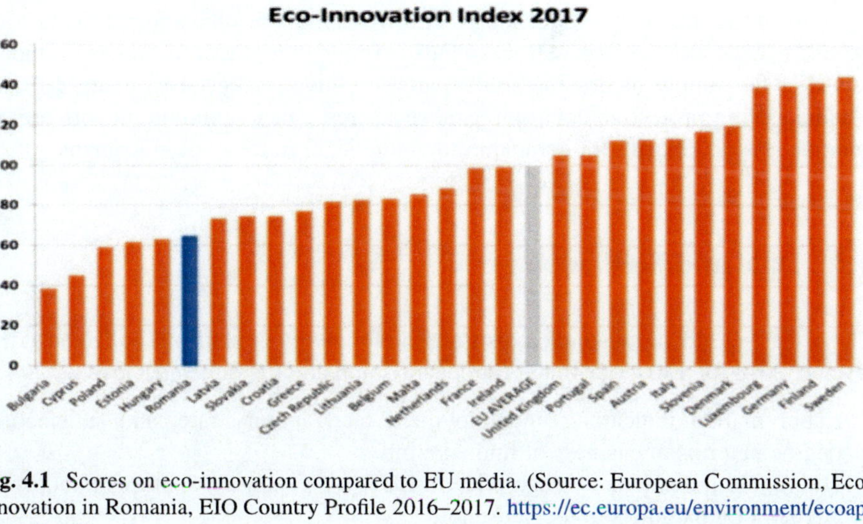

Fig. 4.1 Scores on eco-innovation compared to EU media. (Source: European Commission, Eco-innovation in Romania, EIO Country Profile 2016–2017. https://ec.europa.eu/environment/ecoap/romania_en)

Generally, Romanian companies do not worry about the environment and are mainly determined by the compliance with the regulations in their environmental practices, but they think opportunistically and consider the costs in their choices. However, there are signs that businesses are becoming more and more involved in self-auditing their waste management practices, trying to find potential opportunities and improve waste management, and thus also raise awareness of the fact that the environment must be protected. A percentage of 70% of the companies monitored by Green Business Index Romania collect more than 75% of the waste, although their number decreases.

Lately, Romania has had a favorable economic environment, showing more and more potential with economic growth in recent years. The Romanian Government, although unstable, has also imposed and changed taxes for environmental protection in recent years, thus discouraging companies to invest in this branch. In 2017, in one of the surveys carried out by the EIB that targeted the Romanian companies, they faced all kinds of challenges depending on the activity field. About 60% of the construction and manufacturing companies encountered difficulties in finding specialized people, thus causing a barrier to invest in these areas of activity. The common economic factors adopt the practices of the circular economy in Romania.

On one hand, there are clear negative factors due to the costs which are considered barriers to the adoption of environmental protection measures. One in three companies in Romania charges costs for protecting the environment as a burden in adopting the efficiency of the use of resources. Due to the model adopted by the Romanian companies which are based largely on cost competitiveness, they are powerful economic operators, opposing any measures that would lead to higher production costs, the strong increases of the opposition to the legislation regarding the protection of the environment. This is a structural problem in this country which would need a systematic approach to transit to the economic model based on a higher added value.

On the other hand, it is interesting that fewer companies have found the lack of expertise, choosing the right actions to make efficient the use of resources for themselves or the supply of raw materials, parts, products, or services, being difficult when adopting protective environmental measures. Such economic factors are, in general, less of a barrier for companies than the legal framework in Romania.

4.3 Data and Methodology

The research used various indicators from the following dimensions collected at the level of 2018 for 140 cities in the European Union and the Schengen area:

- Labor market indicators: unemployment rate, activity rate, and satisfaction degree in terms of easiness of finding a job
- Household indicators: average price in EUR for buying an apartment and average no. of inhabitants in the household

- Education indicators: the number of students in higher education (per 1000 people) and the satisfaction degree in terms of education
- Social inclusion indicators: the satisfaction degree in terms of expats' social integration, the satisfaction degree in terms of the life people lead, and the satisfaction degree in terms of discrimination
- Health indicators: the satisfaction degree in terms of health care services
- Safety-related indicators: the number of murders per year and satisfaction degree in terms of citizens safety
- Transport indicators: the satisfaction degree in terms of public transportation
- Administrative service-related indicators: the satisfaction degree in terms of administrative services
- Sport-related indicators: the satisfaction degree in terms of sports facilities
- Culture indicators: satisfaction degree in terms of concert halls, theatres, museums, and libraries and satisfaction degree in terms of markets and squares
- Cleanliness indicators: satisfaction degree in terms of cleanliness of the city and satisfaction degree in terms of the beauty of the streets and buildings
- Green areas indicators: satisfaction degree in terms of green spaces

The cities chosen within the study are either the largest in terms of population in Europe (in the case of several smart cities from the same country), either cities with historical and cultural importance or small cities from countries with a low population, which ranks secondly in the population classification within that country. The main data sources used for all indicators are the Eurostat Urban Audit database and Numbeo databases.

Starting from our main objective, the chapter proposes building a composite index of smart city performance at the European level using two of the most commonly used techniques – principal component analysis (PCA) and cluster classification method.

In order to build the composite index of smart city performance, we have used the principal component analysis following the main steps proposed by OECD (2008) and allowing attention to the data normalization (Nardo et al., 2005).

PCA is a dimensionality reduction technique, selecting as principal components, the factors that recovered a high amount of cumulative variance from the initial dataset. Each component is a linear weighted combination of the initial variables (Davidescu et al., 2015).

Cluster analysis is an important technique, helping in grouping information about countries on the basis of their similarities. The cluster analysis has been performed using the Ward method and the Euclidean squared distance.

The papers of Nardo et al. (2005), OECD (2008), Davidescu et al. (2015), Davidescu et al. (2013a, b), Abdi and Williams (2010), Mourão (2007), and Nomikos and MacGregor (1994), INRIX (2016) offer valuable information about the process of building composite indices.

Usually, in order to make easier the interpretation of the composite indices, the index can be transformed to take values between 0 and 100 using the percentile rank, stating that 100 is the best performing and 0 is the worst. In order to compute the percentile rank, I will use SPSS software 20.0.

4.4 Empirical Results

The first objective of this section is to develop a composite index of smart city performance for 2018, as well as for other countries using principal component analysis (PCA).

The data was normalized in the first step in which the problem of the measurement distinct units of the indicators was solved. The method used was to standardize the variables obtaining Z scores. One of the essential steps is the standardization for bringing all the variables to the same unit of measurement thus eliminating the data asymmetry.

In order to evaluate the quality of the results provided by the PCA, the empirical results of KMO and Bartlett's test of sphericity revealed satisfactory conclusions. KMO value is 0.833, being above the value of 0.500, the minimum necessary to proceed to the next steps.

The empirical results of Bartlett's test of sphericity revealed the significance of the test, the probability being lower than the threshold of 5% (approximate chi-square = 1902.83) (Table 4.2).

The empirical results of PCA revealed based on the Kaiser criteria the existence of five main principal components, explaining nearly 75.06% of the variability in the original dataset and being selected based on the Kaiser criteria (with their eigenvalues supra unitary) (Table 4.2). Analyzing the distribution of variance by main components, we can mention that the first principal component explains 37.7% of total variance and the second principal component covered an additional 16.4% of the total variance (a total of 54.09% of the initial variance). The last three principal components explained almost the same amount of the remaining variance, about 8% each.

In order to easier identify the main principal components, the Varimax rotation technique was used to obtain components on orthogonal axes, exploring the correlation coefficients calculated between the synthetic components and the original indicators. Thus, each of these principal components can be interpreted in terms of the original variables with which these synthetic indicators registered the highest values of correlation coefficients (the results are presented in Table 4.3).

Based on the information provided by the rotated component matrix, the principal components can be interpreted. The first principal component has high coefficients regarding the variables "satisfaction degree in terms of green spaces" (0.976), "satisfaction degree in terms of life that people lead" (0.967), "satisfaction degree in terms of markets and squares" (0.959), "satisfaction degree in terms of cleanliness of the city" (0.953), and "satisfaction degree in terms of the beauty of the streets and buildings in the city" (0.936). This shows that there is a strong influence on the

Table 4.2 Kaiser-Meyer-Olkin test results and Bartlett sphericity test

Kaiser-Meyer-Olkin measure of	Sampling adequacy.	.833
Bartlett's test of sphericity	Approx. chi-square	3325.170
	df	210
	Sig.	.000

Source: Author's contribution

Table 4.3 The component Eigenvalues

	Initial eigenvalues			Extraction sums of squared loadings		
Component	Total	% of variance	Cumulative %	Total	% of variance	Cumulative %
1	7.916	37.695	37.695	7.916	37.695	37.695
2	3.444	16.399	54.094	3.444	16.399	54.094
3	1.684	8.021	62.115	1.684	8.021	62.115
4	1.580	7.522	69.636	1.580	7.522	69.636
5	1.139	5.425	75.061	1.139	5.425	75.061
6	.997	4.749	79.810			
7	.819	3.899	83.709			
8	.604	2.878	86.587			
9	.576	2.743	89.330			
10	.527	2.508	91.838			
11	.369	1.755	93.593			
12	.311	1.483	95.076			
13	.272	1.295	96.372			
14	.232	1.107	97.479			
15	.190	.903	98.382			
16	.143	.681	99.063			
17	.128	.609	99.672			
18	.035	.169	99.841			
19	.020	.093	99.934			
20	.009	.041	99.975			
21	.005	.025	100			

Source: Author's contribution

beauty of the cities and places of relaxation. A greener, cleaner, and more beautiful city leads to a more fulfilled life.

From the point of view of the second principal components, the key variable is "satisfaction degree in terms of easiness of finding a job" (0.755), this component being a proxy for a labor market indicator.

The third principal component can be interpreted in terms of satisfaction degree in terms of education" (0.859); people prefer cities where the emphasis is placed on the quality of education. Additionally, we can mention the relative importance here of "satisfaction degree in terms of sports facilities" (0.859) and "health care services" (0.657).

The fourth principal component can be interpreted in terms of "satisfaction degree of citizens' safety" (0.721), thus showing that citizens want to live together in a safe place, without problems with crimes.

The fifth principal component can be defined as "the satisfaction degree in terms of expats' social integration" (0.848). Resuming the thread of recent years, where in the European space have appeared many immigrants and refugees, they must be integrated as soon as possible in the host country in order to bring their own contribution to the area. If the countries do not invest in their integration, it can appear many social, educational barriers which can worsen the condition of the population.

Putting it all together, it is worth mentioning that a smart city involves many aspects and a circular economy based on recycling represents a way of living in which you have easy access to education, health, and a job. A smart city is therefore a full city of development opportunities on all levels – socially, culturally, technologically, and, not least, safely (Table 4.4).

In the last step, we have constructed the composite index of smart city taking into account each of the five main principal components, as weight share of the deviation explained by all the factors. The nonstandardized smart city index is:

$$\text{Smart City Index} = \frac{37{,}695}{75{,}061}\text{CP1} + \frac{16{,}399}{75.061}\text{CP2} + \frac{8{,}021}{75{,}061}\text{CP3} + \frac{7{,}522}{75{,}061}\text{CP4} + \frac{5{,}525}{75{,}061}\text{CP5} \quad (4.1)$$

The aggregate index of smart cities has been transformed using the percentile rank showing how a city performs to other cities for the same year 2018. The smart city index takes values between 100 (highest level of smart city performance), up to 0 (lowest level of smart city performance). The value of 50 represents the average performance of a smart city (Fig. 4.2).

Figure 4.2 presented the performance registered by all 140 cities according to the smart city index, as follows:

- Cities with a very high value of the index: Zurich, Oslo, Bergen, Bern, Vienna, Munich, Stockholm, Basel, Cologne, Stuttgart, Salzburg, Linz, Lucerne, Hamburg, Düsseldorf, Luxembourg, Frankfurt, Arhus, Alborg, Helsinki, Innsbruck, Dresden, Hannover, Cardiff, Riga, and Nurnberg.
- Cities with high value of index: Groningen, Belfast, Gothenburg, Graz, Edinburgh, Vilnius, Lodz, Prague, Glasgow, Timisoara, Kaunas, Leeds, Cluj-Napoca, Leipzig, Odense, Bristol, Utrecht, Geneve, Sheffield, Warsaw, Gdansk, Krakow, Tallinn, Turku, Bremen, Manchester, Wroclaw, Tartu, Amsterdam, Bradford, Zagreb, Tampere, Liverpool, Paris, Tilburg, Bordeaux, Rotterdam, Oradea, Birmingham, Eindhoven, Poznan, Burgas, Antwerp, Gent, Leuven, and Ljubljana.
- Cities with average value of the index: Dublin, Strasbourg, Brasov, Malmo, Bruges, The Hague, Brno, Split, Berlin, Maribor, Iasi, Toulouse, Seville, Malaga, Barcelona, Plovdiv, Valencia, Lille, Zadar, Lyon, Dortmund, Braga, Nice, Nantes,

Table 4.4 The rotated component matrix

	Components				
	1	2	3	4	5
Zscore: Average price for buying an apartment – EUR	.194	.066	.404	.361	.040
Zscore: Number of murderers	–.002	.140	–.428	.721	–.118
Zscore: Average size of HH	–.148	–.380	–.248	–.022	.680
Zscore: Share of students in higher education in the total population (per 1000 persons)	–.080	–.065	.506	–.054	.004
Zscore: Unemployment rate	–.257	–.742	.171	.175	–.114
Zscore: Activity rate	.110	.522	.178	.493	–.030
Zscore: Satisfaction: Public transport	.225	.628	.366	.294	–.096
Zscore: Satisfaction: Schools	.007	.094	.859	.049	.048
Zscore: Satisfaction: Health care services	.214	.102	.657	.452	–.274
Zscore: Satisfaction: Green spaces	.976	.699	.428	.166	–.122
Zscore: Satisfaction: Sports facilities	.137	.401	.740	.022	–.049
Zscore: Satisfaction: Concert halls, theatres, museums, and libraries	.043	.627	.421	.191	–.210
Zscore: Satisfaction: Easy to find a job	.298	.755	–.080	.106	.062
Zscore: Satisfaction: Integration of foreign	–.066	.171	.169	–.076	.848
Zscore: Satisfaction: Administrative services	.220	.442	.593	.151	.291
Zscore: Satisfaction: Beauty of streets and buildings	.936	.192	.108	.171	–.042
Zscore: Satisfaction: Markets, squares	.959	.189	.096	.088	–.086
Zscore: Satisfaction: Safety	.945	.205	.121	.053	–.056
Zscore: Satisfaction: Cleanliness	.953	.225	.078	.087	–.043
Zscore: Satisfaction: Life you lead	.967	.189	.051	.086	–.077
Zscore: Satisfaction: Discrimination	.829	.054	–.131	–.047	.013

Source: Author's contribution

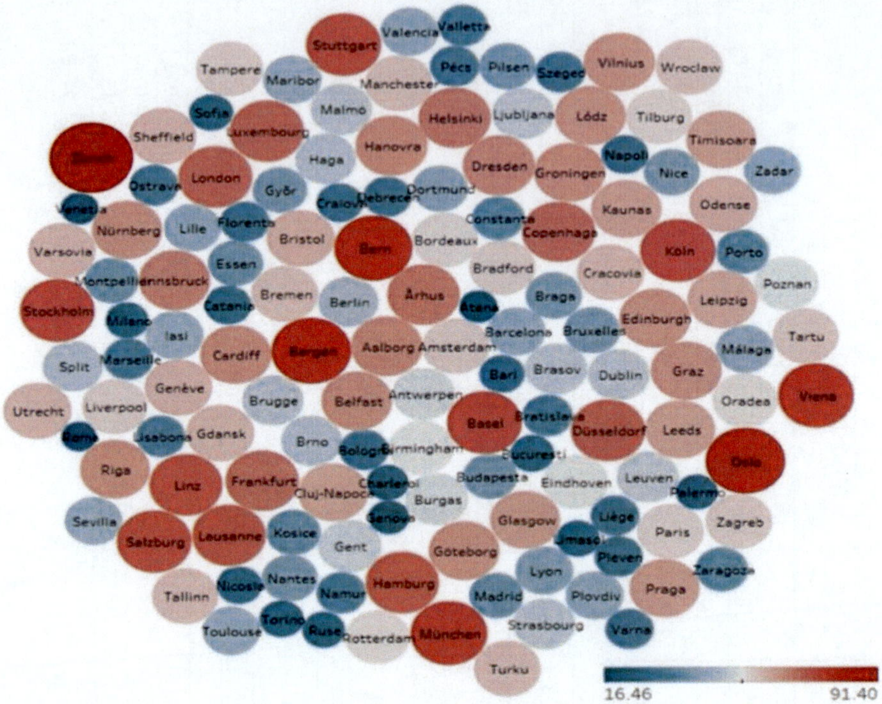

Fig. 4.2 Smart city index for the 140 cities. (Source: Authors' contribution)

Brussels, Plzen, Budapest, Gyor, Montpellier, Madrid, Essen, Kosice, Zaragoza, Constanta, and Porto.

- Cities with low value of the index: Lisbon, Namur, Bratislava, Marseille, Valletta, Pécs, Szeged, Ostrava, Varna, Liege, Florence, Debrecen, Pleven, Bologna, Craiova, Catania, Naples, Bari, Nicosia, Bucharest, Sofia, Turin, Limassol, Milan, Ruse, Palermo, Charleroi, Genoa, Athens, Venice, and Rome.

It is worth mentioning that cities from the Schengen area but outside the European Union are far from the cities of the Union. Switzerland and Norway are the countries with the best overall performance in terms of smart city performance, all cities of these two countries belonging to the first category. In addition, most cities from the Nordic countries, along with some from Austria and Germany, got the best performance.

On the opposite side, there are the cities of Italy, Greece, Bulgaria, and Cyprus. An interesting finding is the fact that Italy as a whole performs poorly; four of the cities from the last positions in the ranking are Italian cities, namely, Rome, Venice, Genoa, and Palermo. The lowest performance has been registered by the capital – Rome – followed by the capital of Greece, Athens. There is a slight correlation between the geographical area and the level of smart city performance, since the

South of Europe, highlighted by the cities of Portugal, Romania, or Hungary, performed poorly.

In the particular case of Romania, things seem to be divided. On the one hand, there are Bucharest and Craiova, with modest performance, and on the other hand, there are Cluj-Napoca, Timişoara, and Oradea with an acceptable level of performance and Iaşi, Constanța, and Braşov registering average values.

The map of Europe captures most of the cities in terms of performance (Fig. 4.3). This can be divided from the point of view of the cardinal points. The south and southeast of the continent present the lowest level of city performance. The Southwest and the West have cities with average and good performances. The same can be said about Central and Eastern Europe. The best performances, on the other hand, are found in the North, mentioning the cities of Norway, Sweden, and Denmark. The country with the best performances regarding smart cities, however, remains Switzerland. The Swiss city of Zurich is the founder of a smart hub in association with SBB, Swisscom, and the Swiss Post. This foundation aims to support and promote the concept of smart city through concrete projects.

Analyzing the distribution of cities in terms of the first two principal components (Fig. 4.4), satisfaction degree in terms of green spaces and satisfaction degree in terms of easiness of finding a job, recovering more than half of the initial variance, four main classes of cities can be highlighted, as follows:

Fig. 4.3 Smart city index map for 140 cities

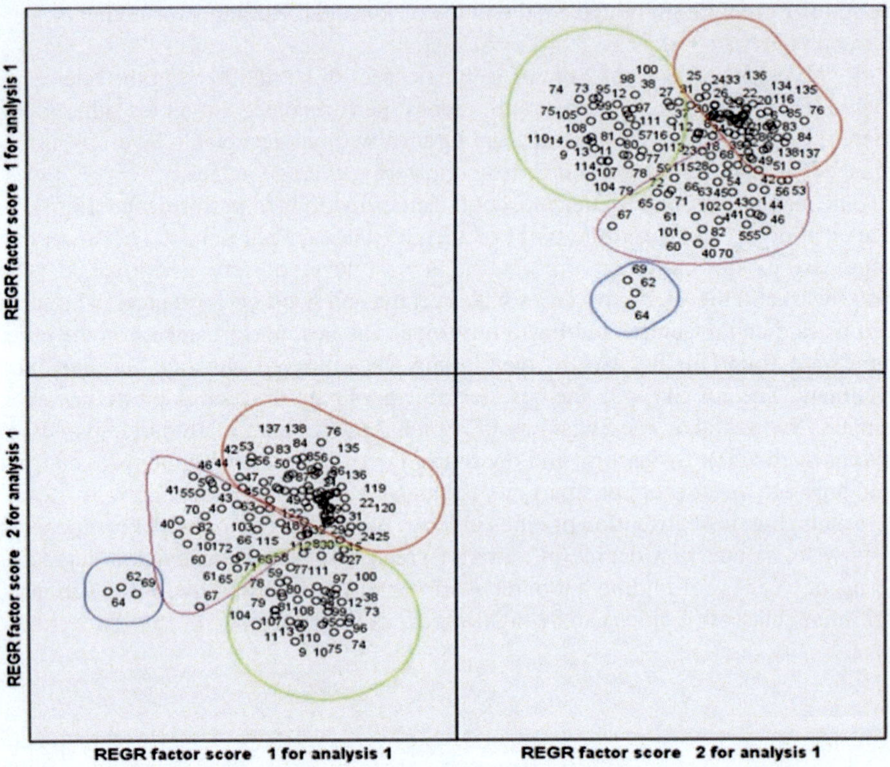

Fig. 4.4 City scores according to the first two components

- Class 1: Naples, Palermo, and Catania
- Class 2: Genoa, Catania, Valletta, Athens, Bratislava, Nicosia, Limassol, Bari, Milan, Malaga, Bucharest, Rome, Lisbon, Sofia, Constanta, Porto, Barcelona, Braga, Oradea, and Craiova
- Class 3: Geneve, Utrecht, Nantes, Pécs, Montpellier, Kaunas, Plzen, Zagreb, Essen, Gyor, Debrecen, Lille, Marseille, Groningen, Dortmund, Liege, Ljubljana, Bologna, Szeged, Maribor, Valletta, Split, Ostrava, Kosice, Porto, Zadar, Valencia, Seville, Madrid, Rome, Zaragoza, and Turin
- Class 4: Prague, Stuttgart, Cluj-Napoca, Frankfurt, Munich, Bratislava, Cologne, Oslo, Stockholm, Antwerp, Düsseldorf, Warsaw, Timisoara, Hamburg, Zurich, Nurnberg, Copenhagen, Vilnius, Liverpool, London, Dresden, Gent, Lodz, Hannover, Paris, Brno, Luxembourg, Arhus, Riga, Sheffield, Birmingham, Leeds, Dublin, Gothenburg, Wien, Cardiff, Manchester, Graz, Edinburgh, Alborg, Tallinn, Gdansk, Bremen, Krakow, Bergen, Helsinki, Brasov, Bristol, Burgas, and Cluj-Napoca

The first class is represented only by Italian cities: Naples, Palermo, and Catania had low scores both on the part of green spaces and labor market. According to

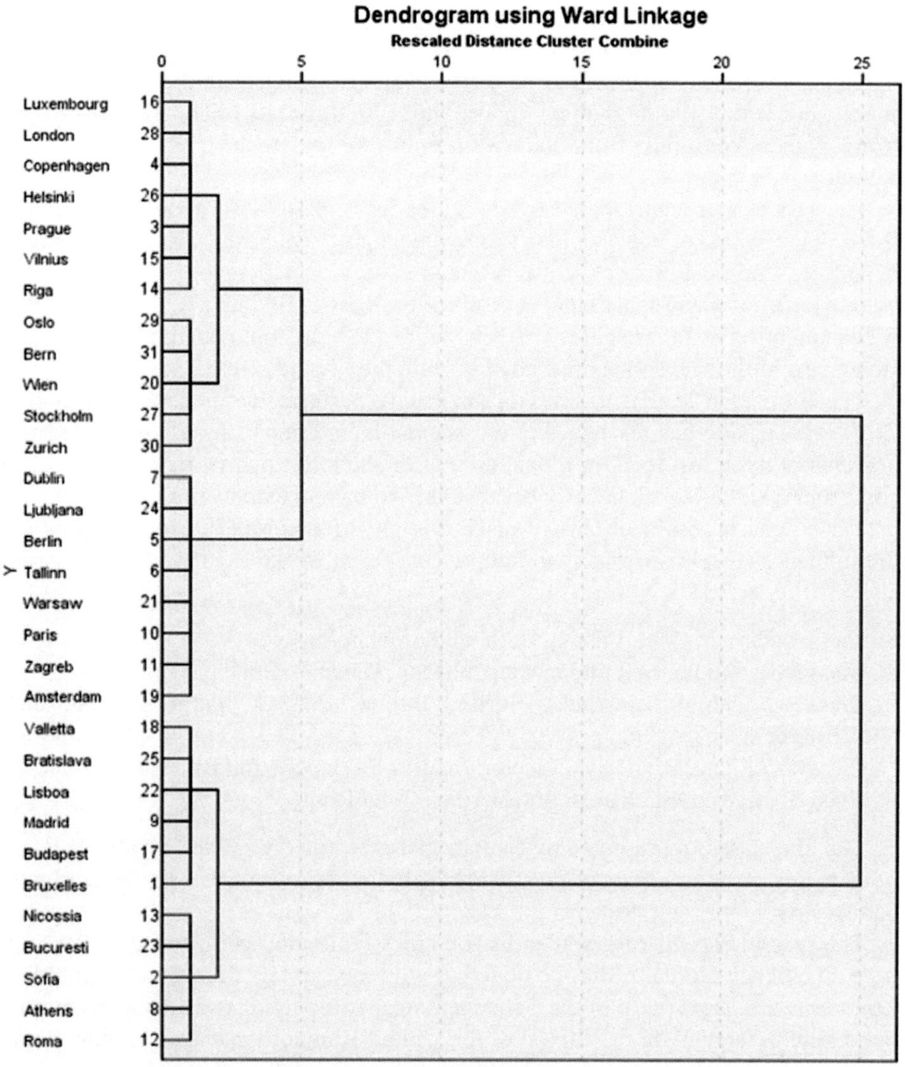

Fig. 4.5 Smart city index value map for European capitals

recent statistics, there is a high unemployment rate in Southern Italy. In fact, a simple analysis of the city maps will show that there is a small part inside the cities that is green. All three cities receive low scores on both components, and thus, they had a very poor performance.

The second class is represented by cities that have poor performance in terms of green spaces, but they had decent career opportunities. A concrete example is Bucharest. The capital of Romania has shown a great expansion in the last years in the IT field. Multinationals are increasingly attracted to the Romanian capital lately.

In terms of green spaces, there are many parks in Bucharest, but at the same time, the traffic is increasing, which makes it feel that more and more greenery is needed.

The third class is represented by cities that perform well on the side of green spaces, but with few employment opportunities. In this class, there are many cities from Spain and generally from Southwestern Europe, where the unemployment rate is high.

The last class is represented by the cities that registered a good performance from both points of view. Cities from the Nordic countries, from the United Kingdom, Central Europe, such as Vienna, Zurich, and Prague, performed well, both in terms of green spaces and in terms of easiness of finding a job. Additionally, we can mention that these cities are clean, with a low unemployment rate, beautiful streets and buildings, and people satisfied with the life they live.

The Romanian leader in terms of smart city performance is considered to be Cluj-Napoca. Cluj has reached Western standards in terms of smart cities. Being a university city, it invests a lot in that area of the country; many foreign companies come and open offices in the city because the Romanian exodus is a quality one.

The empirical results of cluster analysis applied for European capitals based on the influence of all five principal components revealed the existence of five main classes (Fig. 4.5):

- Class 1: Zurich, Oslo, Vienna, Bern, and Stockholm
- Class 2: Luxembourg, London, Copenhagen, Helsinki, Prague, Vilnius, and Riga
- Class 3: Dublin, Ljubljana, Berlin, Tallinn, Warsaw, Paris, Zagreb, and Amsterdam
- Class 4: Valletta, Bratislava, Lisbon, Madrid, Budapest, and Brussels
- Class 5: Nicosia, Bucharest, Sofia, Athens, and Rome

The first class is represented by capitals that performed very well on all levels. In other words, besides the city of Zurich, the capitals of Norway, Sweden, Switzerland, and Austria are the smartest cities at European level.

The second class is represented by the cities with good performances. We find here all cities in Northern Europe, together with the capital of the Czech Republic. London is the largest city in the Schengen area. Although it is difficult, when the population is very high, the capital of the United Kingdom manages to maintain a good position, besides the rest of very large cities, such as Madrid, Rome, and Bucharest.

The third class includes cities with average performances. In terms of latitude, most of the cities in this class are from Central Europe.

The fourth class contains cities with poor performances in terms of smart city. We can mention here not only Southern cities, such as Valletta, Madrid, and Lisbon, but also a city that would not normally have anything to do with the rest, Brussels. The Belgian capital does not perform very well, especially on the integration side of foreigners, and consequently, it falls much in the ranking.

The cities of the last class perform poorly in terms of smart city performance. Here, we find cities like Bucharest, Rome, Athens, and Sofia. Although in Bucharest it is relatively easy to find a job, this did not matter much in the rankings. It remains in a weak position being among the most underperforming capitals in the European Union. However, Sofia, Nicosia, Athens, and Rome have a much lower performance than Bucharest, which is on the border between the last two performance classes.

4.5 Conclusions

Circular economics and artificial intelligence are two areas where massive investment must be made in order to achieve high results in terms of city intelligence. Lately, there is a focus on the technologies of circular economy and artificial intelligence to optimize dead times, to recycle, and to help the economy and many other aspects.

The research aimed to evaluate the performance of European smart cities by building a composite index based on two main multidimensional techniques – principal component analysis and cluster analysis.

In terms of smart city determinants, the empirical results pointed out the importance of citizens' satisfaction regarding green spaces, finding a job, schools, safety, and integrating expats.

The cluster analysis results highlighted Zurich and Oslo as the smartest cities in Europe, while at the opposite side there were Athens and Rome.

Switzerland and Norway are the countries with the best overall performance in terms of smart city performance, all cities of these two countries belonging to the first category. In addition, most cities from the Nordic countries, along with some from Austria and Germany got the best performance.

On the opposite side, there are the cities of Italy, Greece, Bulgaria, and Cyprus. An interesting finding is the fact that Italy as a whole performs poorly; four of the cities from the last positions in the ranking are Italian cities, namely, Rome, Venice, Genoa, and Palermo.

In the case of Romanian cities, the results were divided. On the one hand, there are Bucharest and Craiova, with modest performance, and on the other hand, there are Cluj-Napoca, Timişoara, and Oradea with an acceptable level of performance and Iaşi, Constanţa, and Braşov registering average values. The Romanian leader in terms of smart city performance is considered to be Cluj-Napoca. Cluj has reached Western standards in terms of smart cities. Being a university city, it invests a lot in that area of the country; many foreign companies come and open offices in the city because the Romanian exodus is a quality one.

The circular economy and artificial intelligence should be the investment priorities now in Europe. There are many steps in this regard, which means that we will have an increasingly developed Europe (Roven, 2019).

As main recommendations, we can mention the following:

- Implement the infrastructure (network) for the "first time." Create IP infrastructure and broadband internet that is scalable, easy to manage, and secure by design.

- Remember to lay the foundation for all governments, from government to fortress, business to citizen, government to business, citizen to citizen, person to car, car to person, and machine to car communication applications.
- Incorporate smart requirements into publicly funded infrastructure programs in areas such as transportation, health, security, lighting, environment, energy, construction, and communications.
- Build or fund the "must have" infrastructure for citizens and be sure that applications are wrapped by private partnerships and initiatives.
- Stimulate ecosystems and the culture of collaboration. Private partners, like project developers, communications service providers, utility companies, and technologies, play an essential role in the development of smart cities.
- Apply free data and free government policies. Free information and data from government and other sources can help solve civic problems and create new business opportunities.
- Governments should stimulate innovation and collaboration through initiatives such as innovation laboratories, competitions for developers, and applied playgrounds. Think in perspective but start from the bottom. If the government is not a technocrat one or there are unlimited resources available, do not give up, but act. Rome (even if it is not a smart city) was built in one day. It must begin with testing and then implementation.

References

Abdi, H., & Williams, L. J. (2010). *Principal component analysis*.

Banks, I., Gravis, L., Iles, J., & Waldegrave, L. (2018). *What does a circular economy bring to the cities*, pp. 9–10.

Davidescu, A. A., Strat, V. A., & Gogonea, R. M. (2013a). An empirical analysis of regional poles from the perspective of Romanian sustainable development. *Procedia Economics and Finance, pages*, 116–122.

Davidescu, A. A., Strat, V. A., & Gogonea, R. M. (2013b). Statistical analysis of Romanian insurance market. A gross written premiums perspective. *JSES*, 75–79.

Davidescu, A. A., Paul, A. M. V., Gogonea, R.-M., & Zaharia, M. (2015). Evaluating Romanian eco-innovation performances in European context. *Sustainability, 2015*(7), 12723–12757.

Guesed, A. L. (2018). *Advances in orchestrating sustainable smart cities*.

Hollands, R. G. (2008). *Will the real smart city please stand up?* Available online: https://www.tandfonline.com/doi/full/10.1080/13604810802479126?scroll=top&needAccess=true

INRIX. (2016). *Europe tops INRIX global congestion ranking – Multivariate analyze and predictions*, pp. 3–4.

Kumar, V., 2017. *Smart economy in smart cities*. International Collaborative Research: Ottawa, St. Louis, Stuttgart, Bologna, Cape Town, Nairobi, Dakar, Lagos, New Delhi, Varanasi, Vijayawada, Kozhikode, Hong Kong. Available online: http://dspace.conacyt.gov.py/xmlui/handle/123456789/25546

Mac Arhtur, E., De Vries, J., Bleriot, J., & Yangjinqi Yu, V. (2015). *Growth within: A circular economy vision for a competitive Europe*, p. 21.

Mac Arhtur, E., De Vries, J., Bleriot, J., & Yangjinqi Yu, V. (2018). *Circular economy in cities: Project guide*, pp. 9–10.

Mourão, P. (2007). *Towards a Fiscal Illusion Index*. Available online: http://mpra.ub.uni-muenchen.de/9760/

Nardo, et al. (2005). *Tools for composite indicators building*.

Nomikos, P., & MacGregor, J. F. (1994). *Monitoring batch processes using multiway principal component analysis*, p. 40.

Novo, P., & Da Silva, A. N. (2017). *Hubgrade smart monitoring centers: Measuring resource consumption and moving towards a circular economy.*

OECD. *Handbook on constructing composite indicators: methodology and user guide*. Available online: https://www.oecd.org/sdd/42495745.pdf

Organizația pentru Cercetare și Dezvoltare Economică. (2008). *Manualul pentru Construirea Indicatorilor Agregați*. OECD. http://www.oecd.org/std/42495745.pdf. Accessed 28 May 2019.

Prieto-Sandoval, V., Jaca, C., & Ormazabal, M. (2017). *Towards a consensus on the circular economy.*

Roman, L., Parvu, A., & Turtureanu, A. (2018). *Scoreboard de eco-inovare*.

Roven, A. (2019). *Artificial intelligence in smart cities from a neurulation investor relations analyst point of view*. https://medium.com/neuromation-blog/ai-in-smart-cities-dfe2fa7d2829. Accessed 26 July 2019.

Walker, J. (2019). *Smart city artificial intelligence application and trends*. https://emerj.com/ai-sector-overviews/smart-city-artificial-intelligence-applications-trends/. Accessed 2 June 2019.

William, A. (2017). *The circular economy and benefits for society: Jobs and climate clear winners in an economy based on renewable energy and resource efficiency.*

Williams, J. (2019). *Circular cities: Challenges to implementing looping actions*. Available online: https://www.mdpi.com/2071-1050/11/2/423/htm

World Bank. (2016). *Urban solid waste management*. http://www.worldbank.org/en/topic/urbandevelopment/brief/solid-waste-management. Accessed 8 May 2019.

***Quality of life API, Numbeo. https://www.numbeo.com/common/api.jsp

***Urban Audit Database, Eurostat. https://ec.europa.eu/eurostat/web/cities/data/database

Chapter 5
Cybersecurity Threats and Vulnerabilities in Energy Transition to Smart Electricity Grids

Vlad Daniel Savin

Abstract National electricity grids and their respective system operators play a critical role in the modernisation and digitisation of our societies. The ongoing transition to smarter grids and demand response systems, the integration of new technologies and also new consumer behaviours, as well as other challenges such as the need to improve efficiency and connect to more intermittent types of generations are all part of a plethora of opportunities which also embed a large variety of new vulnerabilities and risks. In particular, with most systems being in the digital world, this exponentially increases the risks of cyberattacks, putting at risk entire systems of smart grids and creating new challenges for the national grid to manage these threats as it moves to a more system operation-focused entity from previously a more static, distribution-focused role. This calls for the need to improve or create new defence strategies, capabilities and mechanisms. This chapter first identifies the most exploited vulnerabilities in the software, hardware and network layers of national electricity grids. It then explores the threats these systems are exposed to, based on their respective vulnerabilities. Finally, it aims to offer a view of the most efficient current defence solutions – as well as a glimpse into the need for the development of new protective solutions and mechanisms.

Keywords Cybersecurity · Industrial control systems · Smart grids · Malware

5.1 Introduction

The economics of the ongoing Fourth Industrial Revolution force companies to adapt by incorporating new technologies and big-data-driven IT solutions. As more operations move into the digital world, cybersecurity becomes a priority for

V. D. Savin (✉)
The Bucharest University of Economic Studies, Bucharest, Romania
e-mail: Vlad.Savin@Ager.Ro

S. L. Fotea et al. (eds.), *Navigating Through the Crisis: Business, Technological and Ethical Considerations*, Springer Proceedings in Business and Economics,
https://doi.org/10.1007/978-3-030-82751-9_5

companies during this period of unprecedented change. Given the levels of complexity and ramification of digitalisation, cybersecurity becomes part of everyone's job. The hazards are inseminated via new forms of viruses and malwares. These and other aspects are at the centre of an enlarging cybercriminal economy that is highly complicated to defend against. The World Economic Forum highlighted that cyberattacks are one of the top five international risks (Brende, 2020), with estimated damages of $6 trillion in 2021 (Walker, 2019), if defence solutions do not evolve with the speed of technological development. The relative speed at which each move – cybersecurity defence tools vs new forms of malware – will dictate who wins and who loses. As malwares develop fast and threats become more sophisticated, defence solutions need to be a step ahead, and the cybersecurity protection mechanisms need to become more complex themselves.

The national electricity grids face some of the most critical challenges as mentioned by President Trump (Winder, 2020). A power outage generated by a successful cyberattack, in its chain reaction, has the power to bring large-scale disruptive impacts, not only to the powered equipment in residential homes but also to the outside world, to the national critical infrastructures like lighting, water providers and national health services, and to the whole business environment – all would be left in the dark. Beyond power outages, connecting more smart appliances, with their respective demand response systems, intelligent cars and other new technologies to the grid exposes the national electricity grid and the system operator to a wider array of safety and privacy-related risks.

National distribution grids, as critical infrastructures, have sustained and provided energy for decades. The integrated and almost closed architecture has factually brought efficiencies in equipment and operations. However, beyond the distribution function, national grids have been developing more and more their system operator role. The role has primarily been to balance the electricity markets' demands, but national grids – as well as distribution grids in some regions and countries – are playing an increasingly important part also in the integration of

Table 5.1 Summary the focus of the chapter

	Hardware	Software	Network
Common threat	Trojan Hardware	Program bugs	Protocol attacks
	Clones	Design bugs	Monitoring and sniffing
	Side channel attacks	Errors in deployment	
Defense mechanism	Hardware that is tamper resistant	Secure coding practice	Firewall
	Hardware watermarking	Secure design and development	Intrusion detection systems
		Formal methods	VPN
			Encryption

smarter technologies and solutions (microgrids, batteries and demand-response systems). These come as digital operational solutions, and with that, they present new cyber vulnerabilities to the system (Knowles et al., 2015).

As the grid expands its role and reach to respond to fresh demands on infrastructure from economic agents and customers, its protection tools need to be compatible with its new digitalised architecture. (Obodoeze et al., 2018).

New ambitions, driven either by businesses or by governments – such as climate-neutral targets – may require even further integration between smart energy systems; the national electricity grid may have, for instance, to communicate more and better with the gas grid and its supply sources, to ensure more flexibility for the take up of renewables. Building more connections between different systems in a digital manner means also, there will be a greater need to secure these connections and to identify potential vulnerabilities and threats before malwares attack these assets (Lonsdale, 2004).

Operational technology (OT) needs to integrate with information technology (IT) to drive digitalisation, automation, efficiency gains and indeed for systems to be able to deliver the new flexible solutions that consumers, businesses and governments are asking for – such as more electricity and gas systems integration, better visibility and balancing between national grids and micro, smarter grids (Ginter, 2018).

Whilst OT is a very secure, solid, tested-and-tried system and hence harder to attack and hack, IT is a lot more permeable to cyber vulnerabilities and threats. Integrating OT with IT means not only the creation of more connectivity – it needs to involve also the creation of new security and defence systems. Only by respecting this, a full integration between OT and IT can be achieved. The challenge is a completely new one – OT was conceived initially to solve an operational problem, to act as an isolated system; it did not need sophisticated protection systems. IT brings a new dimension to these operational solutions – an opportunity to make the system more efficient and a fresh threat to its safe operation – in the form of cyberattacks.

As the barriers between information technology (IT) and operations technology (OT) disappear, industrial control systems (ICS) environments are increasingly exposed to an increasing volume and complexity of cyberattacks (Alexander, 2013). Recently, cyberattacks have been very aggressive on industrial control systems. These have included the development of new malwares to take advantage of identified vulnerabilities, as well as advanced persistent threats driven by national interests (Jang-Jaccard & Nepal, 2013). At the same time, counter-espionage services, along with organized groups driven by internal and external interests – and often financially motivated – have started to engage in terrorist cyberattacks targeting critical infrastructures such as industrial networks, especially the networks of national electricity grids. Given the extensive development on the integration of the OT with IT systems, the volume of cyberattacks can only intensify in time, possibly disturbing the operations of the industrial control systems (Potlapally, 2011).

Several ICS studies have been reviewed for the purpose of this chapter, to identify current as well as emerging cybersecurity threats and vulnerabilities. The consensus is that ICSs have evolved from an isolated type of platform to an open one, which is highly vulnerable to the expanding IT vulnerabilities and threats. In 1997, Kaspersky, an antivirus software developer, discovered just two cyber vulnerabilities (ICS, 2019). In 2010, the number increased to 19. After another 5 years, in 2015, the number of vulnerabilities multiplied by 10, to 189, which shows the amount of interest the domain receives from the different stakeholders.

The changing technological environment brought by the Fourth Industrial Revolution creates the need for technological systems to monitor and control ICSs. These were previously isolated types of infrastructure. However, with more communication channels between the infrastructure capabilities, with monitoring and controlling now more linked together, the risks of the new cyber vectors like malware, phishing, ransomware, DDoS or zero-day exploits also increases (Howard, 2009).

Cyber operating systems are here and will only expand in time. With them, cyber challenges will also develop and enlarge, and there is no single silver bullet to address them – challenges are operation-system-specific, and they change as rapidly as or more than the systems themselves. The attention that is given to such topics needs to reflect the risks posed by the expansion of systems in the cyberspace. The fact that many businesses have been built on singular, isolated OT systems means the practice of giving enhanced attention to cybersecurity issues has not developed as thoroughly as the new technological wave would need it to. Understanding the risk and preventing it has to be entrenched in the building out of smarter, cyber-systems. The cyberattacks will bring new responsibilities for those in charge of security. The critical industrial infrastructures are experiencing alterations to become "smart". In contrast to traditional systems, a smart system enables the grid to incorporate new technologies and resources. By adopting new emerging data transfer systems that allow information flows between the grid and its different external stakeholders, the grid will become more exposed to cyberattacks. The advantages of the smart grid with its technological tools are clear, but the modernisation process will not be a straightforward one. Modernisation will probably happen in stages; the full process probably will be at least a decade lasting one. There will be challenges and vulnerabilities for the ICSs operators during the transition process because the new systems will interfere with the existing ones and probably other ICSs plant operators will be at different stages in their OT and IT integration – this will only further increase the complexity of the upgrade process. Meanwhile, when an ICS cannot be shut down during the upgrade process, the associated risks increase.

In order to understand the cyberattacks threat vectors, this chapter analyses the most commonly exploited vulnerabilities in existing ICS software, hardware and network layers, as well as analyses the proposed defence methods against such exploitations.

5.2 Software Vulnerabilities

Program errors create software vulnerabilities. A software fault is a common indication used to define a deficiency in a computer program. Cyberattacks usually use software imperfections such as design flows, missing data encryption, SQL injection, buffer overflows, issues with libraries and other types of bugs in order to control the systems in unintended ways from the original design, thus obtaining unauthorised access to data, compromising it or causing denial of service (DoS). The majority of cyberattacks continue to use system bugs and design flows – making these the key vulnerabilities in information security. Programming errors can open the door for attackers even in front of firewalls, intrusion detection systems (IDS) or other defence protocols. Thus, it is imperative to prevent, detect and react to the software imperfections. In this section, the chapter describes the main software vulnerabilities.

- Types of Software Vulnerabilities
  - Buffer Overflow

  Software exploitation happens when a software is abused. The majority of cyberattacks target software vulnerabilities by taking advantage of snags in memory, user validation and access privileges (Howard et al., 2005). The attack on memory safety is executed by modifying the contents of memory. One of the common ways of achieving this is by buffer overflow. The attack on buffer overflow happens when a program stores more information in a buffer than it was built to hold. Since the buffer is programmed to keep a certain amount of data, the extra information can overflow and corrupt by overwriting valid data in other adjacent buffers.

  - Data Validation

  The process of input validation refers to the process of data flowing in a certain way. Misleading data validation can drive data to corrupt SQL databases. SQL injection is one of the most common attacks on a website's database. An attacker inserts SQL commands to alter the database. The attacker exploits a defect knowing that the output is reliant on the successful application of other successive events.

  - Other Types

  Race condition error is the attack that causes changes in the system between the checking of a condition and the usage of the outcomes of that check.

Privilege confusion is another attack exploit by getting access to information that is normally protected. The result is that attackers gain access to confidential data.

- Existing Defence Software Solutions

The attempts to solve these software vulnerabilities can be grouped in:

(a) Detection of malicious code
(b) Detection of programming flaws, errors and patch releases to solve flaws
(c) Sandboxing

The primary objective for all is to develop solutions and to create a safe programming environment and context. Engineers look and discover the common errors that lead to software threats and vulnerabilities and try to establish a better-secured software code.

– IDS and Anti-malware

IDS and antivirus software are the most common tools for detecting attacks. IDS detect exploits or interactive attackers while antivirus scanners detect malware. Antivirus scanners are the most popular defence mechanisms. They detect known codes of malware (signatures).

– Type-Safe Programming Languages

Secure design and development is a technique that verifies that the program is defect-free. The testing software errors is a tool developed to uncover flaws in programming languages. The testing software module was designed to check and ensure that the application performs as expected, meets the security requirements and does not contain errors or bugs. The testing process consists of trying to identify defects, which are considered variances between the actual and the expected results. A type-safe language program also prevents memory management errors. Reducing programming errors aims to limit the privileges a program has while running. The mechanism follows the principle of least privilege – an old design principle. The main idea is to offer the program only the rights needed to operate. By limiting these privileges, the possible damages are restricted in case of an attack.

– Sandboxing

Another emerging cyber defence tool is sandboxing, which executes and verifies the code in a restricted virtual environment, limiting the initial access to the operating system, before granting the access of the code to be executed on the physical system.

5.3 Hardware Vulnerabilities

Hardware components represent the physical parts of a computer. Through exploitation of the hardware vulnerabilities, attackers can make use of known weaknesses to control the system (Constantin, 2020). In comparison with software-level attacks where updates, patches, newly developed detection tools for intrusion and antivirus programs search to identify malware, the majority of the hardware-based cyberattacks are susceptible to escape such detections. Taking advantage of these deficiencies, hardware-based attacks targeting the weaknesses are on the rise (Potlapally, 2011).

- Types of Hardware Vulnerabilities
  - Trojans

Trojans for hardware equipment are the most common hardware malwares. A hardware Trojan maliciously modifies the logic behind the electronic circuits in order to alter the planned process of the system. They have a variety of troublesome effects. A hardware Trojan might change, when triggered, an electronic circuit to provide remote unauthorised permission or to accept commands that otherwise should be rejected. Another type of Trojan might attach the chip's buffets and hence consume more power than normal. In a more serious scenario, Trojans might prevent operations of a resource. A DoS Trojan could affect the target module to exhaust its scarce resources. It could also physically affect the device's settings, including to ignore commands from other peripherals or simply to destroy the components.

– Illegitimate Hardware Copies

Illegitimate copies of hardware are another main source of malicious exploitation since they can contain Trojans. The pressures of the current economic context to reduce costs has increased the trend for companies to purchase untrusted hardware from cheaper sources. The current economic model forces outsourcing and buying tampered-off equipment from untrusted factories in low-cost countries. Furthermore, businesses driven by the need of reducing costs may purchase untrusted hardware such as firewalls and access points from untrusted online marketplaces, which do not have any guarantee of being free of malicious Trojans.

These practices also raise the possibility of intellectual property rights to be accessed by unauthorised personnel.

– Side-Channel Attacks

Another example of hardware exploitation is the side-channel type of attack. These materialize when attackers obtain valuable insights about a system's configuration by analysing the physical details of that device including information such as power consumption.

- Existing Security Hardware-oriented Solutions

Different ways have been proposed to divert the attacks on hardware equipment.

- Tamper-Resistant

Hardware equipment that is tamper-resistant has become critical due to its position within the networks as an entry point to the network's security.

- Trusted Computing Base

Another development has been the trusted computing base (TCB), which is considered as the set of hardware components that are valuable to the security of the whole network. Rigorous checks are done to audit these devices to ensure the security of the TCB and thus of the entire network. These safety mechanisms are in place to divert the attackers from getting the critical design elements of the industrial systems.

- Distortions

Other defence measures to protect against hardware vulnerabilities through side attacks include distortions, so that information cannot be replicated, thus reducing any interrelationship between data and the emission of the side channels.

5.4 Network Architecture and Protocol Vulnerabilities

When the network protocols were developed, they were designed to support entirely different environments, which were smaller in scale. Given the complexity and large dimensions of today's industrial networks, they do not properly work in these environments. The weaknesses of the protocols become more evident when the operators and users have narrow knowledge of the architecture of the networks. Examples of this limited knowledge include insufficient encryption schemes, patches not applied in time and lack of properly configured security filters and policies.

- Types of Network Layers and Protocols vulnerabilities

Cyberattacks commonly happen by manipulating the limitations of the following protocols: Internet protocol (IP), transmission control protocol (TCP) and domain name system (DNS).

- IP

The Internet protocol is the main protocol on which the traffic within the network happens. It offers the main data needed for packets to route between computers and routers. However, the IP was not built to check the authenticity and privacy of the data transmitted. This embedded lack of security permitted the packets to be hijacked or changed while they were routing over unknown networks.

- IPSec

To solve this gap, another protocol was developed, IPSec, which provides secured and encrypted IP traffic. This protocol has been used for the establishment of the VPN, which forms a secure route between a computer from outside and a trusted network.

- TCP

The TCP protocol makes sure that the packets are transmitted in a reliable way and directs the order in which the packets are transmitted.

- SSL

SSL protocol was developed to offer security between end-to-end computers.

- DNS

The DNS protocol uses human-readable host names and translates them into IP addresses. The DNS replies are not authenticated – a hacker can send DNS messages to imitate an Internet server. The DNS servers have been one of the common targets of the DoS attacks creating important interruptions on the Internet.

- Existing Security Network and Protocol-Oriented Solutions
  - Cryptography

Cryptography is the most common system to protect information. It aims to offer confidentiality, message integrity and authentication in an unsecured network. It is a principal tool to safeguard the information sent between users by encoding data, so only users with the right keys can decrypt the information.

The emergence of new technologies has allowed attackers to have powerful exploitation tools that are used to decrypt the existing encryption algorithms. Given the dangers, the American National Institute of Standards and Technologies has changed the SHA-1 (Secure Hash Algorithm) protocol with the SHA-3, a more advanced encrypting protocol (Bryson, 2015).

Skilled attackers use refined techniques to camouflage traffic loads to look more like genuine traffic. Furthermore, big data flowing on networks requires new analysis algorithms to analyse the uncertainty of information attached. This has led to the creation of a new domain of research, where network security experts collaborate with the design community to elaborate better ways for visualizing the traffic in order to understand the breaches. The resulting data is then analysed by network experts.

- Firewalls and IDS

Typical network defence tools include firewalls and intrusion detection systems (IDS). The firewall is the most common tool to protect the systems within the internal network from external attacks. The way it works is by analysing the data packets and determining whether they should be allowed, based on the rules set by the network administrator.

Firewalls can be placed in many layers in the network infrastructure. Network layer firewalls filter traffic at the edge of the network and block packets unless they match certain rules defined by the network administrator. The next-generation firewalls (NGFW) have become more sophisticated in order to keep pace with the new threats, being able to protect against more complex types of malware, like advanced malware payloads (Alto, 2020).

The proxy server is similar to a firewall by responding to the input packets and blocking depending on the policies set by the administrator. Both layering tools, firewalls and proxies, make it more difficult to manipulate the internal system.

The emergence of new technology increased the capability of the attackers to create more advanced cyber malwares. The intrusion detection systems (IDS) analyse any suspicious activity over the network. These detection systems are extremely valuable that they detect attacks in the early stages and then can protect further the system from subsequent attacks. In addition, these systems help detect any sign of suspicious activity generated by a user, application or a malware.

The system analyses the normal traffic by examining the pattern and reporting abnormal traffic. Such detections are either anomaly-based or signature-based. In the signature-based analysis, the system detects the malicious packets based on their signatures as they route. However, signature-based IDS have been considered ineffective as the sophistication of malware has developed – and hence, advanced anomaly-based IDSs have been designed. In anomaly-based signature analysis, the system has no expertise of how the malicious packets look like but analyses the changes in the behaviour of the system, thus alerting immediately when detecting suspicious software behaviour. These systems learn with the help of artificial intelligence and machine learning technology what is supposed to be normal and legit traffic for an extended period.

Still, more holistic approaches to better protect networks are needed, instead of focusing only on configuring specific assets such as Firewalls or IDS.

Best practices identified by network forensic studies include understanding the traffic attack patterns and locating the hackers (Ayodeji et al., 2020).

Another way is to create honeypots (Baykara & Das, 2018). A honeypot is a defence tool that mitigates cyberattacks by attracting hackers to parts of the system that appear to contain legitimate information. Honeypots trap the attackers into them in order to understand their techniques better. All the attack information captured by the honeypots is analysed in order to improve protection against future attackers.

5.5 Conclusions

The recent digitalization of the world economy, coupled with the growing penetration of smart machines and industrial systems, has led to operating systems being increasingly exposed to cyberattacks. There is a plethora of ways to protect against such attacks; however, more holistic approaches need to build on existing IT solutions. As the world continues to modernise and as it becomes more technological, cyber malware solutions need to keep pace with all developments and continuously evolve. OT and IT have long started to become more integrated, but new ambitions continue to arise. The previously more static and isolated systems belonging to the traditional architecture of most businesses, including that of large bodies like the national grid, for instance, is changing as they adapt to more automation and as they increase efficiencies. This creates a wider array of safety-related and privacy-related risks. In building out the new architectures, these risks need to be accounted for, in order to be one step ahead of malware systems. Adapting old architecture to new cybersecurity solutions may be burdensome or impossible. Legacy equipment, safety regulations that may prohibit any modifications being made to equipment and compliance regulations that require sensitive data to be made available to third parties are further challenges. Whilst further efficiencies and developments represent a significant gain for industries, creating new structures without their protective shell poses considerable risks (Vacca, 2013).

As cybersecurity vulnerabilities and threats expand for critical infrastructures, the industry's resilience to defence against such threats also needs further development. Different techniques and tools exist to remedy vulnerabilities in software, hardware and networks; however, the consensus is that the best technique is the one that protects everything from inside out (David & Thomas, 2019). The overwhelming majority of companies protect their perimeters to guard their networks from any outside possible attack.

This research chapter has focused on the cyber vulnerabilities and threats that pose risks to the modern national electricity grid. Based on the research done, it presented the main vulnerabilities facing the software, hardware and networks layers of the industrial control systems and presented the existing defence solutions to address these.

The results provide administrators in charge of the ICS cybersecurity an insight into the key elements that need protection and the means to achieve such protection for the successful deployment of a holistic cybersecurity strategy.

However, whilst the chapter discusses the existing cyber risks and defence mechanisms and solutions, significant challenges are presented by the constantly evolving and developing of cyber threats, so ICS administrators have to continuously monitor and deploy the latest defence tools to secure their assets. Further research is needed to identify threats before they emerge and hence keep a step ahead of possible attackers to best protect and fully integrate OT and IT systems within the more digitalised and ultimately more customer-responsive ICS infrastructures. Finally, emerging technologies, as they face their own new, unique cyber threats, will need fresh defensive mechanisms – for which research and investments will be needed.

Acknowledgements I would like to express my gratitude to Professor Silvia Fotea and Professor Ioan Fotea for the valuable support and guidance provided.

References

Alexander, D. (2013). Information security management principles. BCS, The Chartered Institute for IT.

Alto, P. (2020). Firewall feature overview datasheet [WWW Document]. Palo Alto Networks. URL https://www.paloaltonetworks.com/resources/datasheets/firewall-feature-overview-datasheet. Accessed 7.31.2020.

Ayodeji, A., Liu, Y., Chao, N., & Yang, L. (2020). A new perspective towards the development of robust data-driven intrusion detection for industrial control systems. *Nuclear Engineering and Technology*. https://doi.org/10.1016/j.net.2020.05.012

Baykara, M., & Das, R. (2018). A novel honeypot based security approach for real-time intrusion detection and prevention systems. *Journal of Information Security and Applications, 41*, 103–116. https://doi.org/10.1016/j.jisa.2018.06.004

Brende, B. (2020). The global risks report 2020 [WWW Document]. World Economic Forum. https://www.weforum.org/reports/the-global-risks-report-2020. Accessed 7.29.2020.

Bryson, J. (2015). Hash functions | CSRC [WWW Document]. NIST. https://csrc.nist.rip/publications/fips/fips180-4/fips-180-4.pdf. Accessed 7.31.2020.

Constantin, L. (2020). 32 hardware and firmware vulnerabilities: A guide to the threats [WWW Document]. CSO Online. https://www.csoonline.com/article/3410046/31-hardware-and-firmware-vulnerabilities-a-guide-to-the-threats.html. Accessed 7.31.2020.

David, J., & Thomas, C. (2019). Efficient DDoS flood attack detection using dynamic thresholding on flow-based network traffic. *Computers & Security, 82*, 284–295. https://doi.org/10.1016/j.cose.2019.01.002

Ginter, A. (2018). *Secure Operations Technology*, Abterra Technologies INC, Alberta, Canada, ISBN 978-0-9952984-2-2.

Howard, M. (2009). *24 deadly sins of software security*. McGraw Hill Professional.

ICS, K. (2019). Threat landscape for industrial automation systems, H1 2019 | Kaspersky ICS CERT [WWW Document]. Kaspersky. https://ics-cert.kaspersky.com/reports/2019/09/30/threat-landscape-for-industrial-automation-systems-h1-2019/. Accessed 7.31.2020.

Knowles, W., Prince, D., Hutchison, D., Disso, J. F. P., & Jones, K. (2015). A survey of cyber security management in industrial control systems. *International Journal of Critical Infrastructure Protection, 9*, 52–80. https://doi.org/10.1016/j.ijcip.2015.02.002

Jang-Jaccard, J., & Nepal, S. (2013). A survey of emerging threats in cybersecurity. *Journal of Computer and System Sciences, 80*(2014), 973–993.

Lonsdale, D. J. (2004). *The nature of war in the information age*. Psychology Press.

Obodoeze, F. C., Obiokafor, I. N., & Asogwa, T. C. (2018). SCADA for national critical infrastructures: Review of the security threats, vulnerabilities and countermeasures. *IJTSRD, 2*, 974–982. https://doi.org/10.31142/ijtsrd9556

Potlapally, N. (2011). Hardware security in practice: Challenges and opportunities. *2011 IEEE International Symposium on Hardware-Oriented Security and Trust*. https://doi.org/10.1109/hst.2011.5955003

Vacca, J. R. (2013). *Cyber security and IT infrastructure protection*. Syngress.

Walker, I. (2019). Cybercriminals have your business in their crosshairs and your employees are in cahoots with them [WWW Document]. URL. https://www.forbes.com/sites/

ivywalker/2019/01/31/cybercriminals-have-your-business-their-crosshairs-and-your-employees-are-in-cahoots-with-them/#47311ea31953. Accessed 7.29.2020.

Winder, D. (2020). Trump declares national emergency as foreign hackers threaten U.S. power grid [WWW Document]. Forbes. URL. https://www.forbes.com/sites/daveywinder/2020/05/02/trump-declares-national-emergency-as-foreign-hackers-threaten-us-power-grid/#5876edf83497. Accessed 7.30.2020.

Chapter 6
Study of Knowledge Management Impact on Sustainable Higher Education Institutions: A Business Process Modelling Approach

Diana Ivana, Mihaela Drăgan, Mihaela Maftei, Uwe Götze, and Daniel Metz

Abstract Sustainability in higher education institutions should mostly be achieved and/or enhanced with concrete actions. This chapter examines the role of knowledge management for sustainable development in universities. Based on the literature synthesis and trends, the aim of this chapter is to propose a conceptual framework for knowledge management in higher education institutions, based on business process modelling principles. The study´s methodology is based on the idea of measuring graduates perception regarding the transferred knowledge by using statistical data and business process management tools. The study was supported by the development of a process framework for knowledge management in order to meet stakeholders' needs and to improve quality. The framework could be applied in higher education institutions in order to assure sustainable development and to create knowledge and skills for future generations. Also, sustainable universities could be a model for any organization that wants to embark knowledge generation in the process of continuous improvement in its relation with society.

Keywords Knowledge management system · Sustainable university · HEIs · University stakeholders · Sustainable development

D. Ivana (✉) · M. Drăgan
Babeş-Bolyai University, Cluj-Napoca, Romania
e-mail: diana.ivana@econ.ubbcluj.ro

M. Maftei
The Bucharest University of Economic Studies, Bucharest, Romania

U. Götze
TU Chemnitz, Chemnitz, Germany

D. Metz
Babeş -Bolyai University, Cluj-Napoca, Romania

S. L. Fotea et al. (eds.), *Navigating Through the Crisis: Business, Technological and Ethical Considerations*, Springer Proceedings in Business and Economics,
https://doi.org/10.1007/978-3-030-82751-9_6

6.1 Introduction

Sustainable development is nowadays one of the biggest challenges in the academic sector. Therefore, several universities have begun the debate about the content of sustainable development and the circumstances in which to integrate it into the university policy, organization and activities (van Weenen, 2000; Disterheft et al., 2015; Mahdi et al., 2019)). The chapter presents an example regarding the impact of knowledge management on a sustainable university. While a wealth research investigates the activities of a "traditional" sustainable university, very little focuses on the sustainable university in relation to knowledge management and concerning the sustainable development of the academic curricula in order to meet students' and business organizations' expectations. In the lack of sufficient study to investigate the role of knowledge management within the university and its relation with the stakeholders, the current study investigates the perceptions of university graduates towards sustainable university by developing and applying a reliable knowledge management model.

Moreover, the subject of the sustainable university was separately discussed from knowledge management, and most research is traditionally focused only on one of these major themes. Therefore, we attempt to address this gap by highlighting the impact of knowledge management on sustainable higher education institutions by using an innovative business process management approach.

In the last decade, many universities have started to develop their own knowledge management system (KMS) in order to assess the quality and increase performance, while pressure coming from society and stakeholders have undoubtedly changed the guidelines for higher education institutions (HEIs), mainly regarding the measurement of academic performance (Karagiannis et al., 2006). Under the influence of specific tools, the chapter brings to the fore the importance of organizations' capacity to develop a sustainable development (Schmid et al., 2017) based on a KMS. Such a system provides an environment that facilitates the creation and usage of knowledge and also the communication and collaboration between the organizations' workers (Pinto, 2012). The KMS consist of four activities, namely, knowledge creation, knowledge retention, knowledge sharing and knowledge innovation (Hameed & Badii, 2012). These activities build a model based on three entities or engines, namely (Oprean et al., 2008; Piccoli et al., 2000; Oprean et al., 2008), faculty and researchers in the research engine provide guidance and set goals for the organization while monitoring progress and evaluation results (knowledge acquisition and knowledge generation/creation). Graduate students in the production engine, under supervision of those managing the research engine, produce and codify knowledge as part of their training (knowledge sharing/generation and knowledge storage/retention). Finally, students in the learning engine, under faculty direction, absorb and apply the storage knowledge (knowledge application).

Moreover, the chapter illustrates how KMS and sustainability are building a unified vision for the organization. The activities embedded in KMS refer to the following processes: knowledge planning, knowledge capture, knowledge organization, knowledge application, knowledge maintenance and knowledge evaluation (Cranfield & Taylor, 2008). Actually, these activities are, in our opinion, the linking point to sustainable development in HEIs, because they represent the basis of a knowledge lifecycle that contributes to the organizations' performance. After illustrating all the activities related to KMS and knowledge management activities, it is important to differentiate those which are relevant for the present chapter. Actually, the dimensions of KMS, which will be discussed in this chapter, refer to knowledge sharing and knowledge retention, and the knowledge management activities refer to knowledge evaluation. This means that from the whole KMS, the knowledge evaluation will be discussed, regarding knowledge sharing and knowledge retention. Further, according to (Pinto, 2012), HEIs are learning organizations which are able to extend knowledge skills and produce top-quality graduates, enhance innovation and creativity and contribute effectively to knowledge production and intellectual property development.

The embedded issue initiated in this definition is the starting point for the case study proposed in this chapter. Therefore, the chapter illustrates the process of measuring graduates' perception regarding the transferred knowledge as part of knowledge sharing and knowledge retention. The chapter brings to the limelight a framework for continuous sustainable development and for knowledge management evaluation in universities. The framework illustrated as a scorecard map in ADOSCORE is based on knowledge sharing and knowledge retention, which refers to graduates' perception regarding the developed competencies (Fig. 6.1). It is important here to highlight the relationship between knowledge and competencies, which refers to the fact that competence is actually knowledge put in action, especially by graduates. The aim of using business process management tools such as ADOSCORE is to increase an institution's efficiency and effectiveness and to improve specific processes in a context of financial stringency, internationalization and growing expectations.

The improvement measures, which are proposed as a result of the empirical study are embedded in a simulation modelling (in ADONIS) as part of a knowledge management spiral. The spiral incorporates the systematization of knowledge practices and tools to linking people and promoting knowledge sharing across the key processes in HEIs, which facilitates an environment and a culture of knowledge collaboration.

6.2 Literature Review: The Role of Knowledge Management in Sustainable Universities

As a first step in the data triangulation, a literature review was conducted in order to highlight the importance of knowledge management in sustainable universities. Sustainability in higher education is a complex concept. The concept of sustainability in HEIs consists of three dimensions: the protection of the natural environment

(Pamfilie et al., 2018), the maintenance of economic vitality and observance of specific social considerations (Bedawy, 2014). The chapter illustrates some organizational strategies in order to meet stakeholders' and social needs and to assure the development of a sustainable curriculum in the context of a KMS.

Zaptcioglu Celikdemir et al. (2017) defined sustainable universities as those that, beyond working for the well-being of the society, support their students and graduates for the future professional life through career planning actions, providing real information about the industrial and economic environment both in classes and in internships and including sustainability as a course in curricula. According to (Viegas et al., 2016), higher education for sustainable development plays a crucial role in the transformation of society towards a more sustainable pathway to development. Higher education patterns are digitally transforming, as the growing use of free and massive open online courses, social media and networking, cloud sourcing and open source codes have enabled an outstanding degree of intelligence generation and knowledge sharing (Hu et al., 2019). Nevertheless, universities can contribute to the changes required by facilitating new approaches that encourage innovative and sustainable ideas, in order to integrate sustainability throughout the world (Lozano et al., 2013). Moreover, a study performed by (Brudermann et al., 2019) at the University of Graz shows that the element of sustainable development is given by the following dimensions: international perspective (international working staff, international students and international topic), disciplines (interdisciplinarity, transdisciplinarity, practitioners' engagement and student engagement) and complex systems (big data, artificial intelligence AI, machine learning, webinars and e-learning). Another study conducted by (Grybauskienė et al., 2019) on the impact of knowledge management on sustainable activities of Vilniaus kolegija/University of Applied Science emphasized some deficiencies in knowledge management that may limit the implementation of management processes knowledge within the institution regarding virtual repository use, personalized professors'activity evaluation and competence development systems and application of innovations in the professional activities. While not traditionally used in the environmental sector, knowledge management has great potential for being applied to achieve sustainable targets. Moreover, knowledge management builds core capacities and knowledge competencies, helping to achieve sustainable higher education in all aspects of campus life (McNeil, 2011). Nevertheless, it is important to mention the strong connection between sustainability and quality assurance in higher education, which can be achieved through knowledge management. (Karatzoglou, 2013) argued that sustainable universities are based on the entire Deming cycle (planning, feedback, measurement and corrective actions or "plan, do, check and act"). The Deming cycle is based on total quality management principles, which means continuous improvement and systematic thinking involving all stakeholders.

According to other authors, quality assurance systems have yet to be integrated into the body of sustainability actions (Ryan and Tilbury, 2013). It remains to be studied whether a KMS based on stakeholders' perception helps to build a sustainable development in HEIs and if it can be applied to identify relevant quality assurance dimensions. Knowledge management has increased in popularity and credibility as a management tool as well as research discipline over the past decade (Cranfield & Taylor, 2008). According to (Sedziuviene & Vveinhardt, 2009), information and knowledge move to an important level in HEIs and become an important resource. Universities are actually the main instruments of society for the constant pursuit of knowledge. Knowledge management in higher education setting, considered by (Petrova et al., 2015) being a management strategy relevant to the society of knowledge, should provide a set of designs for linking people, processes and technologies and discuss how organizations can promote policies and practices that help people share and manage knowledge (Yeh, 2005). According to this author, one could distinguish two perspectives of knowledge management in higher education institutions: (1) academic knowledge, resulting from learning and teaching activities, the primary purpose of universities and (2) organizational knowledge, which refers to knowledge of the overall business of an institution: its strengths, weakness strategies and critical factors of success and relationship with the university as a research centre itself. HEIs must identify and focus on academic knowledge dimensions required to deliver quality educational programs (Brewer & Brewer, 2010) since the main asset which determines the employability of individuals is their knowledge (Rowley, 2000). The role of HEIs in modern information society requires a new innovative way into knowledge management and the creation of KMS, where knowledge management combines the parts of an organization into one unit: process, people and technologies (Sedziuviene & Vveinhardt, 2009). Further, one of the main objectives of this chapter is to analyse the main features related to knowledge management and sustainable development in HEIs embedded in a framework, because the assessment of sustainability invites academia to cross boundaries in order to create new lines among institutions and their basic unit regarding quality assurance (Zaki & Zubairi, 2012). Concerning this, there exists a knowledge spiral, which produces dynamic interactions between tacit and explicit knowledge and distinguishes four methods, namely, socialization, externalization, blending and integration, and endows separate distribution of knowledge to magnify results of knowledge crystallization (Zaki & Zubairi, 2012).

The spiral model choosed for this research proposes, according to the authors Picolli et al., 2000, a recount flow of knowledge through a rightly administered official environment and determine the existence of interventions that enhance the flow of knowledge for maintaining sustainable development. Moreover, (Yeh, 2005) and (Omona et al., 2010) adopted a framework to integrate knowledge management in HEIs. (Trivella & Dimitrios, 2015) also proposed a dynamic simulation model, which shows that developing the knowledge management strategy within the universities of Greece improves quality services and will enable them to respond correctly to the changing demands of the knowledge society, European standards and global market.

Actually, to create a comprehensive and working knowledge management framework, an organization has to provide for the whole knowledge lifecycle. To achieve this, the key processes that contribute to the organizations' effectiveness and efficiency are knowledge planning, knowledge capture, knowledge organization, knowledge utilization, knowledge maintenance and knowledge evaluation (Omona et al., 2010).

6.2.1 Research Methodology

With research methodology based on the review and synthesis of relevant literature, this chapter proposes a conceptual framework to enhance knowledge management in sustainable HEIs. For this chapter, knowledge sharing and knowledge evaluation are taken into consideration by highlighting the graduates' perception regarding the quality of the academic service, represented by achieved competencies and knowledge. In his proposition of a knowledge-based view, (Grant, 1996) points out that competitive success is governed by the capability of an organization to develop new knowledge-based assets that create core competencies. These core competencies are actually, in our opinion, the knowledge that HEIs transfer to their graduates (knowledge sharing).

This chapter brings to the fore also the idea of measuring graduates' perception regarding the transferred knowledge, seen as customers or stakeholders in HEIs, by using business process management tools (ADONIS and ADOSCORE). Understanding the graduates' perception implies a lot of benefits for HEIs regarding student retention and graduates' level of employability. We begin by outlining the benefits of measuring graduates' perception regarding their level of satisfaction related to the transferred competencies. The existing empirical evidences reveal the connection between graduates' satisfaction and sustainability in HEIs, and according to these, the graduates' satisfaction might be a performance dimension in universities. It is remarkable that in many countries the students'/graduates' perception has become a measure used for rankings and from this point of view higher-ranked institutions benefit by attracting top students and high levels of external funding (Wilkins & Huisman, 2011).

In a study performed in HEIs in Spain (Serrano et al., 2015) shows that graduates perceived the utility of their acquired competencies and their employability level to be greater than their educational content, while both levels were reasonably high. Also, the results illustrate that a qualification framework might be connected with sustainability in HEIs, but it depends on a continuous monitoring process by HEIs' interest groups. Therefore, education centres could thus adapt their mission, study plans, and any other plans of action to respond to the needs identified. (Natek & Zwilling, 2014) encourage HEIs to improve the student's success rates by incorporating data mining tools into their KMS.

According to (Westerheijden et al., 2007) today's knowledge economy requires highly skilled personnel at all levels to deal with all the rapid technological changes. In order to meet current needs, HEIs across the world are striving to reconstruct curriculum and assessment policies to ensure that graduates have the desired attributes and competencies.

Further, according to (Kearns, 2001), important developments in society have led to a different view of knowledge, accompanied by increased attention for the acquisition of competencies and competency-based education and training. There are several applications of knowledge management for graduates, namely, the portal of career placement services, portal for alumni and development services to capture contact reports and link to curriculum, research and career development efforts (Kidwell et al., 2000). By using these portals, HEIs contact their graduates in order to evaluate the educational quality, regarding the transferred knowledge by integrating the elements of knowledge management appraisal tool (KMAT), namely, institution's culture and leadership, that supports universities' mission in order to develop the curriculum in accordance to the market requirements, institutional strategies regarding strategic planning in alignment with the customer requirements on how well the service helped the graduates to achieve their goals, institutional technology and knowledge management processes regarding infrastructures to communicate with students and graduates through ICT and institutional measurement tools. (Peng et al., 2013) designed and implemented such KMS ICT tool to support university web-based learning platform, where professors and students could manage course resources during the web-learning process. Further, there will be proposed a conceptual model based on building a balanced scorecard map in order to follow our research objectives, namely, to assess sustainable development in HEIs by evaluating knowledge management through graduates' feedback, regarding the developed competencies (Fig. 6.1). Besides, in order to acknowledge the research methodology, the last level of the proposed model will be analysed, namely:

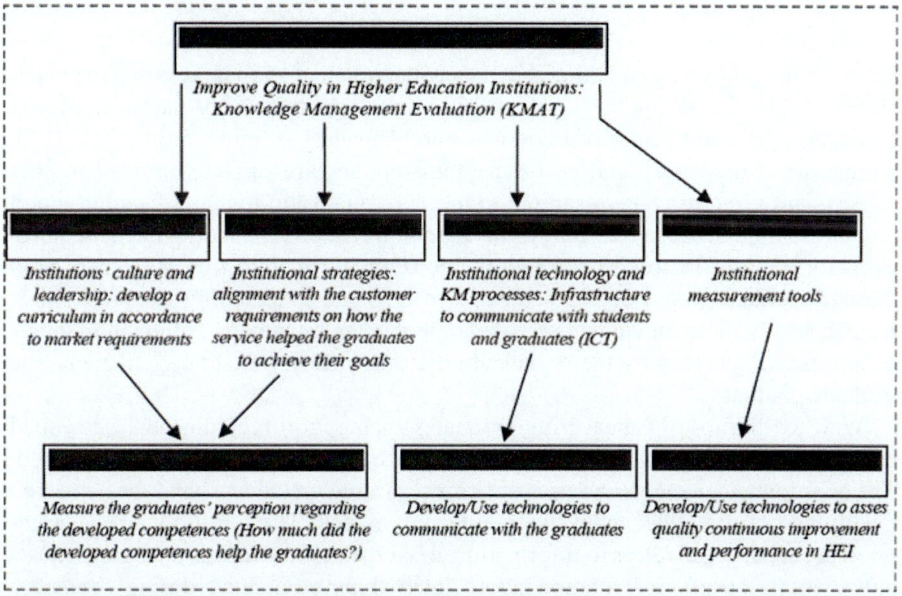

Fig. 6.1 Conceptual model for improving quality in higher education area through knowledge management evaluation. (Source: Own representation)

- Measure the graduates' perception regarding the developed competencies (How much did the developed competencies helped the graduates?): for this to be achieved, a questionnaire was developed. The questionnaire was focused on achieving a feedback from the graduates regarding the developed competencies. Furthermore, the study illustrates a performance-importance analysis, namely, the graduates had to give a feedback regarding the quality of the delivered academic quality and regarding how much the competencies achieved in the university help the graduates at the current job. The competencies, which are highlighted in the study refer to specific competencies in the economic field and transversal competencies, which are transferable to many occupations area. The target group for this study was the graduates of an international study program (German) in Romania. A number of 103 respondents participated in the study (N =103) and the pilot study, which took place in the initial phase included 25 graduates (some of the items were rewarded but most of the items were retained).
- Develop/use technologies to communicate with the graduates: in order to communicate with the graduates, a database on salesforce.com was built, where the contact information about the graduates was registered by the university administration.
- Develop/use technologies to assess sustainable development HEIs: the ADOSCORE instrument was used in order to assess performance and to build a continuous quality improvement model.

6.3 Results and Discussions

Firstly, it is important to mention that data collection had as a target group the bachelor graduates in an international study program. In this study participated 103 graduates from the Faculty of Economics and Business Administration (N = 103), within one of the largest and best-ranked universities in Romania. In this case, the subjects are a representative sample to measure quality in higher education, not a random sample because the survey was based on real understanding of the requirements of internal customers through the constant communication with them both through workshops and events dedicated to graduates. According to (Motwani & Kumar, 1997), there may be other stakeholders in the university, but the individuals most directly serviced by the organization are its primary customers, namely, the students/graduates.

With the purpose of measuring graduates' perception regarding the developed competencies and abilities during the study, a questionnaire has been developed. The questionnaire suggests a series of items regarding on the one hand the perceived quality and on the other hand the quality importance. The questionnaire is structured in six parts and refers to information about the graduated study program (qualitative information), information about internships completed during the study (qualitative information), information about the quality of the graduated study program and about the developed competencies and abilities during the study (quantitative information, five-point Likert Scale), information about the graduates' employment status (qualitative information and quantitative information, five-point Likert Scale), and information about future events dedicated to alumni/graduates and socio-demographic information.

For this study, there were taken into consideration information about the quality of the graduated study program and about the developed competencies and abilities during the study, embedded in an importance-performance analysis. According to the importance-performance analysis (Table 6.1) based on paired sample t test, there exists a remarkable difference between the performance (quality) of the delivered competencies and the importance of these competencies at the job. In order to illustrate the above-mentioned differences, namely, between the perceived quality and the quality importance, there was used as a statistical method the paired sample t test based on mean and standard deviation results. The paired sample t test is based on the idea of focusing on the differences between two values.

$$t = \frac{\sum d}{\sqrt{\frac{n\left(\sum d^2\right)-\left(\sum d\right)^2}{n-1}}} \quad (6.1)$$

Significant differences between the perceived quality regarding the specific and transversal competencies and their importance in the labour market refer to dimensions such as the ability to work in complex and multicultural teams, ability to effectively manage working time, ability to mobilize others, critical and analytical thinking (Table 6.1). According to the European Higher Education Area Report (EACEA et al., 2012; European Commission/EACEA/Eurydice, 2018), the need to improve curricula and the development of specific and transversal skills required in the labour must be included in any HEI. Actually, the graduates stated that the transferred knowledge is not always the important one in accordance with the requirements of the companies they work in, which means that there should be implemented knowledge management-based strategies to continuously improve quality and assess quality and performance (Marquardt et al., 2017).

The relevance of this study consists actually in the idea that higher education performance is based on the fact that students/graduates (as primary customers) participate in performance and sustainability achievement and should play an active role. The performance in the higher education sector requires the active participation of students/graduates to obtain consumer experience, which is actually education, embedded in competencies. Therefore, according to (Hartman & Schmidt, 1995), performance is the interaction between an HEI (as academic service provider) and student/graduate as an active participant in creating educational process performance.

It is important to mention that the data in this table highlight graduates' perception about the 14 competencies that were identified according to the national framework as being the most relevant competencies to obtain after graduating from the study program. The data analysis shows that the graduates perceived a real gap

Table 6.1 Paired sample test

Importance		Paired differences					t	df	Sig. (2-tailed)
		Mean	Std. deviation	Std. error mean	95% Confidence interval of the difference				
					Lower	Upper			
Pair 1	**Competence 1**	−.46078	1.14036	.11291	−.68477	−.23680	−4.081	101	.000
	Knowledge of basic investigative methods specific to market economy								
Pair 2	**Competence 2**	−.41176	1.05636	.10460	−.61925	−.20428	−3.937	101	.000
	Explanation and interpretation of specific processes of economic activities								
Pair 3	**Competence 3**	−.65686	1.25466	.12423	−.90330	−.41043	−5.287	101	.000
	The ability to view, interpret and apply rules and regulations in the economic and social field								
Pair 4	**Competence 4**	−.81373	1.36237	.13489	−1.08132	−.54613	−6.032	101	.000
	Use of specific technology and tools in the economic and social activities								
Pair 5	**Competence 5**	−.79412	1.16329	.11518	−1.02261	−.56563	−6.894	101	.000
	Data collection, processing and analysis for decision making processes								
Pair 6	**Competence 6**	−.94118	1.33367	.13205	−1.20313	−.67922	−7.127	101	.000
	Ability to work in complex and multicultural teams								
Pair 7	**Competence 7**	−.77451	1.39948	.13857	−1.04939	−.49963	−5.589	101	.000

(continued)

Table 6.1 (continued)

Importance		Paired differences					t	df	Sig. (2-tailed)
		Mean	Std. deviation	Std. error mean	95% Confidence interval of the difference Lower	Upper			
	Business initiation and development in the global economy								
Pair 8	**Competence 8**	−.56863	1.43168	.14176	−.84984	−.28742	−4.011	101	.000
	Supporting management activity through studies, summaries and forecasts at micro and macro level								
Pair 9	**Competence 9**	−.68627	1.11675	.11057	−.90563	−.46692	−6.206	101	.000
	Effective communication (in German/ English) and effective conducting comparative of studies in the area of business								
Pair 10	**Competence 10**	−1.24510	1.56342	.15480	−1.55218	−.93801	−8.043	101	.000
	Ability to effectively manage working time								
Pair 11	**Competence 11**	−.90196	1.40374	.13899	−1.17768	−.62624	−6.489	101	.000
	Rhetorical and presentation skills								
Pair 12	**Competence 12**	−1.19608	1.49613	.14814	−1.48995	−.90221	−8.074	101	.000
	Ability to mobilize others								
Pair 13	**Competence 13**	−.94118	1.46120	.14468	−1.22818	−.65417	−6.505	101	.000
	Critical thinking								
Pair 14	**Competence 14**	−1.08824	1.34314	.13299	−1.35205	−.82442	−8.183	101	.000
	Analytical thinking								

Source: Data analysis using the Statistical Package for the Social Sciences (SPSS) between the way in which these competencies were transferred and their actual value in the market, namely, their importance at the workplace. Therefore, Fig. 6.2 illustrates a complex model on how universities could enhance this gap in order to meet graduates' and other stakeholders' expectations (e.g., companies) and achieve performance.

Likewise any organization, which is aware that knowledge is among their valuable strategic assets, the education program mentioned in this case study should re-evaluate the way in which the organization engages with the source of knowledge in order to underpin sustainable development (Minonne & Turner, 2009). This will, actually, create a fundamental change to establish practices and a potential framework to shift from the traditional strategic approach to an operational one. Therefore, in order to evaluate the knowledge management and continuously improve quality, there should be built a knowledge spiral model, which illustrates the dynamic interaction between the organization's culture and the way in which knowledge is transferred to graduates.

Moreover, Fig. 6.2 illustrates the knowledge spiral model, which embeds a simulation modelling in ADONIS of the activities, which are thought to improve quality and assess a model of knowledge management evaluation. The model is based on the transformation of tacit knowledge into explicit knowledge, which includes not only the epistemological perspective but also the ontological perspective, which refers to individuals, groups, organizations and inter-organizations.

Actually, the model begins with the focus on knowledge management evaluation and quality improvement and is structured in four stages, namely:

(1) The objective of measuring graduates' perception about the transferred knowledge is becoming an embedded activity of the university's culture/organizational culture.
(2) The measures, which are taken to transfer this in the organization, refer to the development of a quality management team for the study program, the development of tools to communicate with graduates and the organization of a solid database of graduates.
(3) On the next swim lane, the measures involve the consideration of the performance-importance analysis and the adaptation of the curriculum in accordance with the market requirements (mostly where the gap between importance and performance is significant).
(4) Further, there should be organized workshops with the companies to discuss their requirements regarding the graduates' competencies and with graduates to discuss their career development. The study program coordinators and the professors should be informed about the graduates' perception, and this model of continuous quality improvement and sustainable development as a cyclical (spiral) model should be transferred to the next swim lane, which engages, actually, the university's culture.

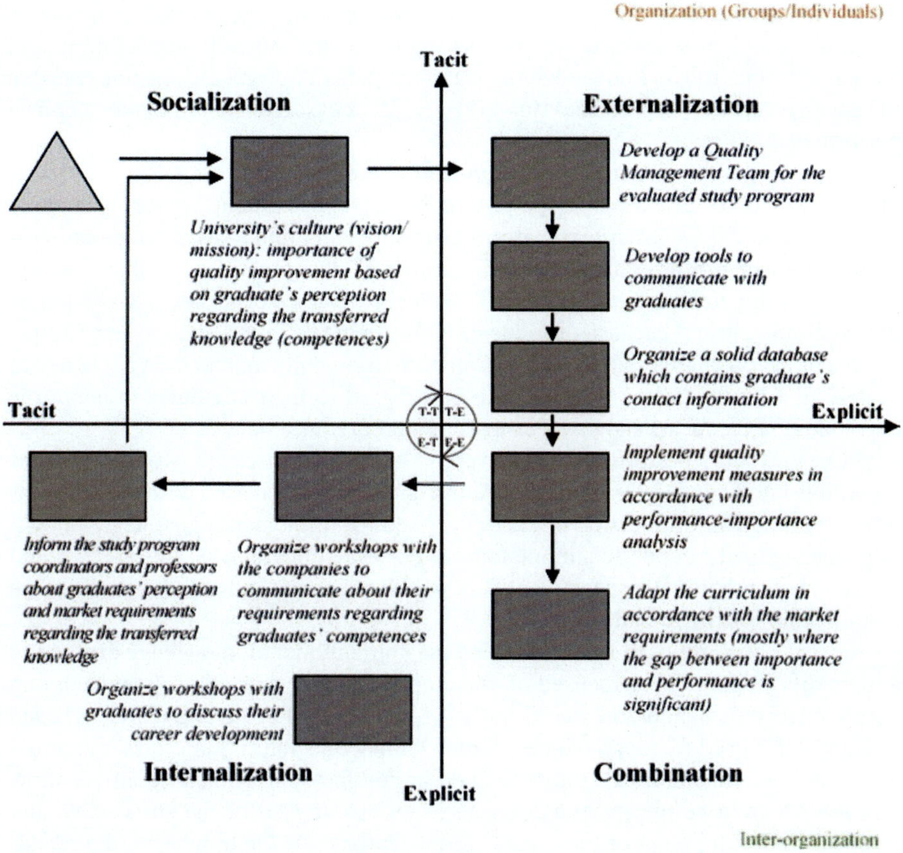

Fig. 6.2 Spiral model to assess knowledge management. (Source: Own representation)

6.4 Conclusions

HEIs are part of the flourishing knowledge business and their core activities. Actually, the knowledge is an end itself in each university. From this point of view, it is necessary to search strategies and approaches to manage knowledge and increase collaboration, communication and interaction between actors, promoting at the same time the creation and sharing of knowledge (Pinto, 2012).

The proposed framework establishes the relationship between process and tools, facilitating the selection of the most valuable knowledge management strategies in accordance with the organization's needs to evaluate the knowledge management related to the graduates' perception regarding the transferred knowledge. This case study demonstrates also the use of a spiral model to achieve performance in HEIs which may be a framework also regarding other objectives in order to develop valuable methods to achieve excellence. Therefore, measuring graduates' perception seen as a sustainability indicator by using knowledge management system activities and a spiral model is suitable for process improvement. Actually, the spiral model has an important role in knowledge management, and therefore, the positive changes in an organization could be quantified and measured in order to achieve performance.

Other models of sustainable development (Velazquez et al., 2006) were developed in order to offer a deep perspective on what people responsible for sustainable initiatives could do in order to transform their university into a sustainable one. This model was organized by using a benchmarking of best practices to foster sustainability in eighty universities. Further, the target group for the empirical evaluation is not randomly chosen because the educational system in Central and Eastern Europe has experienced changes and massive transformation and embarked on a journey to "catch up with the West" (Kwiek, 2014) in regard to their strategies to adapt the curriculum and educational services to the market requirements.

Also, in a study performed by Guerrero et al. (2019), there are two implications regarding knowledge management in university: a practical and a social implication. The practical implication refers to the need for implementing strategic knowledge management in public administration. For the policymakers, this study could present an insight into the effectiveness of public resources and to redefine the value chain within the organization.

However, the proposed framework and the spiral model of knowledge evaluation and quality improvement focused on the empirical evidences allows knowledge to be effectively managed and stored in the organization. Further, ADOSCORE and ADONIS are used as tools, which enables knowledge sharing and dissemination. The results of the empirical study based on importance-performance analysis show that there should be implemented measures and strategies for the sustainable and continuous development of the organization. The knowledge transfer to the graduates through specific and transversal competencies is the key issue in HEIs, facilitating knowledge sharing (tacit and explicit) and knowledge acquisition (between individuals, groups, organization and inter-organization) and supporting the continuous transfer of knowledge in the society. Developing a framework and a spiral model for knowledge management evaluation and quality improvement is vital for the strategic value of knowledge, which disseminates the culture, values and mission of HEIs.

Nevertheless, according to (Grecu & Ipina, 2014), knowledge, skills and values are part of a developed model for sustainability in HEIs. Actually, knowledge, skills and values that a university creates and promotes will influence and shape the future society, because the main means available for sustainable universities to equip their students with knowledge, skills and values are the core academic functions given by education and research.

Acknowledgement We would like to acknowledge the support of BOC Group Wien by providing the business process management (BPM) tools.

References

Bedawy, R. E. L. (2014). Embedding sustainable development into higher education: A casestudy from Egypt. *International Review of Management and Business Research, 3*(1), 465–484.

Brewer, P. D., & Brewer, K. L. (2010). Knowledge management, human resource management, and higher education: A theoretical model. *Journal of Education for Business, 85*(6), 330–335. https://doi.org/10.1080/08832321003604938

Brudermann, T., Aschemann, R., Füllsack, M., & Posch, A. (2019). Education for sustainable development 4.0: Lessons learned from the University of Graz, Austria. *Sustainability (Switzerland), 11*(8), 1–14. https://doi.org/10.3390/su11082347

Cranfield, D., & Taylor, J. (2008). Knowledge management and higher education: A UK case study. *The Electronic Journal of Knowledge Management, 6*(2), 85–99. http://www.ejkm.com/volume6/issue2

Disterheft, A., Caeiro, S., Azeiteiro, U. M., & Filho, W. L. (2015). Sustainable universities – A study of critical success factors for participatory approaches. *Journal of Cleaner Production, 106*, 11–21. https://doi.org/10.1016/j.jclepro.2014.01.030

EACEA, Eurydice, Eurostat, & Eurostudent. (2012). *The European higher education area in 2012: Bologna process implementation report. Eurydice.* https://doi.org/10.2797/81203

European Commission/EACEA/Eurydice. (2018). *The European higher education area in 2018: Bologna process implementation report. Publications Office of the European Union.* https://doi.org/10.2797/63509

Grant, R. M. (1996). Toward a knowledge-based theory of the firm. *Strategic Management Journal, 17*(S2), 109–122. https://doi.org/10.1002/smj.4250171110

Guerrero, M., Herrera, F., & Urbano, D. (2019). Strategic knowledge management within subsidised entrepreneurial university-industry partnerships. *Management Decision, 57*(12), 3280–3300. https://doi.org/10.1108/MD-10-2018-1126

Grecu, V., & Ipina, N. (2014). The sustainable university-a model for the sustainable organization. *Romania, 6*(2), 15–24. https://doi.org/10.1515/msd-2015-0002

Grybauskienė, I., Jankauskienė, Ž., & Kubilienė, E. (2019). The impact of knowledge management on sustainable activities of higher education institution. *EUREKA: Social and Humanities, 3*(3), 17–29. https://doi.org/10.21303/2504-5571.2019.00891

Hameed, S., & Badii, A. (2012). Effectiveness of knowledge management functions in improving the quality of education in higher education institutions. *International Journal of Information and Education Technology, 2*(4), 319–323. https://doi.org/10.7763/ijiet.2012.v2.141

Hartman, D. E., & Schmidt, S. L. (1995). Understanding student/alumni satisfaction from a consumer's perspective: The effects of institutional performance and program outcomes. *Research in Higher Education, 36*(2), 197–217. https://doi.org/10.1007/BF02207788

Hu, Y. F., Hou, J. L., & Chien, C. F. (2019). A UNISON framework for knowledge management of university–industry collaboration and an illustration. *Computers and Industrial Engineering, 129*(November 2018), 31–43. https://doi.org/10.1016/j.cie.2018.12.072

Karagiannis, D., Lichka, C., & Rieger, B. (2006). Von der Balanced Scorecard zu universitüren Wissensbilanzen. In D. Karagiannis & B. Rieger (Eds.), *Herausforderungen in der Wirtschaftsinformatik* (pp. 209–220). Springer. https://doi.org/10.1007/3-540-28907-0_14

Karatzoglou, B. (2013). An in-depth literature review of the evolving roles and contributions of universities to Education for Sustainable Development. *Journal of Cleaner Production, 49*(June), 44–53. https://doi.org/10.1016/j.jclepro.2012.07.043

Kearns, P. (2001). *Review of research generic new economy.* NCVER Ltd.. www.ncver.edu.au

Kidwell, J. J., Vander Linde, K. M., & Johnson, S. L. (2000). Applying corporate knowledge management practices in higher education. *EDUCAUSE Quarterly, 4*, 28–33. http://net.educause.edu/ir/library/pdf/EQM0044.pdf

Kwiek, M. (2014). Changing higher education and welfare states in postcommunist Central Europe: New contexts leading to new typologies? *Human Affairs, 24*(1), 48–67. https://doi.org/10.2478/s13374-014-0205-1

Lozano, R., Lozano, F. J., Mulder, K., Huisingh, D., & Waas, T. (2013). Advancing higher education for sustainable development: international insights and critical reflections. *Journal of Cleaner Production, 48*(2013), 3–9. https://doi.org/10.1016/j.jclepro.2013.03.034

Mahdi, O. R., Nassar, I. A., & Almsafi, M. K. (2019). Knowledge management processes and sustainable competitive advantage : An empirical examination in private universities. *Journal of Business Research Journal, 94*(February 2018), 320–334. https://doi.org/10.1016/j.jbusres.2018.02.013

Marquardt, K., Olaru, M., & Ceausu, I. (2017). Study on the development of quality measurements models for Steering business services in Relation to customer satisfaction. *Amfiteatru Economic, 19*(44), 95–109. https://www.amfiteatrueconomic.ro/temp/Article_2596.pdf

McNeil, R. (2011). Application of knowledge management for sustainable development in institutions of higher education. *Dalhousie Journal of Interdisciplinary Management, 7*(Spring 2011), 1–13. https://doi.org/10.5931/djim.v7i1.82

Minonne, C., & Turner, G. (2009). Evaluating knowledge management performance. *Electronic Journal of Knowledge Management, 7*(5), 583–592. http://www.ejkm.com/volume7/issue5

Motwani, J., & Kumar, A. (1997). The need for implementing total quality management in education. *International Journal of Educational Management, 11*(3), 131–135. https://doi.org/10.1108/09513549710164023

Natek, S., & Zwilling, M. (2014). Student data mining solution-knowledge management system related to higher education institutions. *Expert Systems with Applications, 41*(2014), 6400–6407. https://doi.org/10.1016/j.eswa.2014.04.024

Omona, W., Van Der Weide, T., & Lubega, J. (2010). Using ICT to enhance Knowledge Management in higher education: A conceptual framework and research agenda. *International Journal of Education and Development Using Information and Communication Technology, 6*(4), 83–101. https://files.eric.ed.gov/fulltext/EJ1085009.pdf

Oprean, C., Lobont, L., Kifor, C., & Negulescu, S. C. (2008). How to integrate knowledge and quality in higher education systems. In *3rd North-East Asia International Conference on Engineering & Technology Education* (pp. 193–200) https://www.researchgate.net/publication/238524023_How_to_integrate_Knowledge_and_Quality_in_Higher_Education_Systems

Pamfilie, R., Firoiu, D., Croitoru, A. G., & Ioan Ionescu, G. H. (2018). Circular economy – A new direction for the sustainability of the hotel industry in Romania? *Amfiteatru Economic, 20*(48), 388–404. https://doi.org/10.24818/EA/2018/48/388

Peng, J., Jiang, D., & Zhang, X. (2013). Design and implement a knowledge management system to support web-based learning in higher education. *Procedia Computer Science, 22*, 95–103. https://doi.org/10.1016/j.procs.2013.09.085

Petrova, G. I., Smokotin, V. M., Kornienko, A. A., Ershova, I. A., & Kachalov, N. A. (2015). Knowledge management as a strategy for the administration of education in the Research University. *Procedia – Social and Behavioral Sciences.* https://doi.org/10.1016/j.sbspro.2014.12.552

Piccoli, G., Ahmad, R., & Ives, B. (2000). Knowledge management in Academia: A proposed framework. *Information Technology and Management, 1*(4), 229–245. https://doi.org/10.1023/A:1019129226227

Pinto, M. (2012). A framework for knowledge management systems implementation in Higher Education. In *International conference on Advanced Research in Scientific Fields (ARSA-2012)* (pp. 2078–2081) https://www.arsa-conf.com/archive/?vid=1&aid=2&kid=60101-13

Rowley, J. (2000). Is higher education ready for knowledge management? *International Journal of Educational Management, 14*(7), 325–333. https://doi.org/10.1108/09513540010378978

Ryan, A., & Tilbury, D. (2013). Uncharted waters: Voyages for Education for Sustainable Development in the higher education curriculum. *Curriculum Journal, 24*(2), 272–294. https://doi.org/10.1080/09585176.2013.779287

Schmid, J., Olaru, M., & Verjel, A. M. (2017). The effect of sustainable investments to the economic objectives of the company in relation to the total quality management. *Amfiteatru Economic, 19*(Specialissue11), 939–950. https://www.amfiteatrueconomic.ro/temp/Article_2675.pdf

Sedziuviene, N., & Vveinhardt, J. (2009). The paradigm of knowledge management in higher educational institutions. *Engineering Economics, 5*(65), 79–90. https://doi.org/10.5755/j01.ee.65.5.11627

Serrano, G., Llamazares, F., & Javier Otamendi, F. (2015). Measurement and sustainability of the qualifications frameworks in the european higher education area through an employment survey on access to the labour market. *Sustainability (Switzerland), 7*(10), 13777–13812. https://doi.org/10.3390/su71013777

Trivella, L., & Dimitrios, N. K. (2015). Knowledge management strategy within the higher education. The case of Greece. *Procedia - Social and Behavioral Sciences, 175*(2015), 488–495. https://doi.org/10.1016/J.SBSPRO.2015.01.1227

van Weenen, H. (2000). Towards a vision of a sustainable university. *International Journal of Sustainability in Higher Education, 1*(1), 20–34. https://doi.org/10.1108/1467630010307075

Velazquez, L., Munguia, N., Platt, A., & Taddei, J. (2006). Sustainable university: What can be the matter? *Journal of Cleaner Production, 14*(9), 810–819. https://doi.org/10.1016/j.jclepro.2005.12.008

Viegas, C. V., Bond, A. J., Vaz, C. R., Borchardt, M., Pereira, G. M., Selig, P. M., & Varvakis, G. (2016). Critical attributes of sustainability in higher education: A categorisation from literature review. *Journal of Cleaner Production, 126*(2016), 260–276. https://doi.org/10.1016/j.jclepro.2016.02.106

Westerheijden, D. F., Stensaker, B., & Rosa, M. J. (2007). *Quality assurance in higher education : trends in regulation, translation and transformation*. Springer.

Wilkins, S., & Huisman, J. (2011). Student recruitment at international branch campuses: Can they compete in the global market? *Journal of Studies in International Education, 15*(3), 299–316. https://doi.org/10.1177/1028315310385461

Yeh, Y. M. C. (2005). The implementation of knowledge management system in Taiwans Higher Education. *Journal of College Teaching & Learning (TLC), 2*(9), 35–42. https://doi.org/10.19030/tlc.v2i9.1861

Zaki, A. R., & Zubairi, S. A. (2012). Role of knowledge management in higher education – A qualitative model. *Interdisciplinary Journal of Contemporary Research in Business, 4*(6), 1104–1118. https://journal-archieves24.webs.com/1104-1118.pdf

Zaptcioglu Celikdemir, D., Gunay, G., Katrinli, A., & Penbek Alpbaz, S. (2017). Defining sustainable universities following public opinion formation process. *International Journal of Sustainability in Higher Education, 18*(3), 294–306. https://doi.org/10.1108/IJSHE-06-2015-0105

Chapter 7
Public Pension Systems' Financial Sustainability in Central and Eastern European Countries

Florin Cornel Dumiter and Ştefania Amalia Jimon

Abstract In the context of demographic aspects revealed by decreasing the birth rate, diminishing the active population average, life expectancy increases, and population aging trend, the public pension systems are confronting the financial sustainability gaps. Moreover, globalization and the free movement of people around the world can lead to several divergencies regarding the assurance of citizens' social protection at the international level. Regarding these issues, Central and Eastern European countries are subject to the assessment of a fundamental reconstruction and settlement shift towards avoiding financial failure. In this chapter, we have conducted an empirical study towards modeling the financial sustainability of pension systems in Central and Eastern Europe. In this sense, we have created a panel data model in which the financial sustainability of pension systems in five Central and Eastern European countries has been tested. The conclusion of this chapter which is highlighted by the empirical testing results reveals the need for a structural change in the structure of pension systems in Central and Eastern European countries by tackling some important financial, legal, and social reforms.

Keywords Financial sustainability · Social protection · Employment · Pension reforms · Descriptive data

7.1 Introduction

Pension systems are the main instrument used to ensure the financial protection of the citizens of a state against the risk of reduction the ability to obtain the incomes necessary for a decent living, due to accidents, pathologies, or disabilities, as well

F. C. Dumiter (✉) · Ş. A. Jimon
Vasile Goldiş" Western University of Arad, Arad, Romania

S. L. Fotea et al. (eds.), *Navigating Through the Crisis: Business, Technological and Ethical Considerations*, Springer Proceedings in Business and Economics,
https://doi.org/10.1007/978-3-030-82751-9_7

as aging and diminishing the body's ability to carry out professional activities. Globally, pension systems are found either as public schemes or as private schemes.

Public pension systems are organized and managed by state, their financing being different depending on their typology. Thus, in the case of systems based on the Beveridgian principles, the financing is made from the resources of the general state budget, and the provision of benefits is universal, based on residence, once the standard retirement age is reached. On the other hand, *pay-as-you-go* pension systems, based on Bismarckian principles, are financed based on the contributions and solidarity of insured persons, the distribution of benefits being made only if the eligibility criteria regarding the standard retirement age and the minimum period of contribution are met.

Forecasting regarding the future trend of the population made by Eurostat predicts a reduction of the population by 2080; the population structure will face aging by an increase of people aged over 80 years, and the rate of the population active on labor market will decline, with an increase of the share of people aged over 65 years. In these conditions, it is expected that the socio-financial dependency rate of the elderly population to double by 2080.

The approach of this topic was chosen due to the importance of ensuring the social protection of citizens, especially for the vulnerable categories. The difficulties encountered by the current pension systems, both at national and international level, bring this subject up to date and attract the attention of specialists and international and national organizations, due to the fact that these are centered on the human persons and the need to meet their basic needs, as well as the request to ensure the long-term financial sustainability of social protection systems.

The aim of this chapter is to present the general framework of the pension systems in Central and Eastern Europe, their functioning, and the main problems confronted, given the influence of new socio-economic and demographic conditions.

This chapter is structured as follows: the introduction presents the main aspects regarding the motivation to approach the topic, the actuality and importance of the research subject, purpose, and objectives; the review of the specialized literature serves as a *quid pro quo* in order to "place" the research within the national and international debates in the field; the third part aims to describe the research methodology and the descriptive data used; the fourth part describes the main results of econometric tests and their implications regarding the pension systems; the last part presents the main final considerations of the research topic.

7.2 Literature Review

In Central and Eastern European countries, the right to the social and financial protection of the elderly and other categories of citizens unable to perform a professional activity to obtain the needed income for daily life is mainly made through *pay-as-you-go* public pension systems. Their functioning is based on contributions and on the principle of solidarity between generations. Therefore, there is a strong connection between pension systems, and the structure of the population, labor market, and the mismatch between employed population – payers of social contributions – and the number of pensioners, beneficiaries of pension system provisions, represent a threat for the budgetary sustainability of public pension systems.

The connections between sociodemographic features, health, and well-being aspects and public pension systems are an important topic of researches conducted in the social, economic, and medical fields. Many empirical researches focus on the correlations between demographic indicators, such as fertility, life expectancy or dependency rate of the elderly population, and the parameters of pension systems.

Fenge and Scheubel (2017) showed that the implementation of the Bismarckian pension system in Germany has led to a reduction in the fertility rate. On the contrary, Wang (2015) argues that the distributions of pensions by social protection systems can have a positive effect on fertility, and Fenge and von Weizsäcker (2010) agree that if the eligibility criteria establish preferential conditions for accessing the benefits in accordance with the number of births, the birth rate may increase.

Dieppe and Guarda (2015) point out that in order to cope with demographic changes, the employment rate must be increased; Verbic and Spruk (2011) show that by raising the fertility rate and by increasing the standard retirement age, the spending on public pension benefits will decrease. Haan and Prowse (2012) demonstrate that in order to obtain adequate future benefits, the population must work longer and postpone retirement, a specific aspect that is supported also by Cipriani (2018). However, Heijdra and Romp (2009) point out the negative effects of early retirement for the social insurance budget and suggest the need for harsher reforms regarding the eligibility criteria for early retirement.

Staubli and Zweimüller (2013) highlight that raising the retirement age in Australia has had a modest effect on the employment rate and at the same time on the social protection systems, as low-income employees and those with medical conditions have requested either early retirement or disability pension or choose to become unemployed. Similar results were obtained by Engels, Geyer, and Haan (2017) for Germany and by Jimon, Balteş, and Dumiter (2020) for Central and Eastern European countries.

A study conducted by Heller-Sahlgren (2017) on a sample of 10 European countries shows the positive effect of continuing the professional activity on mental health of people; Krumins et al. (2019) identifying the professional activity as a significant factor for reducing mortality. On the other hand, Brockmann et al. (2009) and Hallberg et al. (2015) highlight the positive effects of early retirement on the physical and mental health of employees working in fields with high risk of accidents and occupational diseases.

The effects of retirement on health were also studied by Coe and Zamarro (2011), the authors highlighting that retirement has positive effects on maintaining health. A similar conclusion can be drawn from the study conducted by Eibich (2015). Contrary, Shin (2012) argues that pension systems do not improve the quality of life under all circumstances, a conclusion also supported by Fitzpatrick and Moore (2018) and by Fe and Hollingsworth (2016), who show that retirement can have negative effects on health, by encouraging sedentarism and social isolation.

Labor migration represents another issue for maintaining the equilibrium between the payers of social contribution and the beneficiaries. The effects of labor migration on pension systems were studied by Han (2013), which concluded that a negative net migration will diminish the benefits and will increase the budgetary pressure, especially in the case of Bismarckian systems. Lacomba and Lagos (2010) focus on the impact of the immigrant population on the labor market and pension systems in the host country, showing the positive effects of immigration. Di Liddo (2018) completed this study, demonstrating that in conditions of budgetary pressure and "unsustainability," only immigrants with high professional skills bring a real benefit to the economy and pension systems.

From the perspective of the right to social protection, the free movement of the population may lead to the incidence of multiple legislative systems and generate disputes regarding the obligation to ensure the social protection of nonresident people. The principle of territoriality eliminates the provision of social benefits at the international level, and, on the other hand, according to the principle of residence, the host state has no obligation towards the nonresidents present on its territory.

The occurrence of such events is most often eliminated by signing bilateral social protection agreements and conventions to avoid international double taxation in the social field. Through these legislative instruments, the contracting states have made compromises regarding fiscal sovereignty and established the circumstances of the taxation (Kirsch, 2009) and the conditions to provide social protection for the nonresident population. According to the United Nations Conference on Trade and Development, there are only seven agreements to avoid international double taxation in the case of contributions to social protection systems, and among the countries of Central and Eastern Europe, Poland concluded such an agreement in 2006 with Macedonia, and the Czech Republic signed a treaty in 2007 to avoid double taxation of social security contributions with the USA (Dumiter and Jimon, 2016).

Holzmann and Koettle (2015) argue the importance of ensuring social protection at the international level, highlighting that the right to social security is a universal right and it must be respected, as well as the positive effects of the absence of obstacles of transferability of social protection rights on economic development and well-being of beneficiaries. The role of financial transfers through public pension systems in maintaining the quality of life of the elderly has been studied by authors such as Mitruț and Wolf (2011), Mentzakis and Moro (2009), Cheng et al. (2018), and Ju et al. (2017), which highlights the positive influence, satisfaction, and increase in quality of life, especially in the case of the population with a modest socio-economic level.

7.3 Research Methodology and Empirical Data

The econometric modeling of the public pension systems implemented by countries of Central and Eastern Europe aimed to study the correlations established between the level of social protection expenditures and different socio-economic and demographic factors. Thus, based on data published by Eurostat, a database for the time period 2013–2017 was set up, consisting of the following variables:

- Public expenditure with social protection (CHHPS)
- Level of GDP per inhabitant (PIBLOC)
- Number of births per year (NN)
- Birth rate (RN)
- Fertility rate (RF)
- Total population (POPT)
- Mortality rate (RM)
- Activity rate (PAT)
- Employment rate (PAG)
- Average duration of working life (DMA)
- Unemployment rate (SOM)

The descriptive analysis of the variables (Table 7.1) shows, according to the Jarque-Bera test, that the variables have an abnormal distribution ($p > 5\%$), except

Table 7.1 Descriptive analysis of variables

	CHHPS?	PIBLOC?	NN?	RN?	RF?	POPT?
Mean	14.06800	12283.60	167836.6	10.08400	1.485600	16733925
Median	14.50000	11740.00	110764.0	10.20000	1.480000	10538275
Maximum	16.60000	18100.00	401982.0	10.80000	1.710000	38062535
Minimum	11.40000	7190.000	54823.00	9.000000	1.290000	5410836
Std. Dev.	1.812852	2981.139	118471.0	0.474060	0.122613	11866021
Skewness	−0.254444	0.062926	0.976398	−0.429902	0.227049	0.972840
Kurtosis	1.613953	2.077269	2.482029	2.380799	2.105611	2.461967
Jarque-Bera	2.270930	0.903407	4.251779	1.169451	1.048060	4.244948
Probability	0.321273	0.636543	0.119327	0.557259	0.592129	0.119735
Sum	351.7000	307090.0	4195915.	252.1000	37.14000	4.18E+08
Sum sq. dev.	78.87440	2.13E+08	3.37E+11	5.393600	0.360816	3.38E+15

	RM?	PAT?	PAG?	DMA?	SOM?
Mean	11.26800	7652720.	7100040.	33.35200	554160.0
Median	10.50000	5213000.	4934000.	33.20000	370000.0
Maximum	13.50000	17153000	16079000	35.90000	1793000.
Minimum	9.500000	2703000.	2318000.	30.80000	155000.0
Std. Dev.	1.507404	5206720.	4815833.	1.198304	438241.9
Skewness	0.363776	1.000711	0.969296	0.398382	1.607481
Kurtosis	1.338003	2.519996	2.496120	2.970318	4.595747
Jarque-Bera	3.428712	4.412600	4.179204	0.662201	13.41915
Probability	0.180080	0.110107	0.123736	0.718133	0.001219
Sum	281.7000	1.91E+08	1.78E+08	833.8000	13854000
Sum sq. dev.	54.53440	6.51E+14	5.57E+14	34.46240	4.61E+12

Source: Author's processing using EViews 10 Academic Edition software

for the unemployment rate. The asymmetry coefficient reflects the negative asymmetry of budget expenditures with social protection and of the birth rate (Skewness < 0), the other variables showing a positive asymmetry (Skewness > 0). The coefficient of kurtosis shows the platykurtic kurtosis of all variables (Kurtosis < 3), except for the level of unemployment which presents a leptokurtic kurtosis (Kurtosis > 3).

The econometric tests were performed by the ordinary least squares method (OLS) using the econometric software EViews 10 University Edition. This econometric method analyzes the variables by pool-data regression models, respectively, not only in a cross-section but also in the temporal section. There are three forms of OLS method for data testing, depending on the relationship between predictors and the dependent variable, respectively: no effects, fixed effects, and random effects. Fixed effects assume the existence of a country and/or period-specific constants which explain the differences between the variances of the variables, while the random effects reflect the existence of an independent random variable that explains these differences.

This chapter aims to explore the correlations established between expenditures with social protection and different socio-economic and demographic indicators by all three forms of the OLS method. However, due to the relatively short time horizon, the OLS method with random effects was unable to be proceeded by econometric soft, and therefore was applied only in the version without effects and with fixed effects.

The regression equations used for the empirical study regarding public pension systems are:`

$$\begin{aligned} CHHPS_{it} &= \alpha + \beta_1 xPIBLOC_{it} + \beta_2 xNN_{it} + \beta_3 xRN_{it} + \beta_4 xRF_{it} \\ &+\beta_5 xPOPT_{it} + \beta_6 xRM_{it} + \beta_7 xPAT_{it} + \beta_8 xPAG_{it} + \beta_9 xDMA_{it} \\ &+\beta_{10} xSOM_{it} + \varepsilon_{it} \end{aligned} \tag{7.1}$$

$$\begin{aligned} CHHPS_{it} &= 34,04 + 0,01xPIBLOC_{it} - 1,42xNN_{it} + 1,90xRN_{it} \\ &-14,46xRF_{it} + 1,27xPOPT_{it} + 0,65xRM_{it} - 0,01xPAT_{it} \\ &+0,01xPAG_{it} - 0,99xDMA_{it} + 0,01xSOM_{it} + \varepsilon_{it} \end{aligned} \tag{7.1a}$$

$$\begin{aligned} CHHPS_{it} &= 88,01 - 4,77xPIBLOC_{it} + 3,31xNN_{it} + 0,13xRN_{it} \\ &-2,89xRF_{it} - 1,95xPOPT_{it} - 0,31xRM_{it} - 0,01xPAT_{it} \\ &+0,01xPAG_{it} - 0,22xDMA_{it} + 0,01xSOM_{it} + \varepsilon_{it} \end{aligned} \tag{7.1b}$$

$$\begin{aligned} CHHPS_{it} &= 71,69 + 0,01xPIBLOC_{it} + 7,96xNN_{it} - 0,97xRN_{it} \\ &-12,34xRF_{it} - 1,74xPOPT_{it} + 0,12xRM_{it} - 0,01xPAT_{it} \\ &+0,01xPAG_{it} - 1,05xDMA_{it} + 0,01xSOM_{it} + \varepsilon_{it} \end{aligned} \tag{7.1c}$$

$CHHPS_{it} = 92, 77 - 0, 01xPIBLOC_{it} + 2, 24xNN_{it} + 0, 57xRN_{it} - 5, 31xRF_{it} - 2, 04xPOPT_{it} - 0, 60xRM_{it} - 0, 01xPAT_{it} + 0, 01xPAG_{it} - 0, 51xDMA_{it} + 0, 01xSOM_{it} + \varepsilon_{it}$ (1d)Where

α – free coefficient
$\beta_{1,2,3,4,5,6,7,8,9,10}$ – predictor coefficients
CHHPS – public expenditure with social protection
PIBLOC – level of GDP per inhabitant
NN – number of births per year
RN – birth rate
RF – fertility rate
POPT – total population
RM – mortality rate
PAT – activity rate
PAG – employment rate
DMA – average duration of working life
SOM – unemployment rate
ε_{it} – regression error

7.4 Empirical Findings

The first econometric model for the study of public pension systems applied equation (7.1a) using the OLS method without effects (Table 7.2). The test results show that the model is significant (R-squared = 0.94, and adjusted R-squared = 0.90), being validated by the F test (Prob F-statistic = 0.00).

The empirical results reflect a positive correlation between social protection expenditures and GDP per capita, birth rate, total population, mortality rate, employment rate, and unemployment rate but also a negative correlation between social protection expenditures and births, fertility rate, activity rate, and the average duration of working life. These results mean that the level of public spending on social protection increases by growing the level of GDP per capita, birth rate, total population, mortality rate, employment, and unemployment rate, as well as by reducing the number of births, fertility rate, activity rate, and average duration of activity on the labor market.

To apply the method OLS with cross-section fixed effects requires to establish the effectiveness of the method by testing redundant fixed effects. The test results reflect the acceptance of the individual cross-section effects in the test by the F test and the chi-square test ($p < 5\%$). Therefore, the tests by the OLS method with fixed cross-section effects used Eq. (7.1b) (Table 7.3), the results showing that the model is significant (R-squared = 0.99 and adjusted R-squared = 0.98) and valid according to F test (Prob F-statistic = 0.00).

The empirical results reflect the negative correlation between social protection expenditure and GDP per capita, fertility rate, total population, mortality rate,

Table 7.2 Results of econometric tests – OLS method without effects

Dependent variable: CHHPS?				
Method: Pooled least squares				
Date: 05/27/20 Time: 13:06				
Sample: 2013 2017				
Included observations: 5				
Cross-sections included: 5				
Total pool (balanced) observations: 25				
Variable	Coefficient	Std. error	t-Statistic	Prob.
C	34.03797	19.84059	1.715572	0.1083
PIBLOC?	0.000641	0.000137	4.667293	0.0004
NN?	−1.42E-05	5.56E-05	−0.255757	0.8019
RN?	1.901524	1.454058	1.307736	0.2120
RF?	−14.46221	4.691130	−3.082885	0.0081
POPT?	1.27E-06	1.49E-06	0.850896	0.4091
RM?	0.651750	0.375332	1.736465	0.1044
PAT?	−0.000282	0.000252	−1.121269	0.2810
PAG?	0.000280	0.000251	1.115779	0.2833
DMA?	−0.989864	0.569348	−1.738593	0.1040
SOM?	0.000278	0.000250	1.110691	0.2854
Root MSE	0.429400	R-squared		0.941558
Mean dependent var	14.06800	Adjusted R-squared		0.899813
S.D. dependent var	1.812852	S.E. of regression		0.573809
Akaike info criterion	2.027143	Sum squared resid		4.609602
Schwarz criterion	2.563448	Log likelihood		−14.33928
Hannan-Quinn criter.	2.175891	F-statistic		22.55525
Durbin-Watson stat	2.628888	Prob (F-statistic)		0.000001

Source: Author's processing using EViews 10 Academic Edition software

activity rate, and average duration of working life but the positive correlation between social protection expenditure and the number of births, birth rate, level employment, and unemployment. In other words, social protection expenditures are increased by a higher number of births, birth rate, employment rate, and unemployment, as well as by a lower GDP per capita, fertility rate, activity and mortality, total population, and average duration of activity on the labor market.

The model was also extended to fixed period effects, which according to the F test and the chi-square test for redundant effects are accepted in the test ($p < 5\%$). Empirical tests using the OLS method with temporal fixed effects used the regression equation (7.1c) (Table 7.4), the results showing that the model is significant (R-squared = 0.98 and adjusted R-squared = 0.95) and was validated by F test (Prob F-statistic = 0.00).

The results of empirical tests with OLS fixed period effects reflect the positive correlation between social protection expenditure and GDP per capita, number of births, mortality rate, employment rate, and unemployment level but the negative

Table 7.3 Results of econometric tests - OLS method with fixed cross-section effects

Dependent variable: CHHPS?				
Method: Pooled least squares				
Date: 05/27/20 Time: 13:11				
Sample: 2013–2017				
Included observations: 5				
Cross-sections included: 5				
Total pool (balanced) observations: 25				
Variable	Coefficient	Std. error	t-Statistic	Prob.
C	88.00543	24.29952	3.621694	0.0047
PIBLOC?	−4.77E-05	0.000313	−0.152422	0.8819
NN?	3.31E-06	3.91E-05	0.084658	0.9342
RN?	0.134565	1.957135	0.068756	0.9465
RF?	−2.894367	8.542920	−0.338803	0.7418
POPT?	−1.95E-06	1.25E-06	−1.567673	0.1480
RM?	−0.313538	0.379463	−0.826267	0.4279
PAT?	−0.000180	0.000128	−1.407002	0.1897
PAG?	0.000177	0.000128	1.379926	0.1977
DMA?	−0.219031	0.386086	−0.567312	0.5830
SOM?	0.000176	0.000128	1.378528	0.1981
Fixed effects (cross)				
_CZ--C	−21.69034			
_HU--C	−23.28109			
_PL--C	75.58612			
_RO--C	8.384599			
_SK--C	−38.99929			
	Effect specification			
Cross-section fixed (dummy variables)				
Root MSE	0.177487	R-squared		0.990015
Mean dependent var	14.06800	Adjusted R-squared		0.976037
S.D. dependent var	1.812852	S.E. of regression		0.280631
Akaike info criterion	0.580160	Sum squared resid		0.787540
Schwarz criterion	1.311486	Log likelihood		7.747994
Hannan-Quinn criter.	0.782999	F-statistic		70.82346
Durbin-Watson stat	2.274550	Prob (F-statistic)		0.000000

Source: Author's processing using EViews 10 Academic Edition software

correlation between social protection expenditure and birth rate, population fertility rate total, active population, and average duration of professional activity. Thus, the social protection expenditures increase if the level of GDP per inhabitant, number of births, mortality rate, employment rate, and unemployment rate increase, as well as if the birth rate, fertility rate total population, active population, and average duration of professional activity will decrease.

Table 7.4 Results of econometric tests – OLS method with fixed period effects

Dependent variable: CHHPS?				
Method: Pooled least squares				
Date: 05/27/20 Time: 13:13				
Sample: 2013–2017				
Included observations: 5				
Cross-sections included: 5				
Total pool (balanced) observations: 25				
Variable	Coefficient	Std. error	t-Statistic	Prob.
C	71.69400	21.69374	3.304825	0.0079
PIBLOC?	0.000289	0.000179	1.618238	0.1367
NN?	7.96E-05	5.51E-05	1.445012	0.1791
RN?	−0.970831	1.685964	−0.575831	0.5775
RF?	−12.33834	4.407642	−2.799307	0.0188
POPT?	−1.74E-06	1.59E-06	−1.093515	0.2998
RM?	0.119741	0.447449	0.267607	0.7944
PAT?	−0.000166	0.000242	−0.687008	0.5077
PAG?	0.000168	0.000241	0.699129	0.5004
DMA?	−1.053087	0.443877	−2.372474	0.0391
SOM?	0.000168	0.000240	0.699143	0.5004
Fixed effects (period)				
2013--C	−1.057001			
2014--C	−0.412865			
2015--C	−0.348397			
2016--C	0.797899			
2017--C	1.020364			
	Effect specification			

Table 7.4 (continued)

Period fixed (dummy variables)			
Root MSE	0.251533	R-squared	0.979946
Mean dependent var	14.06800	Adjusted R-squared	0.951871
S.D. dependent var	1.812852	S.E. of regression	0.397709
Akaike info criterion	1.277515	Sum squared resid	1.581721
Schwarz criterion	2.008840	Log likelihood	−0.968937
Hannan-Quinn criter.	1.480354	F-statistic	34.90441
Durbin-Watson stat	2.234631	Prob (F-statistic)	0.000001

Source: Author's processing using EViews 10 Academic Edition software

The econometric model was performed by applying the OLS method with cross-section and period fixed effects. After testing the redundant fixed effects, the F test and the chi-square test show the acceptance of cross-section and period effects in the tests (p <5%).

Table 7.5 Economy test results – OLS method with cross-section and period fixed effects

Dependent variable: CHHPS?				
Method: Pooled least squares				
Date: 05/27/20 Time: 13:08				
Sample: 2013–2017				
Included observations: 5				
Cross-sections included: 5				
Total pool (balanced) observations: 25				
Variable	Coefficient	Std. error	t-Statistic	Prob.
C	92.76665	36.49650	2.541796	0.0440
PIBLOC?	−0.000318	0.000425	−0.747128	0.4832
NN?	2.24E-06	6.35E-05	0.035288	0.9730
RN?	0.573495	2.671284	0.214689	0.8371
RF?	−5.305898	11.67263	−0.454559	0.6654
POPT?	−2.04E-06	1.77E-06	−1.154949	0.2920
RM?	−0.604434	0.937330	−0.644847	0.5429
PAT?	−0.000229	0.000203	−1.129000	0.3020
PAG?	0.000227	0.000201	1.131244	0.3011
DMA?	−0.506391	0.630155	−0.803598	0.4523
SOM?	0.000226	0.000200	1.129514	0.3018
Fixed effects (cross)				
_CZ--C	−17.11069			
_HU--C	−18.60604			
_PL--C	61.56620			
_RO--C	6.446715			
_SK--C	−32.29618			
Fixed effects (period)				
2013--C	−0.542700			
2014--C	−0.430199			
2015--C	−0.033585			
2016--C	0.151857			
2017--C	0.854627			
	Effect specification			
Cross-section fixed (dummy variables)				
Period fixed (dummy variables)				
Root MSE	0.151910	R-squared		0.992686
Mean dependent var	14.06800	Adjusted R-squared		0.970743
S.D. dependent var	1.812852	S.E. of regression		0.310084
Akaike info criterion	0.588938	Sum squared resid		0.576913
Schwarz criterion	1.515283	Log likelihood		11.63828
Hannan-Quinn criter.	0.845867	F-statistic		45.23933
Durbin-Watson stat	2.633260	Prob (F-statistic)		0.000062

Source: Author's processing using EViews 10 Academic Edition software

Tests by the OLS method with cross-section and period fixed effects used the regression equation (7.1d) (Table 7.5), and the results reflect that the model is significant (R-squared = 0.99 and adjusted R-squared = 0.97) and valid according with F test (Prob F-statistic = 0.00).

The results of the tests included in equation (7.1d) by the OLS method with cross-section and period fixed effects highlight the existence of a positive correlation between social protection expenditure and the number of births, birth rate, employment rate, and unemployment level, as well as the existence of a negative correlation in social protection expenditure and the level of GDP per capita, fertility rate, total population, mortality rate, activity rate, and average duration of professional activity. These correlations reflect the fact that social protection expenditures grow not only with increasing births, birth rate, employment rate, and unemployment rate but also with decreasing GDP per capita, fertility rate, total population, mortality rate, activity rate, and average duration of working life.

7.5 Conclusions

The foundation of pension systems represents the right of the population to social protection, in the framework of income inequality, which will lead to poverty. The manner to respect this right has been different between countries, depending on the government system and political ideology. The Czech Republic, Hungary, Poland, Slovakia, and Romania have descending structures of paternalistic socialist systems but in recent decades have adopted numerous regulations on the field of social protection in order to maintain the sustainability of public pension systems.

The reforms adopted by the five Central and Eastern European countries aimed at the maintaining of financial sustainability of public pension systems and the adequacy of benefits. In this regard, the eligibility criteria for accessing benefits have been redefined, and through parametric reforms, the compulsory social contributions rates have been modified, the minimum contributory period and the standard retirement age have been increased, penalties for early retirement were established, but for continuing activity after reaching retirement age were given extra-benefits, the way of determining the amount of provision was redefined, as well as the way of indexing them.

Efforts to provide adequate benefits through public pension systems in these countries were reflected in increasing the replacement rates of pension income, reducing the poverty rate and severe material deprivation rate, and maintaining the level of consumption and improving the health status of population over the age of 65. On the other hand, expenditures with pension benefits increased. The direct link with the population structure and the contribution of the labor force represents, in the current demographic context, especially for Romania, where emigration is extensive, a threat to the financial sustainability of public pension systems.

The empirical study regarding public pension systems considered the specific situation of these five Central and Eastern European countries, for a time period between 2013 and 2017. The econometric model had studied the correlations that can be established between the level of social protection expenditures and different socio-economic and demographic factors. The method applied for the econometric study was ordinary least squares (OLS), which allows the analysis of pool data variables, both in cross-section section and period section. Due to the relatively short time horizon, the OLS method was applied only in the version without effects and with fixed effects.

Following the validation of the econometric model, it was highlighted that public spending on social protection is correlated with GDP per capita, number of births per year, birth rate, fertility rate, total population, mortality rate, activity rate, employment rate, average duration of working life, and the unemployment rate.

The results of the tests show that the level of public spending on social protection can be reduced by increasing the birth rate and fertility, the activity rate, and the average duration of working life, as well as by reducing unemployment. These results reflect the dependence of public social protection systems on the structure of the population and labor market. Increasing the share of the active population on labor market and spending on unemployment benefits and other aid to reduce the risk of poverty will decrease, while budget revenues from social contributions will increase, which will strengthen the financial sustainability of the public social protection systems.

The general conclusion of the chapter highlights the need to harmonize the reforms of social protection systems with the general national framework and to consider the determinants of the economic, social, and medical environment, as well as their influence on the parameters of pension systems.

References

Brockmann, H., Muller, R., & Helmert, U. (2009). Time to retire – Time to die? A prospective cohort study of the effects of early retirement on long-term survival. *Social Science & Medicine, 69*, 160–164.

Cheng, L., Liu, H., Zhang, Y., & Zhao, Z. (2018). The health implications of social pensions: Evidence from China's new rural pension scheme. *Journal of Comparative Economics, 46*, 53–77.

Cipriani, G. P. (2018). Aging, retirement, and pay-as-you-go pensions. *Macroeconomic Dynamics, 22*, 1173–1183.

Coe, N. B., & Zamarro, G. (2011). Retirement effects on health in Europe. *Journal of Health Economics, 30*, 77–86.

Di Liddo, G. (2018). Immigration and PAYG pension systems in the presence of increasing life expectancy. *Economics Letters, 162*, 56–61.

Dieppe, A., & Guarda, P. (Eds.). (2015). *Occasional paper series: Public debt, population ageing and medium-term growth*. Occasional Paper No 165, European Central Bank.

Dumiter, F., & Jimon, Ş. (2016). Double taxation conventions in Central and Eastern European countries. *Journal of Legal Studies, 18*(32), 1–12.

Eibich, P. (2015). Understanding the effect of retirement on health: Mechanisms and heterogeneity. *Journal of Health Economics, 43*, 1–12.

Engels, B., Geyer, J., & Haan, P. (2017). Pension incentives and early retirement. *Labour Economics, 47*, 216–231.

Fe, E., & Hollingsworth, B. (2016). Short- and long-run estimates of the local effects of retirement on health. *Journal of the Royal Statistical Society, A, 179*(4), 1051–1067.

Fenge, R., & Scheubel, B. (2017). Pensions and fertility: Back to the roots Bismarck's Pension Scheme and the first demographic transition. *Journal of Population Economics, 30*(1), 93–139.

Fenge, R., & von Weizsäcker, J. (2010). Mixing Bismarck and child pension systems: An optimum taxation approach. *Journal of Population Economics, 23*, 805–823.

Fitzpatrick, M. D., & Moore, T. J. (2018). The mortality effects of retirement: Evidence from Social Security eligibility at age 62. *Journal of Public Economics, 157*, 121–137.

Haan, P., & Prowse, V. (2012). Longevity, life-cycle behavior, and pension reform. MPRA Paper No. 39282. Available at: https://mpra.ub.uni-muenchen.de/39282/

Hallberg, D., Johansson, P., & Josephson, M. (2015). Is an early retirement offer good for your health? Quasi-experimental evidence from the army. *Journal of Health Economics, 44*, 274–285.

Han, K. J. (2013). Saving public pensions: Labor migration effects on pension systems in European countries. *The Social Science Journal, 50*, 152–161.

Heijdra, B. J., & Romp, W. E. (2009). Retirement, pensions, and ageing. *Journal of Public Economics, 93*, 586–604.

Heller-Sahlgren, G. (2017). Retirement blues. *Journal of Health Economics, 54*, 66–78.

Holzmann, R., & Koettl, J. (2015). Stability of pension, health, and other social benefits: Facts, concepts, and issues. *CESifo Economic Studies, 61*(2), 377–415.

Jimon, Ş. A., Balteş, N., & Dumiter, F. (2020). Empirical approaches upon pension systems in Central and Eastern European countries. Triangle assessment: Free movement of people, labor market and population health features. *Studia Universitatis "Vasile Goldis" Economics Series, 30*(1), 1–21.

Ju, Y. J., Han, K. T., Lee, H. J., Lee, J. E., Choi, J. W., Hyun, I. S., & Park, E. C. (2017). Quality of life and national pension receipt after retirement among older adults. *Geriatrics and Gerontology International, 17*, 1205–1213.

Kirsch, M. S. (2009). The limits of administrative guidance in the interpretation of tax treaties. *Texas Law Review, 87*(6), 1063–1135.

Krumins, J., Berzins, A., Dahs, A., Ponomarjova, D., (2019). Healthy and active pre-retirement and retirement ages: Elderly inequality in Latvia. In *11th International scientific conference „New Challenges of Economic and Business Development – 2019: Incentives for Sustainable Economic Growth" Proceedings*, 463–475.

Lacomba, J. A., & Lagos, F. (2010). Immigration and pension benefits in the host country. *Economica, 77*, 283–295.

Mentzakis, E., & Moro, M. (2009). The poor, the rich and the happy: Exploring the link between income and subjective well-being. *The Journal of Socio-Economics, 38*, 147–158.

Mitrut, A., & Wolf, F. C. (2011). Do private and public transfers received affect life satisfaction? Evidence from Romania. *Journal of Economic Psychology, 32*, 969–979.

Shin, I. (2012). The effect of pension on the optimized life expectancy and lifetime utility level. MPRA Paper No. 41374. Available at: http://mpra.ub.uni-muenchen.de/41374/.

Staubli, S., & Zweimüller, J. (2013). Does raising the early retirement age increase employment of older workers? *Journal of Public Economics, 108*, 17–32.

Verbic, M., & Spruk, R. (2011). *Aging population and public pensions: Theory and evidence*. MPRA Paper No. 38914. Available at: https://mpra.ub.uni-muenchen.de/38914/

Wang, L. (2015). Fertility and unemployment in a social security system. *Economics Letters, 133*, 19–23.

Chapter 8
A Bioeconomic Perspective on Agriculture Development in the European Union

Bălan Emilia Mary and Cismaş Laura Mariana

Abstract Bioeconomy and agriculture are two interconnected areas, and each contributes to the development of the other. Agriculture is an important sector of the bioeconomy that can contribute to the economic development of a state. The process of transition to a green and circular economy is a present and future goal for the European Union (EU), particularly on the background of the highly polluting processing technologies of fossil resources.

To determine the role of agriculture in the evolution of the bioeconomy in the Member States of the European Union, we have carried out an analysis of the indicators suggesting the development of the bioeconomy. The analysis relies on quantitative and qualitative methods, focused on the most relevant scientific articles in the field, and the analysis of indicators in the European Commission's data. The indicators that configure the dynamics of bioeconomy in the European Union are the number of persons employed, added value at factor costs, and turnover. We have also calculated the apparent productivity of labor to illustrate the profitability of the bioeconomy sector and agriculture, in particular.

The research highlights the significant contribution of agriculture to the dynamics of the bioeconomy in the Member States of the European Union. Agriculture also supports other economic sectors that are part of the bioeconomy. Concrete and coordinated measures by the Member States are needed to boost all factors involved in the economy based on raw materials, products, and environmentally friendly activities.

Keywords Economics · Development · Bioeconomy · Agriculture · European Union

---

B. E. Mary (✉) · C. L. Mariana
West University of Timisoara, Timisoara, Romania
e-mail: emilia.balan75@e-uvt.ro

S. L. Fotea et al. (eds.), *Navigating Through the Crisis: Business, Technological and Ethical Considerations*, Springer Proceedings in Business and Economics,
https://doi.org/10.1007/978-3-030-82751-9_8

8.1 Introduction

In the 1970s, Georgescu-Roegen used the term bioeconomy as a result of a new approach to the economy: "The term is meant to make us continuously consider the biological origin of the economic process and thus to focus the problem of human existence with limited and unevenly localized accessible resources" (Gowdy & Mesner, 1998, p. 15).

According to the United Nations 2030 Agenda for Sustainable Development (United Nations [UN] 2015), of the seventeen global objectives, two are related to the sustainable economy. Point three of the agenda establishes the population's access to clean energy that could be purchased at low prices, to be achieved in the long term and with modern technologies. Point thirteen recommends that the agenda signatory states take urgent measures to protect the environment in order to curb the effects of climate change (Food and Agriculture Organization of the United Nations [FAO], 2016).

The need for all the countries of the world to adopt the bioeconomy model also derives from the inevitable reduction of resources (soil erosion, gas, oil), as well as from the recent effects of climate change, the trigger of which is the excessive industrialization of the economy. Georgescu-Roegen conceived the bioeconomy with man at the center of economic processes and the bioeconomy being a set of economies, which revolve around it (Pauna et al., 2017).

According to the Organization for Economic Cooperation and Development (OECD), the role that biotechnology can play in addressing the most pressing challenges of national economies and societies in the coming years can be transposed into what is called the bioeconomy as a whole (Organization for Economic Cooperation and Development [OECD], 2009). In order to ensure long-term economic and environmental sustainability, the bioeconomy can have a significant impact on many areas of activity in order to ensure the need for food, water energy, health, and other resources and services to the population. The growing world population, in the near future, is forced to face climate change (OECD, 2009).

Characterization of the concept of bioeconomy has become one of the main aspects of innovation policy development (Wilfried & Frieder, 2014). The definition of the bioeconomy also implies the inclusion or exclusion of certain economic activities and sectors, as well as the identification of driving forces and barriers that arise in the process of future development. The rather large number of definitions relating to the bioeconomy is a disadvantage for this area, not only in terms of economic interests but also in terms of sustainability. According to Wilfried and Frieder (2014), the definitions of the bioeconomy in the early 2000s did not adequately take into account the concept of ecological value. This issue remains, and the solution could be a greater focus on carrying out research activities in the biological field.

As stated by Ronzon et al. (2015), the bioeconomy represents the production of biomass and the transformation of biomass into value-added products such as food, feed, organic products, and bioenergy. The bioeconomy includes agriculture, forestry, fisheries, agri-food, pulp, and paper manufacturing as sub-sectors, as well as specific subgroups in the chemical, biotechnology, and energy industries (European Commission [EC], 2018).

Patermann and Aguilar (2018) think that the concept of a bioeconomy in the European Union (EU) emerged as a necessity and was implemented by the European Commission (EC) through the Framework Programme for Biotechnology and Life Sciences in 2002, which called it the "knowledge-based bioeconomy" (Patermann & Aguilar, 2018, p. 2).

However, the essential issue for the bioeconomy analysis at the European and regional level derives from differences in the definition of bioeconomy for most researchers. Thus, some consider that the bioeconomy is comprising all the economic sectors that use natural raw materials, while others consider that the bioeconomy incorporates only those industries that can generate biomass. Regardless of the opinions of specialists on the definition of the bioeconomy, all the studies consulted include agriculture in the bioeconomy and argue that it is its most important sector.

According to the European Strategy (EC, 2018, p. 6), the bioeconomy is made of those sectors and economic systems that "rely on biological resources (animals, plants, microorganisms, and biomass products, including organic waste), and their functions and principles." The bioeconomy also includes "terrestrial and marine ecosystems and the services that these areas provide, all primary production sectors using and producing biological resources (agriculture, forestry, fisheries, and aquaculture)." In addition, "all economic and industrial sectors using resources and biological processes to produce food, feed, bioproducts, energy, and services (excluding biological medicines and health biotechnology)" are included and interconnected within the bioeconomy.

Through the Strategy "A Sustainable Bioeconomy for Europe: Strengthening the Links between the Economy, Society and the Environment" updated at the end of 2018, the EC proposes to the Member States the achievement of several objectives including ensuring food and nutrition security, sustainable management of natural resources, reducing dependence on conventional and nonviable energy resources of domestic or external origin, mitigating the effects of climate change and adapting to them, strengthening competitiveness, and creating new jobs (EC, 2018).

In this context, the EC positions the bioeconomy among its priorities. The EC also suggests that the bioeconomy should be promoted and that it should benefit from proper market conditions, as well as similar regulations under industries using traditional fuels, in order for the bioeconomy to be used to its full potential.

The bioeconomy can also be defined as the economy that relies on the transformation of renewable resources into biomass and the latter into organic, biosubstance, or bioenergy products. The advantages of the transition to a green economy have been discussed extensively in the literature. A point of the UN 2030 Agenda for Sustainable Development is the long-term and modern technology production of renewable energy that is accessible to the population at a low price. Another point of the agenda recommends that signatories speed up action to protect the environment and restrict the effects of climate change (UN, 2015).

The chapter brings as a novelty the analysis of the bioeconomy from the perspective of the agricultural sector in the European Union, which has often been overlooked as the main driver of the bioeconomy. It also highlights the dynamics of the indicators for assessing the bioeconomy by the Member States, with a focus on the countries at the top of the hierarchy and the lowest performing in terms of relevant indicators. Our study emphasizes the contribution of agriculture to the bioeconomy and the economic development of the Member States. We find that agriculture is a primary sector of the bioeconomy and can contribute much more to the evolution of the green and circular economy of the future in the European Union. Coordinated measures by the Member States are needed to boost all factors involved in the economy based on raw materials, products, and environmentally friendly activities.

8.2 Literature Overview

8.2.1 European Union Policies in the Bioeconomy Fields

In the current context of climate change and limited natural resources, their efficient and sustainable use represents a present and future desire for the EU Member States. The use of renewable resources is one of the solutions to environmental problems, which European Union countries need to apply to their full potential, and biomass from agriculture is of particular importance, as stipulated in the European Directive on the promotion of the use of energy from renewable resources (Schöpe, 2008).

As part of the bioeconomy, renewable energies are covered by the European Strategic Framework through the Renewable Energy Promotion Directive (EU, 2018). The main objective of the directive is that by 2030, the share of renewable energy in the Union's gross final energy consumption will be at least 32%. In order to support the Member States in achieving this objective, the European Commission is proposing the application of support schemes, which consist of providing incentives for electricity production from renewable sources. In order to achieve the objectives of the directive, the European Union Member States are advised to comply with sustainability criteria and not exceed the regulated level of greenhouse gas (GHG) emissions.

Within the framework of the Common Agricultural Policy, cross-compliance requirements regulate sustainable agricultural production (EC, 2010). In this con encompassing biodiversity and the maintenance of carbon stocks, such as those in forests. Since most of the biomass used as heat and electricity comes from wood mass, it is necessary to limit the pressure on forest cutting. At the European Union level, there are concerns about an increase in the use of forest biomass, as this action can exacerbate the effects of climate change (EC, 2016).

At the end of 2019, as a support for its strategy on combating the effects of climate change, the European Union adopted a set of measures transposed into the European Green Pact, which facilitate the community citizens and industry to a green and sustainable economy. The principal objective of the pact is for the European Union to become the first climate-neutral continent by 2050 (European Commission, 2019a). The European project is initiated in the context of the commitments made by the EU through the Paris Agreement on Climate Change, and the Sustainable Development Goals signed as part of the UN 2030 Agenda for Sustainable Development, as well as European Union policies on the synergy between the current and future economies, which contribute directly and effectively to halting climate change, at European and global level.

The roadmap of the European Union strategy set out in the European Green Pact includes a set of measures to boost resource efficiency by switching to the circular economy, restoring biodiversity, and reducing pollution (European Commission, 2019b). Most of the EU-27 Member States have a strategy dedicated to the bioeconomy, and some have defined their concepts in national strategies, while others have adopted the European Commission definition of the 2012 and/or 2018 Strategies.

8.2.2 *The Contribution of the Bioeconomy to the Economic Development of the Member States*

The transition from the current economy, based on exhaustible resources whose manufacturing technologies are highly polluting, to a circular economy, where the value of products, materials, and resources is maintained in the economy for as long as possible is necessary. In this sense, waste generation is an essential effort on the part of the European Union. Through all its institutions, the European Union contributes to the development of a sustainable, competitive, low-carbon, and resource-efficient economy. Such a transition is an opportunity to transform the current economy and generate new and sustainable competitive advantages for the EU (European Commission, 2015). In this context, the bioeconomy offers alternatives to depleting products and energy from mineral resources and contributes to a circular economy.

According to (European Commission, 2015), in order for the bioeconomy to meet its food security objectives, sustainable resource management, reducing dependence on depleting resources, combating climate change, creating jobs, and maintaining competitiveness, stakeholders in this area should strive to respect a set of principles, which are shown in Fig. 8.1:

At the European Union level, the bioeconomy can become the engine of rural development and coastal areas. The EU's vision is to understand that the bioeconomy is based on integrated systems and networks that use biological resources, maximizing added value throughout closed cycles of use of raw materials, water, nutrients, by-products, and energy (Diakosavvas, 2019).

In the forthcoming EU financial program (2021–2027), the Common Agricultural Policy (CAP) provides for increased investment in the development of the

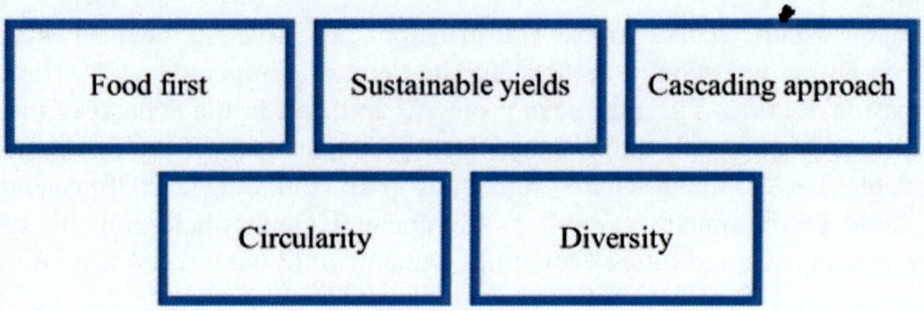

Fig. 8.1 The main principles of sustainable bioeconomy. (Source: Authors representation based on European Commission, 2015)

bioeconomy, which is considered to have enormous economic and job creation potential. The European Fund for Strategic Investments (EFSI) and other financial instruments available to the EU should attract additional support from rural development programs in order to provide advantageous long-term loans to entrepreneurs who are willing to invest in rural areas (Gafo, 2018). The EU Framework for Research and Development Programme – Horizon Europe – allocates a budget of EUR 10.000 million for research and innovation projects in the fields of agri-food, agriculture, forestry, rural development, and the bioeconomy.

Analytical documentation of the bioeconomy is a challenge for scientists and researchers, as official statistics report only data on traditional sectors without differentiating the manufacturing activities of synthetic and organic products. A concrete example is the manufacture of synthetic textiles and organic textiles. For these reasons, indicators relating to the bioeconomy are estimated based on compilations from multiple sources (Ronzon et al., 2015).

Because the bioeconomy is not a clearly defined economic sector, assessing the bioeconomy is the main challenge for researchers. It is difficult to quantify the bioeconomy, as no economic activity is entirely environmentally friendly so that only organic products can be included throughout the production flow. Moreover, almost all economic sectors use environmentally friendly materials to a certain extent (Kuosmanen et al., 2020).

Based on the traditional model of the classification of economic sectors – primary, secondary, and tertiary – Kuosmanen et al. (2020) proposed an alternative classification for the economic sectors included in the bioeconomy (Fig. 8.2).

According to the researchers (Kuosmanen et al., 2020), mathematically, the bioeconomy is the sum of the three productions (primary, secondary, and tertiary) of activities within the environmental industry, respectively:

$$Bioeconomy = IB + IIB + IIIb$$

The classification facilitates the evaluation of the distribution of organic products in the value chain, all the more so given the economic and political debates on the economy focus on quantifying the added value that producers in the processing of organic raw materials achieve in an environmentally friendly, booming economy.

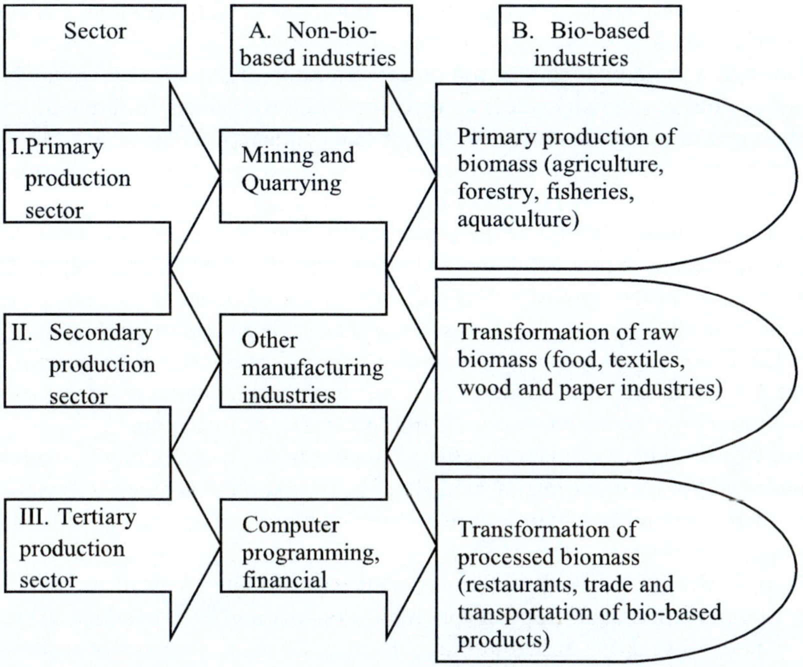

Fig. 8.2 Classification of sectors and industries resulting from the classic model of economic activities. (Source: Authors representation based on Kuosmanen et al., 2020)

8.2.3 Bioeconomy and Agriculture

The concept of bioeconomy brings together the sectors of agriculture, forestry, fisheries, and aquaculture (primary sectors), on the one hand, and sectors producing food, chemicals, materials, and energy, on the other (European Commission, 2015). Referring to sustainable agriculture, Georgescu-Roegen stressed that the economy must take into account both the agroecological conditions in which solar energy is transformed into biomass under the constraints of biodiversity conservation and the limits of energy from recyclable materials, due to the reduced waste processing capacities (Vivien et al., 2019).

Agriculture is essential for the food safety of the population and is also the primary source of income for local entrepreneurship in areas with high agricultural potential. Local agricultural initiatives provide jobs in rural areas and support community development. In close connection with this, the bioeconomy uses renewable biological resources from the use of agricultural land and the exploitation of marine resources. Its objective is to produce both food and energy, to make resources more efficient (European Investment Bank, 2018).

Birner (2018) agrees that agriculture is part of the bioeconomy, and the latter is an integral part of the green economy. From its point of view, the bioeconomy is sustainable and covers the ecological, economic, and social dimensions that agriculture offers (Fig. 8.3).

Through a horizontal connection of agriculture with the renewable energy production sector, ecological cycles can be compressed so that agriculture will become the reservoir of natural resources of the present century (Levidow, 2015).

Agriculture, the food, beverage, and tobacco industries, chemicals, pharmaceuticals, plastics, and rubber products obtained from organic raw materials, the wood and furniture sector, as well as the paper industry, are the five major areas considered by specialists to rely 100% on organic raw materials (Kuosmanen et al., 2020). However, it is complicated to estimate the ecological implications of these products, especially in some marginal sectors such as chemicals and pharmaceuticals. On the other hand, significant sectors of the previous classification, within the tertiary environmental sector, are not currently included in the quantitative assessment of the bioeconomy, such as accommodation and food services (restaurants).

In terms of indicators that can set up a picture of the bioeconomy at the level of a country and/or region, Ronzon and M'barek (2018) note that the NACE classification system does not highlight activities based on the use of ecological and polluting resources (Fig. 8.4).

Ronzon et al. (2020a) show that agriculture contributes 53% to the number of people employed in the European Union bioeconomy and 31% to added value. The same authors reveal that agriculture was the most dynamic component sector of the bioeconomy in 2017, with an increase of EUR 20.5 billion. This data demonstrates that agriculture is a significant sector of the bioeconomy and can contribute to the economic development of the Member States.

On the other hand, the amounts of waste generated by modern agriculture are significant. There are several ways to reintroduce this waste into production chains

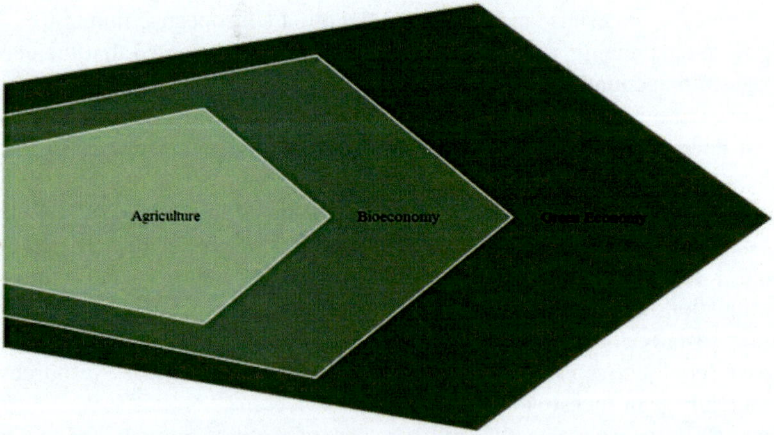

Fig. 8.3 The connection between agriculture, the bioeconomy, and the green economy. (Source: Authors representation based on Birner, 2018)

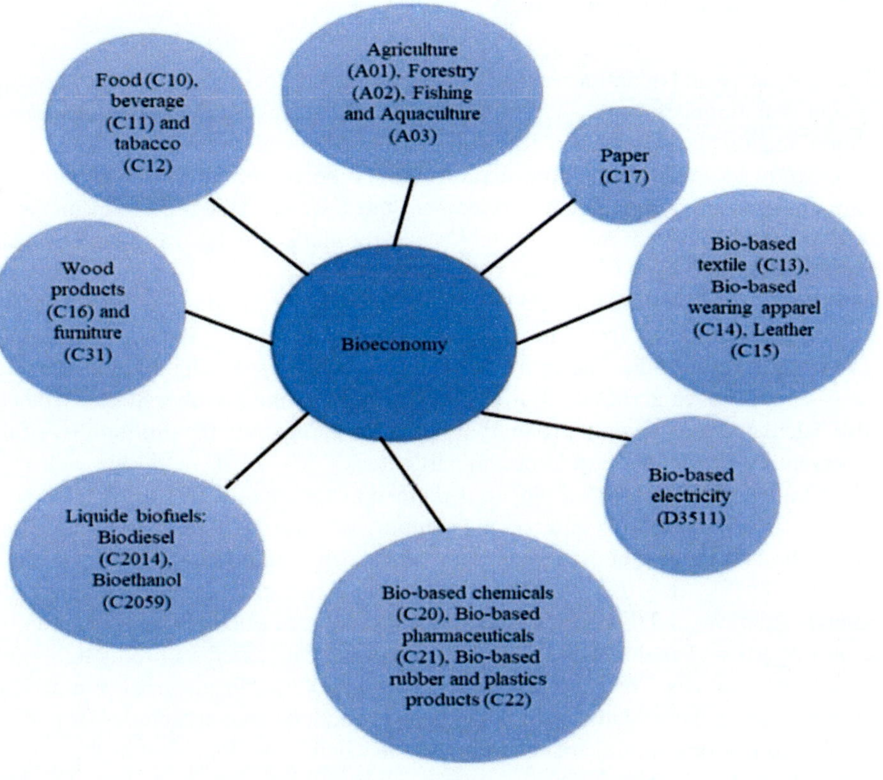

Fig. 8.4 Economic activities (NACE Rev.2) included in the bioeconomy sectors in the European Union. (Source: Author's interpretation based on Ronzon & M'barek, 2018)

in order to generate new organic products, using modern techniques for extracting chemical compounds from agricultural products (Jimenez Lopez et al., 2020).

An important segment of the use of agricultural waste is the production of biomass, which is then converted into energy (Duan et al., 2020). According to Duque-Acevedo et al. (2020), improving the current management models of agricultural waste can lead to an appropriate circularity for efficient use as raw materials for biomass production. Numerous studies (De Corato, 2020; Duan et al., 2020; Gregg et al., 2020) show that agricultural products and waste can be converted into energy as biomass resources.

All these aspects lead to the assumption that the importance of agriculture as a branch of the bioeconomy is necessary to study, as well as to quantify its contribution to the economic development of a state. This topic is insufficiently approached by academia. In this respect, we aim to investigate the role that agriculture can play in the evolution of the bioeconomy and its contribution to the economic development of the Member States of the European Union.

8.3 Research Methodology

The qualitative and quantitative research of the chapter focused on the most relevant scientific documents in the field, both of the official institutions of the European Union and on the specialized research articles retrieved from international databases. In order to shape the contribution of the bioeconomy to the development of agriculture in the European Union Member States, we used the most relevant socio-economic indicators for this purpose. We used the statistical data from the European Commission and Eurostat for the 2008–2019 period in the case of gross domestic product (GDP) values and the 2008–2017 period in case of all the other indicators.

The data extracted from the statistics were processed by types of indicators: gross domestic product, the number of persons employed, added value at factor costs, and turnover, across the European Union and by the Member States. We have also calculated the apparent productivity of labor to illustrate the profitability of the bioeconomy sector and agriculture, in particular.

The number of persons employed is defined as the total number of persons who work in an administrative unit, such as employees who work outside of the enterprise who belong to it and are paid by it (European Union [EU], 2009; Ronzon & M'barek, 2018). Also, turnover is the total invoiced by the economic unit during the reference period, and this corresponds to market sales of goods or services supplied to third parties. The added value at factor costs is calculated as production value minus total purchases of goods and services (EU, 2009). The apparent productivity of labor has been calculated as the ratio between added value at factor costs and the number of persons employed, according to the calculation definition of this indicator (Ronzon & M'barek, 2018).

8.4 Results and Discussion

8.4.1 Gross Domestic Product Analysis

As products and activities considered to be components of the bioeconomy vary widely from one country to another, depending on national priorities and comparative advantages, the possible approaches of the bioeconomy in the European Union Member States are limited. A standard methodology has not been established for calculating the contribution of the bioeconomy to GDP (Bracco et al., 2018).

The average contribution of the bioeconomy to the formation of the European Union GDP was 62% in the tertiary sector (services) of the economy, the share being exceeded only by Spain, by 64% (Fig. 8.5).

In what concerns the secondary sector (economic activities that convert raw materials into finished or semifinished products), Romania had a 40% share, the highest of the Member States, followed by Denmark with 37% and Poland with 33%.

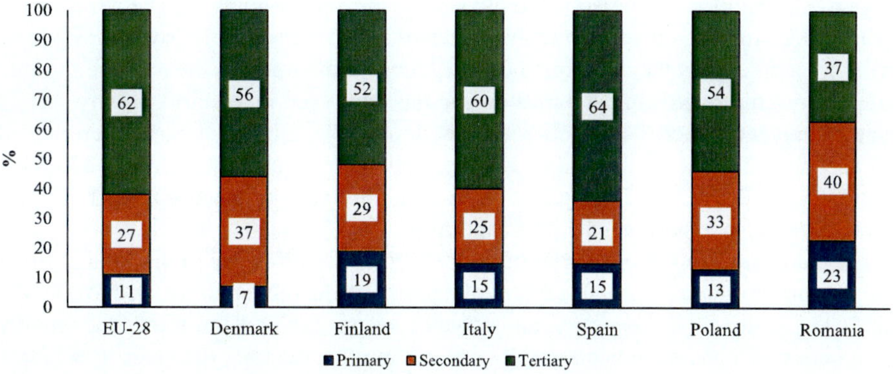

Fig. 8.5 Share of the bioeconomy in GDP in some EU countries, by economic sectors. (Source: Authors representation based on Kuosmanen et al., 2020)

Between 2008 and 2019, agriculture's contribution to the formation of gross domestic product decreased in the European Union – 28 average as a whole, from 1.68% to 1.64%, as the tertiary sector expanded. Bulgaria and Romania recorded the most significant decrease in the share of agriculture in GDP. Bulgaria by 3.28 percentage points (from 6.98% in 2008 to 3.71% in 2019) and Romania by 2.49 percentage points (from 7.03% in 2008 to 4.54% in 2019).

Over the 2008–2019 period, the share of agriculture in GDP has declined over almost all Member States, which shows the migration of agricultural inputs to other sectors of activity with the globalized and consumer economy.

We have tried to find out what is the share of bioeconomy added value at factor costs in the gross value added of all the statistical classification of economic activities in the European Community (NACE) in the Member States of the European Union. The analysis revealed that, between 2008 and 2017, the contribution of the bioeconomy to the GDP across the European Union stagnated, as the increase was only 0.1% points. The most significant increases were in the cases of Latvia (+1.81% points), Lithuania (+1.64% points), and Greece (+1.31% points). Compared to the other countries, Romania and Bulgaria had the most pronounced decreases of 3.24 percentage points and 2.63 percentage points, respectively.

During the same period (2008–2017), Bulgaria, Romania, and Croatia not only contributed an average of the share of the bioeconomy added value to GDP of about 9% each but also recorded the sharpest downward trends, of more than 30%.

8.4.2 Dynamics of the Number of Persons Employed

The number of persons employed in all European Union bioeconomy sectors in the 2008–2017 period was about two million, registering a decreasing trend (−12.07%), down to 1.86 million in 2017. Romania, Poland, and Germany had the most significant number of persons employed in the bioeconomy in the 2008–2017 period. During the ten years, the average number of persons employed was over 2 million people in every mentioned country. Only Romania has the average number of persons employed, almost 3 million persons employed in the bioeconomy sectors in the analyzed period. The deepest contractions in the number of persons employed in the bioeconomy in the 2008–2017 period took place in Croatia (−37.84%). Romania (−29.46%), Portugal (−20.85%), Finland (−19.02%), and Poland (−18.51%) also experienced significant drop.

In the European Union, agriculture contributes significantly to the total number of persons employed from all sectors of activity of the bioeconomy, with over 51% in 2017. In the food, beverage, and tobacco sector, 26% of the total bioeconomy number of persons have been employed, and in other sectors, the share was below ten percentage points (Fig. 8.6).

In the 2008–2017 period, most of the number of persons employed in agriculture were in Romania (about two million persons) and Poland (between 1.5 and 2 million persons), which represented over 40% of the number of persons employed from the EU agriculture sector. The other Member States had below one million persons employed in agriculture. In 2017, the number of persons employed in the European Union agriculture sector down by 17% compared to 2008, at 9.6 million persons, due to drops in Croatia (−50%%), Romania (−31%), Latvia (−28%), Portugal (−27%), and Poland (26.6%).

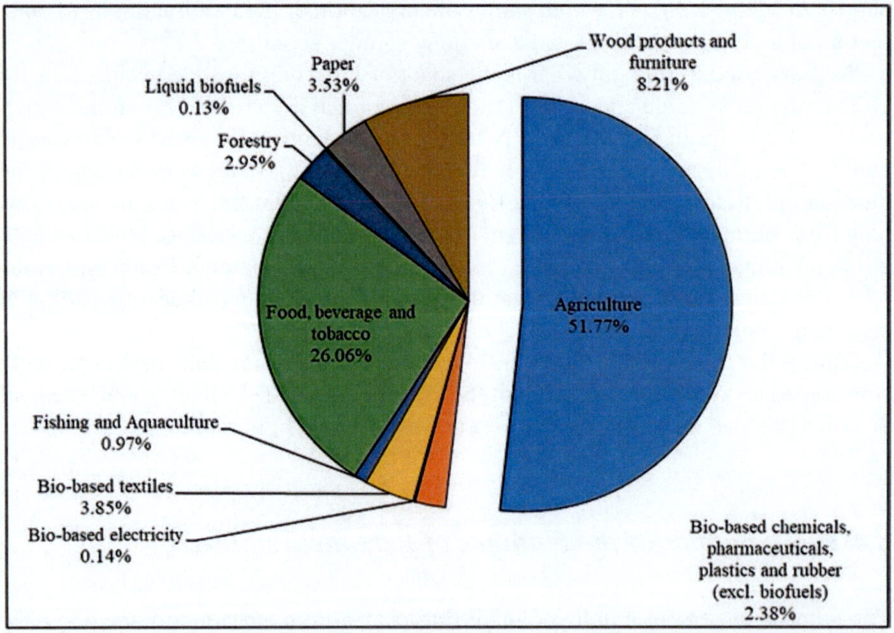

Fig. 8.6 Share of the number of persons employed in EU bioeconomy by economic sectors, in 2017. (Source: Authors representation based on Ronzon et al., 2020a)

Romania, Bulgaria, Greece, Poland, and Portugal had the highest number of persons employed in the agriculture sector of bioeconomy, as an average of the ten years analyzed. The weights by country were Romania 83.73%, Bulgaria 75.15%, Greece 73.1%, Poland 97.21%, and Portugal 63.32%.

8.4.3 Evolution of Added Value at Factor Cost

From the standpoint of the added value at factor costs, all EU bioeconomy sectors amount to around EUR 600 million, an increase of 20% between 2008 and 2017, to EUR 685 million. Substantial contributions to the generation of added value in the bioeconomy are Germany (15.78% of the EU total), France (14.45%), Italy (13.70%), and the United Kingdom (10.58%). Between 2008 and 2017, a significant jump in added value from the bioeconomy was achieved in Lithuania (+57.91%), Ireland (39.10%), Latvia (33.69%), Belgium (+32.99%), and Slovakia (32.68%). Except for Belgium, all these countries have adopted or are in the process of adopting a strategy dedicated to the bioeconomy.

Ronzon and M'Barek (2018) points out that countries that have established a bioeconomy strategy, covering a wide variety of sectors, have achieved an increase in added value, taking into account research and innovation, as well as implementing more efficient and environmentally friendly production processes.

The added value of agriculture had an average value of EUR 17,700 million between 2008 and 2017, across the EU. The share of this sector in the bioeconomy has remained constant, at about 30% (Fig. 8.7), with minor fluctuations ranging from 28.17% (in 2009) to 30.86% (in 2013).

Although it is not the sector that adds high value to outputs, agriculture has had an upward trend of added value at factor costs in the ten years analyzed, marking an increase of 19% to EUR 202,600 million in 2017. In many Member States, agriculture does not support the added value of the bioeconomy, not only as it is a sector that benefits from numerous subsidies and aid from national governments and/or central European institutions but also because it is a sector that is highly dependent on natural environmental factors (Sayari et al., 2018).

The Member States with the highest contributions of added value at factor costs from agriculture to the EU total are France (16.37%), Italy (16.35%), Spain (14.1%), and Germany (11.14%), while the other countries have shares of less than 7%.

Although the added value of agriculture is small, at around EUR 3.3 million in 2017, Ireland has seen a substantial increase compared to the sector in 2008, EUR 1.5 million (+2.2 times). Denmark also managed to double the added value of agriculture from EUR 1.6 million in 2008 to EUR 3.5 million in 2017.

One of the arguments that can be the basis of this development in the added value of agriculture of those two countries can be considered the investment in innovation as a result of the attraction of European funds. Another significant aspect is highlighted by (Nitescu & Murgu, 2020), which shows that in Ireland and Denmark, as

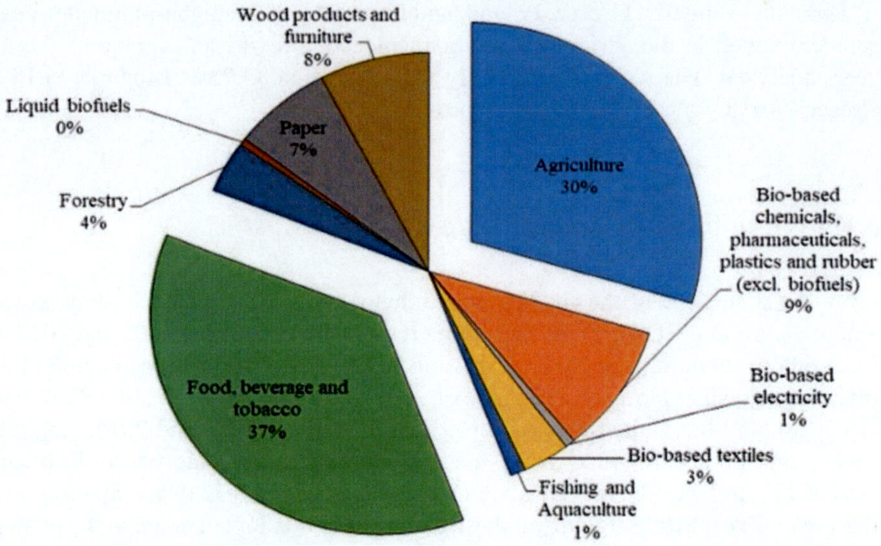

Fig. 8.7 Share of added value in EU bioeconomy by economic sectors in 2017. (Source: Authors representation based on Ronzon et al., 2020a)

well as in other Nordic states, agriculture holds an essential place among the component sectors of the bioeconomy.

8.5 Apparent Labor Productivity

Despite the decrease in the number of people employed in the EU bioeconomy, the value of apparent labor productivity increased by more than 36% between 2008 and 2017, to 36.76 thousand euro/person. In the bio-based chemicals, pharmaceuticals, plastics and rubber, and bio-based electricity and liquid biofuels sectors were registered the highest values (Fig. 8.8), due to advanced technologies used, which create high added value to products. Agriculture generates the lowest apparent labor productivity value of all sectors of the bioeconomy, only EUR 21.00 thousand/person in 2017.

By country, the analysis shows that 13 western European countries achieve apparent labor productivity in the bioeconomy above the EU 2008–2017 average (EU 30.94 thousand). These countries are Ireland, Belgium, Sweden, Denmark, Netherlands, Finland, the United Kingdom, France, Germany, Austria, Spain, Italy, and Luxembourg. In these countries, the average maturity of research and development in the bioeconomy is relatively high. Bio-based chemicals, bio-based pharmaceuticals, and biorefinery sectors have a priority in investing in research and innovation (Ronzon & M'barek, 2018).

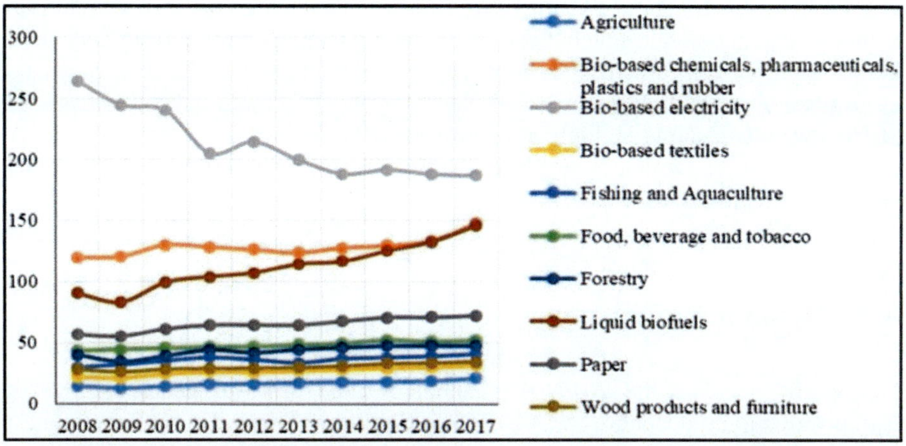

Fig. 8.8 The dynamic of apparent labor productivity in EU bioeconomy by economic sectors in 2008–2017 (EUR 1000). (Source: Authors representation based on Ronzon et al., 2020a)

Bulgaria and Romania had the lowest apparent labor productivity value in the bioeconomy of less than EUR 5 thousand/person during the whole period under review. An exception is represented by Romania, which managed in 2017 to surpass the threshold and recorded an apparent labor productivity value of EUR 5.18 thousand/person. In these two countries, many sectors of the bioeconomy use outdated technology, and the lack of investment and the attraction of EU funds are factors that make the development of a sustainable economy quite difficult

Wydra (2020) suggests that stimulating research and development in the agricultural sector through technological innovation can ensure productivity and lead to an increase in the number of jobs and the expansion of the range of ecological activity methods. Furthermore, better coherence in the implementation of strategies and the reform of national policies on agricultural subsidization can lead farmers to abandon non-environmentally friendly farming practices or crops (Agovino et al., 2019).

In agriculture, the European Union average of apparent labor productivity in the ten years of analysis is 16.77 thousand euro/person, with a steady growth trend, from 14.54 thousand euro/person in 2008 to 21 thousand euro/person in 2017. The Netherlands and Sweden are the only countries in the European Union to have achieved values of more than 50 thousand euros/person in apparent labor productivity in 2017. Romania and Bulgaria show an opposite situation, with approximately 3 thousand euro/person each, due to a modest performance in all bioeconomic sectors.

However, Romania and Bulgaria are part of the group of countries with the highest ecological efficiency in agriculture, as much of the agricultural production is based on field crops and does not use excessive amounts of fertilizers (Rybaczewska-Błazejowska & Gierulski, 2018).

Ireland stands out for doubling its apparent labor productivity from 13.09 thousand euros/person in 2008 to 31.37 thousand euros/person in 2017. The same trend was in the case of Denmark, but the apparent productivity of labor in agricultural countries had significant fluctuations. If, in 2008, Denmark started from a value of almost 25 thousand euros/person, in 2012, it exceeds the threshold of 60 thousand euros/person, after which the trajectory decreases to 31.54 thousand euros/person in 2015. These data show the high competitiveness of agriculture in the bioeconomy of these countries, which have placed particular emphasis on the collection and recycling of agricultural waste.

8.6 Dynamics of Turnover

During the period 2008–2017, the annual average turnover generated by the European Union bioeconomy was EUR 2,200 million. The sector with the highest turnover in the bioeconomy sector was food, beverages, and tobacco, with over 1,100 million euros (50%).

Compared to the food, beverage, and tobacco sector, agriculture holds the largest share of turnover in the European Union bioeconomy, with an average value of EUR 418,000 million, over the period 2008–2017. In the ten years analyzed, the value of turnover in European Union agriculture has increased by 11.84%, from EUR 402,000 million in 2008 to almost EUR 450,000 million in 2017. However, the agriculture share in the bioeconomy decreased moderately by 0.6% point, oscillating between 16.61% in 2013 and 18.32% in 2017 (Fig. 8.9). The fluctuations of turnover in European Union agriculture reflect oscillations in agricultural raw material prices.

Germany, France, Italy, and the United Kingdom recorded the highest turnover values in the bioeconomy of all Member States between 2008 and 2017. The combined contribution of the four countries to total turnover in the European Union bioeconomy was over 50%.

Germany's average contribution to the European Union's turnover in the bioeconomy was 19.30% in 2017, up 2.37 percentage points from 16.92% in 2008. The leadership position between the countries of the European Union reflects the initiation and implementation of bioeconomy strategies at both federal and regional levels. It is important to note that, in Germany, the number of patents in the bioeconomy represents 15% of the total number of patents granted annually (Wydra, 2020).

The high turnover achieved by France reflects a large number of bio-based production plants (European Commission – Joint Research Centre, 2017) and the food, beverage, and tobacco sector.

Croatia, Cyprus, Slovenia, and Romania are the countries of the European Union that marked a decrease in the trend of turnover in the bioeconomy between 2008 and 2017. The cumulative turnover as a share in the total European Union of these four countries is less than 3%, which has not influenced the growth path of this indicator throughout the community.

The role of agriculture in the European Union's bioeconomy is high in terms of turnover in countries such as Romania (41.39%), Greece (36.14%), Bulgaria

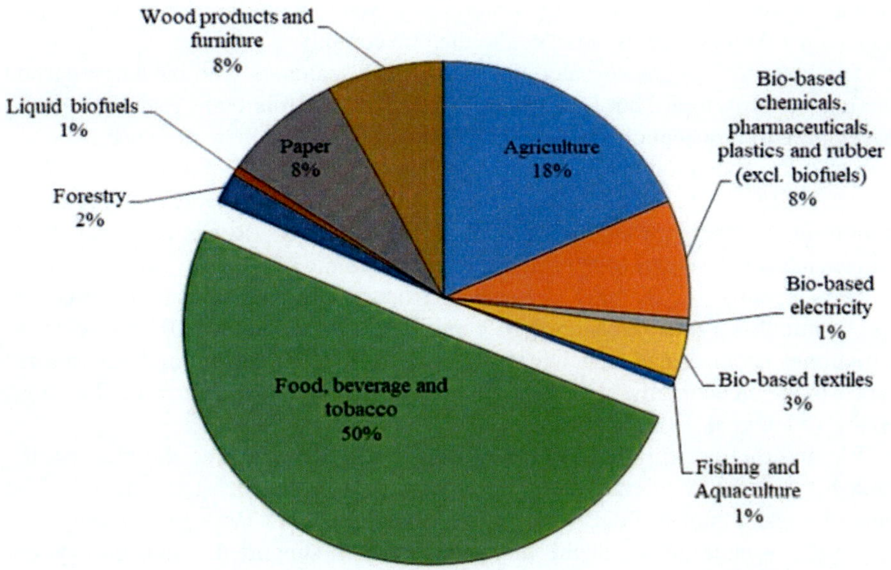

Fig. 8.9 Share of turnover in EU bioeconomy by economic sectors in 2017. (Source: Author's representation based on Ronzon et al. (2020a) data)

(34.75%), Hungary (33.30%), and Luxembourg (30.21%). However, except for Romania and Greece, these countries had a turnover in agriculture of less than EUR 10,000 million.

The increase in turnover in European Union agriculture is held up by Ireland's input (+39.19% in the period 2008–2017), Latvia (+33.20%), Estonia (+32.57%), and Sweden (+30.86%). The sharpest decreases in agricultural turnover between 2008 and 2018 took place in Croatia (−27.07%), Romania (−23.24%), and Bulgaria (−12.10%).

8.7 Conclusion

Bioeconomy is a relatively new field in contemporary research, even though the term emerged decades ago. Scientific analyses, implementation, and development of the bioeconomy are at different stages of application in many countries of the world, and in others, such as Romania, the phenomena of the bioeconomy are at an early stage of understanding and awareness. Between 2000 and 2020, many countries of the world focused their economic policies on the concept of bioeconomy. In its efforts, the European Union has developed a bioeconomy strategy and recommended that the Member States make their efforts to transpose it into national legislation. With the context created, in conjunction with the intensification of climate change in recent decades, many Community States have developed and implemented national strategies dedicated to the bioeconomy.

The literature review revealed that there are researchers who have approached the bioeconomy topic, but few articles investigate the role that agriculture has in developing the bioeconomy. At the European Union level, there are general policy frameworks related to the bioeconomy, such as directives and strategies (EC, 2018; EC, 2010; EC, 2016; EC, 2019a). Several authors tried to analyze and clarify the notion of bioeconomy within the classical economy (Ronzon et al., 2015; Kuosmanen et al., 2020) or to establish those economic sectors that can be included in the bioeconomy so that this area benefits from quantifiable indicators to establish its evolution over time (Ronzon & M'barek, 2018; Ronzon et al., 2020b). As far as agriculture is concerned, specialists agree that it is a component and determinant sector of the bioeconomy, and the two intertwine and influence each other (Levidow, 2015; Vivien et al., 2019).

We find that agriculture in the European Union contributes to the bioeconomy with a large number of employees. In terms of other indicators (the share of added value to agriculture in GDP, gross value added, apparent labor productivity, and turnover), agriculture is not the first sector to help support the bioeconomy, but places second, after the food, drink, and tobacco sector. However, the economic efficiency of agriculture is lower compared to other sectors that add added value to products, but there is a trend of growth in the agriculture apparent labor productivity between 2008 and 2017 in the European Union. Another conclusion that can be drawn is that agriculture can be considered a support sector for the other ones that generates half of the total turnover value in the European Union's bioeconomy, i.e., the food, drink, and tobacco sector. In this respect, it is worth highlighting that the Member States contribute less than a quarter to the turnover in agriculture as the European Union's bioeconomy sector.

Our findings are in line with the previous results of Ronzon and M'barek (2018) who observed that countries that have established a bioeconomy strategy, covering a wide variety of sectors, have achieved an increase in added value, taking into account research and innovation, as well as implementing more efficient and environmentally friendly production processes. Also, Ronzon et al. (2020b) reveal that agriculture has most people employed in the labor force in the bioeconomy and hold a significant share of the added value. Besides, "the development of bioeconomy will create new markets for agricultural commodities and diversify rural economies" (Ronzon & Sanjuan, 2020, pp. 8).

Consequently, we can say that agriculture is an important sector of the bioeconomy and can contribute much more to the evolution of the economy of the future in the European Union. In order to achieve this objective, concrete and sustained measures by the Member States are needed to boost all factors involved in the economy based on raw materials, products, and environmentally friendly activities. The measures may consist in the development and implementation of strategies dedicated to the bioeconomy, as demonstrated by examples of good practice in Germany, France, or Ireland.

References

Agovino, M., Casaccia, M., Ciommi, M., Ferrara, M., & Marchesano, K. (2019). Agriculture, climate change and sustainability: The case of EU-28. *Ecological Indicators, 105*(April 2018), 525–543. https://doi.org/10.1016/j.ecolind.2018.04.064

Birner, R. (2018). *Bioeconomy shaping the transition to a sustainable, biobased economy* (pp. 17–38). Publisher Springer Nature.

Bracco, S., Calicioglu, O., Juan, M. G. S., & Flammini, A. (2018). Assessing the contribution of bioeconomy to the total economy: A review of national frameworks. *Sustainability (Switzerland), 10*(6). https://doi.org/10.3390/su10061698

De Corato, U. (2020). Agricultural waste recycling in horticultural intensive farming systems by on-farm composting and compost-based tea application improves soil quality and plant health: A review under the perspective of a circular economy. *Science of the Total Environment.* https://doi.org/10.1016/j.scitotenv.2020.139840

Diakosavvas, D. (2019). Bio-economy and the sustainability of the agriculture and food system: Opportunities and policy challenges. OECD Food, Agriculture and Fisheries Papers, No. 136, 2018, 104. https://doi.org/10.1787/d0ad045d-en

Duan, Y. M., Pandey, A., Zhang, Z. Q., Awasthi, M. K., Bhatia, S. K., & Taherzadeh, M. J. (2020). *Organic solid waste biorefinery: Sustainable strategy for emerging circular bioeconomy in China.* https://doi.org/10.1016/j.indcrop.2020.112568

Duque-Acevedo, M., Belmonte-Urena, L. J., & Cortes- García, F. J., & Camacho-Ferre, F. (2020). Agricultural waste: Review of the evolution, approaches and perspectives on alternative uses. *Global Ecology and Conservation, 22*, 1–23. https://doi.org/. https://doi.org/10.1016/j.gecco.2020.e00902

European Commission. (2010). *Report from the Commission to the Council and the European Parliament on sustainability requirements for the use of solid and gaseous biomass sources in electricity, heating and cooling*. Publications Office of the European Union. https://eur-lex.europa.eu/legal-content/EN/TXT/?uri=CELEX:52010DC0011. Accessed 7.8.2020.

European Commission. (2015). Sustainable agriculture, forestry and fisheries in the bioeconomy - A challenge for Europe. European Commission, (June), p. 141. https://doi.org/10.2777/179843.

European Commission. (2018). A sustainable Bioeconomy for Europe: strengthening the connection between economy, society and the environment. [WWW Document]. URL. https://doi.org/10.2777/478385. Accessed 7.2.2020.

European Commission. (2019a). The European Green Deal, 53(9), 1689–1699. COM(2019) 640 final. [WWW Document]. URL. https://doi.org/10.1017/CBO9781107415324.004. Accessed 7.14.2020.

European Commission. (2019b). Annex to The European Green Deal. European Commission, 2019–2022. [WWW Document]. URL https://ec.europa.eu/info/sites/info/files/european-green-deal-communication-annex-roadmap_en.pdf. Accessed 7.8.2020.

European Commission – Joint Research Centre. (2017). Bioeconomy Report 2016. *JRC Science for Policy Report.* https://doi.org/10.2760/20166

European Investment Bank. (2018). Agriculture and bioeconomy - Unlocking production potential in a sustainable and resource-efficient way. [WWW Document]. URL www.eib.org/agriculture. Accessed 5.3.2020.

European Union. (2009). Directive 2009/28/EC of the European Parliament and of the Council of 23 April 2009 on the promotion of the use of energy from renewable sources and amending and subsequently repealing Directives 2001/77/EC and 2003/30/EC, Official Journal of the European Union, 2009(L 140), pp. 32–38. [WWW Document]. URL https://eur-lex.europa.eu/legal-content/en/TXT/?uri=CELEX%3A32009L0028. Accessed 5.11.2020.

European Union. (2018). Directive (EU) 2018/2001 of the European Parliament and of the Council on the promotion of the use of energy from renewable sources, Official Journal of the European Union, 2018(L 328), pp. 82–209. [WWW Document]. URL https://eur-lex.europa.eu/legal-content/EN/TXT/PDF/?uri=CELEX:32018L2001&from=EN. Accessed 5.30.2020.

European Commission. (2016). Clean energy for all Europeans. *COM (2016), 860*. 1–13.
Food and Agriculture Organization of the United Nations. (2016). Key to achieving the 2030 agenda for sustainable development. *Food And Agriculture, 32*. https://doi.org/I5499E/2/04.16
Gafo, M. (2018). Bioeconomy in the new Common Agricultural Policy 2021-2027. Bioregions Forum. 13 November 2018. [WWW Document]. URL http://www.ctfc.cat/docs/bioregions/GafoMaria.pdf. Accessed 29.06.2020.
Gowdy, J., & Mesner, S. (1998). The evolution of Georgescu-Roegen's bioeconomics. *Review of Social Economy, 56*(2), 136–156. https://doi.org/10.1080/00346769800000016
Gregg, J. S., Jürgens, J., Happel, M. K., Strøm-Andersen, N., Tanner, A. N., Bolwig, S., & Klitkou, A. (2020). Valorization of bio-residuals in the food and forestry sectors in support of a circular bioeconomy: A review. *Journal of Cleaner Production*. https://doi.org/10.1016/j.jclepro.2020.122093
Jimenez Lopez, C., Fraga-Corral, M., Carpena, M., Garcia-Oliveira, P., Echave, J., Pereira, A., Lourenço-Lopes, C., Prieto, M., & Simal-Gandara, J. (2020). Agriculture wastes valorisation as a source of antioxidant phenolic compounds within a circular and sustainable bioeconomy. *Food & Function*. https://doi.org/10.1039/d0fo00937g
Kuosmanen, T., Kuosmanen, N., & El-Meligi. (2020). How big is the bioeconomy? Reflections from an economic perspective. [WWW Document]. URL https://doi.org/10.2760/144526. Accessed 7.14.2020.
Levidow, L. (2015). European transitions towards a corporate-environmental food regime: Agroecological incorporation or contestation? *Journal of Rural Studies, 40*, 76–89. https://doi.org/10.1016/j.jrurstud.2015.06.001
Nitescu, D. C., & Murgu, V. (2020). The Bioeconomy and foreign trade in food products - A sustainable partnership at the European level? *Sustainability (Switzerland), 12*(6). https://doi.org/10.3390/su12062460
Organization for Economic Cooperation and Development. (2009). The bioeconomy to 2030: Designing a policy agenda. *Main findings and policy conclusions. OECD Publishing, 2009*.
Patermann, C., & Aguilar, A. (2018). 2017. The origins of the bioeconomy in the European Union. *New Biotechnology, 40*, 20–24. https://doi.org/10.1016/j.nbt.2017.04.002
Pauna, C. B., Simionescu, M., Diaconescu, T., & Iorgulescu, I. R. (2017). Bio-Based Economy Sketch : The Case of Romania. Conference Proceedings 7–8 April, 2017, Globalization – Economic, Social and Moral Implications, pp. 112–122. https://doi.org/10.5281/zenodo.581777.
Ronzon, T., & M'barek, R. (2018). Socioeconomic Indicators to Monitor the EU's Bioeconomy in Transition. *Sustainability (Switzerland), 10*(6). https://doi.org/10.3390/su10061745
Ronzon, T., & Sanjuan, A. I. (2020). Friends or foes? A compatibility assessment of bioeconomy-related Sustainable Development Goals for European policy coherence. *Journal of Cleaner Production*. https://doi.org/10.1016/j.jclepro.2019.119832
Ronzon, T., Santini, F., & M'barek, R. (2015). JRC Science for Policy Report – The Bioeconomy in numbers, facts and figures on biomass, turnover and employment. 2012, 2011–2014. https://ec.europa.eu/jrc/sites/jrcsh/files/JRC97789
Ronzon, T., Piotrowski, S., M'barek, R., Carus, M., & Tamošiūnas, S. (2020a). Jobs and wealth in the EU bioeconomy / JRC - Bioeconomics. European Commission, Joint Research Centre (JRC) [WWW Document]. URL. http://data.europa.eu/89h/7d7d5481-2d02-4b36-8e79-697b04fa4278
Ronzon, T., Piotrowski, S., Tamosiunas, S., Dammer, L., Carus, M., & M'barek, R. (2020b). Developments of economic growth and employment in bioeconomy sectors across the EU. *Sustainability (Switzerland), 12*(11). https://doi.org/10.3390/su12114507
Rybaczewska-Błazejowska, M., & Gierulski, W. (2018). Eco-efficiency evaluation of agricultural production in the EU-28. *Sustainability (Switzerland), 10*(12) https://doi.org/10.3390/su10124544
Sayari, N., Sari, R., & Hammoudeh, S. (2018). The impact of value added components of GDP and FDI on economic freedom in Europe. *Economic Systems, 42*(2), 282–294. https://doi.org/10.1016/j.ecosys.2017.03.003

Schöpe, M. (2008). Renewable energy directive. Eur. In *Wind Energy Conf. Exhib* (Vol. 1, pp. 32–38).

United Nations, General Assembly. (2015). Resolution adopted by the General Assembly on 25 September 2015. Transforming our world : the 2030 Agenda for Sustainable Development. [WWW Document]. URL. https://www.refworld.org/docid/57b6e3e44.html. Accessed 28.11.2019).

Vivien, F. D., Nieddu, M., Befort, N., Debref, R., & Giampietro, M. (2019). The Hijacking of the bioeconomy. *Ecological Economics, 159*(June 2018), 189–197. https://doi.org/10.1016/j.ecolecon.2019.01.027

Wilfried, E., & Frieder, K. (2014). Plant-based bioeconomy in Central Germany – Mapping of Actors, Industries and Places, IWH Discussion Papers, No. 7/2014. [WWW Document]. URL http://nbn-resolving.de/urn:nbn:de:101:1-2015011311752. Accessed 5.25.2020.

Wydra, S. (2020). Measuring innovation in the bioeconomy – Conceptual discussion and empirical experiences. Technology in Society. Elsevier Ltd, 61(February), p. 101242. https://doi.org/10.1016/j.techsoc.2020.101242.

Chapter 9
Risk and Solutions for Economic Entities Identified Through Integrated Reporting

Luminiţa Rus, Mărioara Beleneşi, and Dana Simona Gherai

Abstract The professional accountant is the one who verifies accounts, advises, makes an economic and financial diagnosis on the activity carried out by the economic entity, and also supports the management team in the decision-making process. In this time of crisis, more than ever, the professional accountant no longer only responds to the well-known challenges of the current activity but must inform the management team about the new risks that may affect the activity of the entity. By providing solutions to the management team, he must stay focused on respecting the fundamental principles of professional ethics. This chapter focuses on integrated reporting of companies, which aims to present by the economic entity information on the conduct of its business, as well as the steps by which it achieves added value over time. But how many economic entities do this integrated reporting? How many entities provide information about its capitals: human, financial, intellectual, or social? Are certain risks associated with these capitals? These are some questions we want to answer through our study. In this regard, by studying the financial reports of companies listed on the Bucharest Stock Exchange, we have extracted information on the capital used by economic entities, the risks identified by these entities, and the solutions presented by the professional accountants respecting ethical principles. The study concludes with the formulation of conclusions on how information is reported by economic entities and whether there is a link between integrated reporting and the field of activity to which it belongs.

Keywords Integrated reporting · Added value · Intellectual capital · Turnover · Risk

L. Rus (✉) · M. Beleneşi · D. S. Gherai
University of Oradea, Oradea, Romania

S. L. Fotea et al. (eds.), *Navigating Through the Crisis: Business, Technological and Ethical Considerations*, Springer Proceedings in Business and Economics,
https://doi.org/10.1007/978-3-030-82751-9_9

9.1 Introduction

We go through different periods in life, both as individuals and as economic entities. Some periods are more relaxed than others, others more difficult, but we want to increase the value. In terms of increasing personal value, each individual turns to what they see as a priority: spiritual, educational, material, financial, and others.

Similarly, economic entities want to create financial and nonfinancial value. In this respect, each entity moves towards attracting capital that can create this value: human capital, material capital, and financial capital. For reporting information on the activity carried out by the economic entity and the economic growth recorded, the annual accounting reporting best answers the questions of those interested in the economic entity.

Financial reporting aims to present financial information: financial position and performance, indicators of economic and financial analysis, number of employees, and others. Nonfinancial reporting, mandatory in Romania, from 2019, for economic entities with an average number of employees of more than 500, must also provide information on the impact of the entity's activity on the environment, social or personal environment, respect for human rights, or the fight against corruption (OMFP 3456, 2018).

The inclusion of the two types of information in one reporting – financial and nonfinancial – is a new type of reporting of economic entities' business: integrated reporting. This type of reporting contains information presented *today* about *yesterday's* economic entity's activity but with an impact on tomorrow, both the economic entity and future generations.

For this type of reporting to best respond to the general interest, it must be a quality one, developed by professionals, comparable over time, and presented for all at the appropriate time. To this end, the International Federation of Accountants (IFAC) has issued several guidelines for companies' integrated reporting. One of these guides concerning creating value through integrated reporting and published by the Romanian Body of Accounting Experts and Authorized Accountants from Romania (CECCAR). This guide refers to the benefits of integrated reporting. It presents the six capitals found in a small and medium-sized enterprise (SME): financial, manufacturing, intellectual, human, natural, and corporate capital (CECCAR, 2020).

This scientific approach's main objective is to identify the information provided by economic entities on capital used in the creation of value, financial or nonfinancial information, provided voluntarily or involuntarily.

As secondary objectives, we aim to identify the risks that may arise in the use or reduction of working capital and solutions to prevent or mitigate their effects, solutions presented in the annual reports of the economic entities subject to the case study.

In the first part of this chapter is presented the information collected from the financial statements of the companies selected for the case study, information grouped on the capitals presented above, also following the evolution over time of these indicators, during the years 2012–2019, because of the obligation of Romanian companies listed on the stock exchange to report following the provisions of the International Accounting Standards.

In the second part of the chapter, we treat the risks – associated with these capitals – identified by us by our professional reasoning or by collecting the information presented in the explanatory notes attached to the annual financial statements prepared by the companies analyzed.

In the third part, we look at the solutions identified to cover the risks recognized in the accounts of economic entities on account of provisions or impairment adjustments.

The chapter concludes with conclusions on the use of capital, the risks identified, and the solutions found in the integrated reporting of the companies analyzed.

9.2 Literature Review

An economic entity achieves success through sustainable and long-term exploitation of the capital it holds and effective risk management. The entity's successful activity must reflect its high performance. However, the level of performance reported in the financial statements mainly expresses the financial achievements of the entity (Dečman and Rep, 2018), depriving most of those interested in information about its nonfinancial performance. Bobitan and Stefea (2017) believe that integrated reporting is the one that captures the holistic picture of an entity's performance.

The subject of "all comprehensive" reporting appears in the sights of researchers, entities, and professional bodies more than two decades ago, with the growing need of the external environment of the firm to know its actions in the social and environmental interest, in addition to its interest. Corporate governance has been the solution to sustainability-based management, social and environmental performance, beyond financial performance, identifying as accurately as possible the risks and building strategies that limit their negative effect as much as possible. Bobitan and Stefea (2017) believe that corporate governance is at an integrated reporting line.

Since corporate reporting is a benchmark for the concept of sustainable development, in Chersan's opinion (2015), it is necessary to develop more condensed and comprehensive reporting techniques to order to meet the increasingly diverse information needs of stakeholders. Nevertheless, it is also necessary to achieve an integration of financial and nonfinancial factors to achieve the real value of the entity. Furthermore, Hurghiş (2017) believes that the wake-up call of an integrated report is necessary, being the tool that explains how the entity creates value over time. Thus, in 2013, the International Integrated Reporting Committee (IIRC) *publishes* the International Integrated Reporting Framework (IIRC, 2013), which contains several guiding principles and components of an integrated report, explaining the fundamental concepts underlying its development. The purpose of this document is to increase the efficiency of the reporting process and improve the quality of the information provided and the connection between financial and nonfinancial information (Dumitru et al., 2013), the adoption of "integrated thinking" focused on the creation of value following the exploitation of all available capital. Since then, many researchers have been concerned about the degree of compliance of the annual reports published by economic entities with the International Integrated Reporting Framework principles.

Some studies, focusing on a single company, present a thorough analysis of how the integrated report corresponds to integrated reporting principles (Dumitru et al., 2013). Others carry out a sample analysis of several companies (Hurghis, 2017; Chersan, 2015) whose integrated reports are considered representative and are available on the IIRC website (Hurghis, 2017; Dumitru et al., 2013; Chersan, 2015). Chersan, in its 2015 study, notes a global increase in the number of entities whose annual reports are considered representative of integrated reporting, an increase in information quality, and an increase in connectivity between them, an increase in the complexity of reports in a smaller number of pages. Still, although the purpose of integrated reporting is to reveal value creation over time, on this issue in most cases, no information is presented.

Since the publication of annual company reports following the principles of the International Integrated Reporting Framework is the option of the economic entity, not at the moment as an obligation (except for South African entities), some authors such as Hurghiş in 2017 through his study seek a possible correlation between an integrated information disclosure index and the characteristics of the corporate governance structure. He considers that the decision whether or not to issue an integrated report is related to the governance structure, specifically the board of directors. The study results show that only the size of the management board influences the extent to which the integrated report issued is in line with the International Integrated Reporting Framework. Also, for integrated reporting, Massingham et al. (2018) believe that an older tool, such as the balanced scorecard, used in a new conceptual strategy for organizational learning helps integrated thinking and future value creation following the requirements of the International Integrated Reporting Framework. Dečman and Rep (2018) trying to investigate whether Croatian entities recognize the benefits of integrated reporting, believe that financial information is not the only relevant factor in the value creation process. Therefore, they offer in their paper suggestions for improving nonfinancial reporting in Croatia to increase added value to different stakeholders.

Other researchers have also studied the impact of capital used by economic entities in value creation. Stubbs et al., in 2014, conducted a pilot research study investigating the position of Australian financial capital providers in terms of integrated reporting and the six capital in investment decisions and market functioning. They identify differences between information disclosed by entities and information required by financial capital providers to substantiate investment decisions, calling on Australian regulators to encourage entities to report social and environmental sustainability risks. A complete system of operational risk information would be useful for risk management activities, Weeserik and Spruit (2018) believe.

In 2020, Khan et al. realized another research based on testing the links between the size of financial capital and the entity's performance. They reveal that there is a positive relationship between capital structure and socioeconomic performance, sources of funding, and capital structure and sources of funding and socioeconomic performance of entities analyzed (Khan et al., 2020).

More researchers (Toszewska-Czerniej, 2018; Männasoo et al., 2018; Úbeda-García et al., 2018) were interested in making the most efficient use of human capital. Toszewska-Czerniej (2018) believes that human capital offers particular value to the entity due to its complexity and diversity, considering it the critical factor in value creation. The scheme developed, following its research, based on the combination of value flows and processes, allows us to determine the differentiation of human potential and its involvement in various organizational processes. Männasoet et al. (2018) show that human capital endowment has a positive effect on increasing total factor productivity, but its effect on R & D expenditure in regions has been mostly absent. Also concerned with human capital and organizational culture, Úbeda-García et al. (2018) believe that innovation in the hotel sector has become a critical factor for success, demonstrating that hotels' ambidexterity has a positive impact on their performance. Watson et al. (2018) present useful technical methods for managers to evaluate and formulate concrete strategies for the most efficient management of natural resources, with a significant impact on natural capital and human well-being. In terms of intellectual capital, Xu and Wang (2018) believe that it is a generator of wealth, an engine of financial performance, capable of creating competitive advantage and sustainability in business. Their study shows that intellectual capital has a positive impact on companies' financial performance and sustainable growth. The latter two variables show to be positively related to physical capital, human capital, and relational capital (considered the most critical factor).

9.3 The Methodology of Research and Database

This research uses the study of the information presented in the financial statements of the economic entities listed on the BVB being quantitative research. Thus, we aim to identify the capital used by the economic entities studied, the types of risks associated with these capitals, and the solutions by which the effects of these risks have been or will diminish.

First, the companies to be subjected to the case study were selected. The hotel and restaurant sector is an area profoundly affected by the pandemic situation we are going through. This fact has incited our interest in finding information on the prevention of severe effects for economic entities as those estimated now. However, the real effects will only be reflected in the 2020 financial statements.

Of the total of 26 hotels and restaurant companies listed on BVB, a company suspended, and one company has separately listed the preferential shares and is not a separate economic entity. The information published on the www.bvb.ro website is delineated into two categories: *financial statements*, developed on the model required by the Ministry of Public Finance, and *annual reports*, prepared according to their models containing companies' voluntary information.

Of the remaining 24 companies, 16 companies did not publish an annual report with explanatory notes, and four companies published only one, two, or three years. Thus, it resulted in four companies that can be subject to the case study since some of the information needed for this research can only be extracted from the companies' annual reports. For reasons of data confidentiality, we do not provide information on the identification data of the companies analyzed.

Through the content analysis, the information extracted from the reports for the eight years is subject to the case study. They were then not only grouped and examined in value but also presented in graphic evolution using comparative analysis. The results obtained were interpreted in the light of the objectives of the research, conclusions drawn at each stage of the research. Tableau 2020.2 data analysis software was used for the graphics.

9.4 Results and Discussion

In achieving this research's objectives, the presentation of information, results, and discussions, we structured into three sections. In the first section, we discuss the identification of the capitals used by the analyzed companies. In the second section, we present the results regarding identifying the risks associated with the economic entities' capitals. In the last section, we analyze the hedging solutions to cover the risks associated with such capital – the research results presented in the form of conclusions.

9.5 Identification of Capital Used by Companies Analyzed

In carrying out their business, economic entities use several capitals, capital that determines the creation of added value of the company. Since its inception, companies start with a share capital consisting of contributions in cash or contributions in kind. These contributions will be able to be used in the realization of the object of activity, but also the production of profit. Over the years, the profits earned will contribute to the increase in the capital made available to the economic entity. The capital that remains available to shareholders, after deduction of all debts, called equity, is the main accounting information – provided by the financial statements – which has the usefulness of satisfying the interest of shareholders in the economic entity. The nondistribution to shareholders of the realized profit, thereby deferring the payment of dividends, is an important working capital for the economic entity.

Like equity, the economic entity also uses other capital, with some not owning the economic entity or the shareholders. From the multitude of capital used by the economic entity, we submit to the study: financial capital, human capital, manufacturing capital, intellectual capital, natural capital, and relationship capital in society.

Financial capital, the source that the economic entity has at its disposal from a financial point of view, is the possibility of attracting the funds necessary to carry out the activity. Of course, loans are an important financial source for the economic entity, but we cannot eliminate any commercial loans, nor other types of payment deadline. Therefore, the financial capital consists of the economic entity's equity, short-term liabilities, long-term liabilities, and investment subsidies. The graphical evolution of these indicators shown in Fig. 9.1

We not only note that the evolution of the three major elements of financial capital has varied developments that have compared with each other but also compare the economic entities analyzed. At the top of the figure, we note the evolution of equity as an upward one, with slight fluctuations, in all the economic entities analyzed; the equity recorded at the end of 2019 is higher than at the end of 2012.

Concerning the long-term debt situation, we note that their evolution is downward, fluctuating in some cases in all economic entities analyzed; the amount of long-term debt recorded at the end of 2019 is lower than that recorded at the end of 2012.

In contrast, the value of short-term debts is different, either almost linear or suddenly upward or downward, developments. Comparing the situation in the period under review, we find that for a company, the value recorded at the end is lower than the value at the beginning; for the other three, the final value is higher than the original value. We note that for the two companies, the difference between the beginning and the end of the time frame analyzed is significant.

Looking at the financial capital for each entity, we find that its evolution is almost linear in the case of the first company. A slight upward tint for equity and short-term debt, the evolution of long-term debt is a downward one, at the end of 2019, their value being zero.

For the second company under review, we note that the decrease in the value of long-term and short-term debt occurs during the same period in which equity growth occurs. We cannot say the same about the other two economic entities whose equity registers high values with a downward trend in long-term debt.

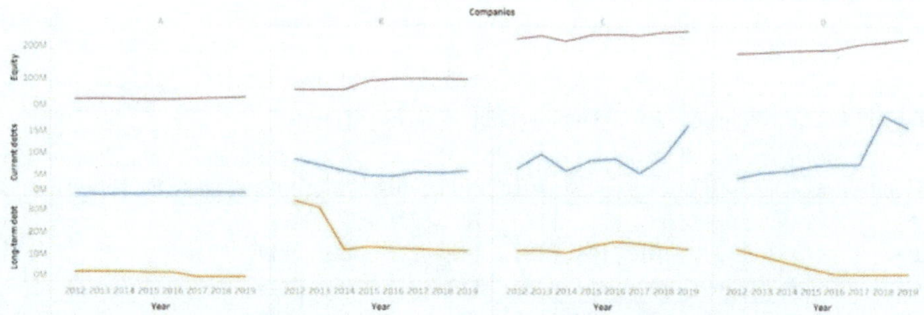

Fig. 9.1 Evolution of financial capital. (Source: Own processing with Tableau 2020.2)

Of course, we must mention that the financial capital structure can determine the economic and financial performance of the economic entity. Nevertheless, the decision-makers of each economic entity will be able to change the value and structure of the financial capital and be able to devise financial strategies to reduce the risks that may arise. They will also be able to assess the risk tolerance for the decrease in financial capital (Khan et al., 2020).

We conclude that Company A maintains a balance in the use of financial capital, perhaps even trying not to engage in long-term debt and Company B increases its independence by reducing debts. Companies C and D are experiencing increases in short-term debt at the same time as the decrease in long-term debt.

Human capital consists of employees through whom economic entities operate, at the expenses generated with them for the work performed, and their loyalty. The average number of employees is shown in Table 9.1, and the graphical development of staff expenditure is shown in Fig. 9.2.

Human capital, made up not only of employees of the company but also of directors or collaborators, is an essential part of the activity carried out by the economic entity in generating added value. The average number of employees experienced oscillations over the period considered, in three cases, the number of employees at the end of 2019 being higher than at the end of 2012.

The increase in value generated by human capital achieved with certain expenses, of which we have identified in the financial statements analyzed the following types of expenditure: expenditure on salaries, expenditure on the salaries of the board of directors, expenditure on meal vouchers, social security expenditure, prizes, and social expenditure.

In Fig. 9.2, these expenditures are detailed compared to the evolution of the number of employees and the value of human capital. We note that the deciding factor in determining human capital is expenditure on wages, the evolving trend being the same for all three indicators mentioned.

We conclude that this capital is predictably used by all economic entities, with an increase in the number of employees leading to an increase in expenditure on wages and social security, with employee benefits granted, we would say, for tax reasons. The granting of meal vouchers is subject only to the calculation of income tax on wages; the increase of wages by the value of meal vouchers would lead to an increase in the income and, thus, also the social contributions due.

Table 9.1 The average number of employees in the analyzed period

Companies	2012	2013	2014	2015	2016	2017	2018	2019	The average number of employees in the period
A	69	68	65	71	78	78	77	81	73
B	151	121	101	108	183	181	172	172	149
C	382	369	329	354	354	322	316	360	348
D	677	635	629	680	725	727	752	756	698

Source: Authors' processing by annual financial statements

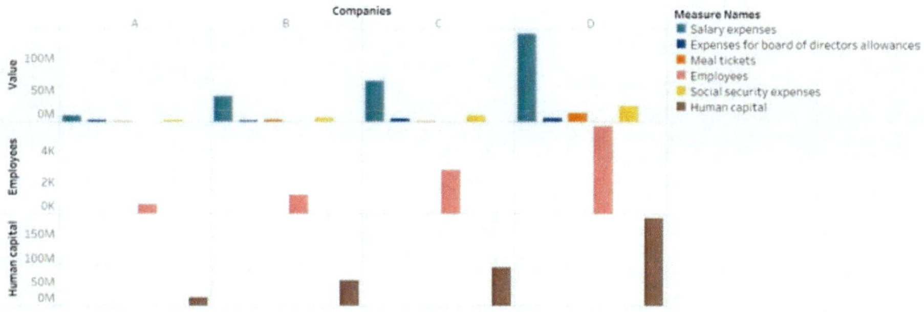

Fig. 9.2 Evolution of staff costs. (Source: own processing with Tableau 2020.2)

Table 9.2 Types of tangible fixed assets

Types	2012	2013	2014	2015	2016	2017	2018	2019
Buildings	A, B, C, D	A, B, C, D	A, B, C, D	A, B, C, D	A, B, C, D	A, B, C, D	A, B, C, D	A, B, C, D
Technical installation and machines	A, B, C, D	A, B, C, D	A, B, C, D	A, B, C, D	A, B, C, D	A, B, C, D	A, B, C, D	A, B, C, D
Other installations, equipment, and furniture	A, B, C, D	A, B, C, D	A, B, C, D	A, B, C, D	A, B, C, D	A, B, C, D	A, B, C, D	A, B, C, D
Real estate investments	B, C, D	B, C, D	C, D	B, C, D	B, C, D	B, C, D	B, C, D	B, C, D

Source: Authors' processing by annual financial statements

Manufacturing capital shall comprise tangible assets that the economic entity uses to realize the object of activity: construction, technological equipment, measuring and control apparatus, means of transport, real estate investments, and other fixed assets. A summary of the types of tangible fixed assets held by the economic entities analyzed is given in Table 9.2. The development in their structure shall be shown graphically in Fig. 9.3.

We note that all economic entities hold tangible assets of the nature of constructions, technological equipment, measuring devices, furniture, and other tangible assets. A single economic entity does not own real estate investments; all fixed assets are used in the realization of the object of activity, unlike the other three companies owning such properties for rental purposes.

Regarding the value of tangible assets held, a company registers an almost linear development of the assets throughout the period under review. One company registers changes in the value of construction slot and technological equipment, with other fixed assets having almost linear developments. The other two economic entities analyzed record upward and downward developments in all types of tangible assets.

We conclude that all economic entities analyzed have manufacturing capital, used in the realization of the object of the activity or leased to third parties, the concern for increasing the degree of modernization being different.

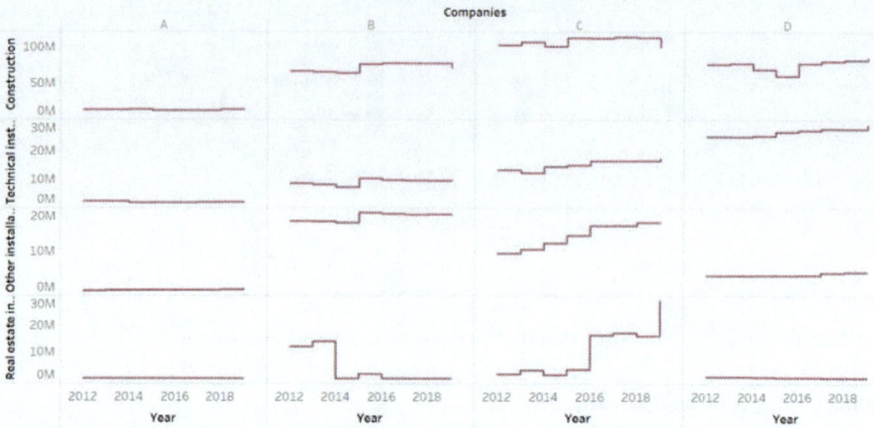

Fig. 9.3 Evolution of tangible assets. (Source: own processing with Tableau 2020.2)

Table 9.3 Types of intangible assets

Types	A	B	C	D
Concessions	No	Yes	No	No
Licenses	No	Yes	Yes	Yes
Trademarks	No	No	No	Yes
Computer program	Yes	Yes	Yes	No

Source: Authors' processing by annual financial statements

Intellectual capital comprises intellectual property rights held by the economic entity in the form of know-how or patents. Their accounts shall show in the category of intangible assets. In Table 9.3, the types of intangible assets used by the economic entities analyzed are presented.

We note the existence, within intangible assets, of software and licenses in most cases. This fact is predictable, given the importance of computer technology in processing information on the achievement of the object of activity.

Software is useful from the reservation of places in hotels and restaurants to the application of marketing policies to the activity of accounting and processing information for other users interested in economic entities.

To our surprise, we have identified only one case that highlights the accounts or provides information about the trademark registered with the State Office for Inventions and Trademarks (OSIM) and a case of highlighting concessions.

We conclude that none of the economic entities analyzed uses intellectual capital, in the form of patents or know-how, which determines intellectual capital presentation as having zero value, throughout the period under review, for all economic entities subject to the case study.

Natural capital is the natural and environmental resources that the economic entity can use in its business, owning or taking over in concession.

Table 9.4 Natural capital elements identified

Types	A	B	C	D
Property lands	Yes	Yes	Yes	Yes
Land in concession	Yes	Yes	No	No
Thermo mineral water resources in concession	No	No	No	Yes
Natural resources – operating license	No	No	Yes	No

Source: Authors' processing by annual financial statements

This capital provides a system of life support, is vital for human well-being, and is irreplaceable with manufacturing, for which there is an increase in the attention given to it worldwide (Buonocore et al., 2018).

The natural capital elements identified in the economic entities analyzed are set out in Table 9.4.

We note that all economic entities own land, two of which also own land taken over in the concession. We also note that there are two situations where these companies use natural resources. One of them uses natural resources in the form of thermo mineral water deposits for which it holds a concession license for exploitation, with possibilities for resale of these deposits. The other economic entity uses natural resources of the spa, mud, seawater, and marine aerosols, which it has taken over in the concession of use.

We conclude that all economic entities analyzed use natural capital, either owned or leased for exploitation or use, to realize the object of activity, which must determine them to protect that capital.

Relationship capital in society is the reputation of the economic entity in the community by highlighting a brand or by participating in the social life of the community by giving donations or supporting charitable actions. The information on the use of this capital by the economic entities analyzed is given in Table 9.5.

Of the companies analyzed, two not only recorded expenditure on donations but also involved in the activity of non-heritage economic entities.

A summary of the evolution of the capital used by economic entities is shown in Fig. 9.4.

We note the various evolution of capital used by the economic entities analyzed; the common element is the absence of intellectual capital information. The other five capitals show different developments during the period under review and between the economic entities studied.

9.6 Identification of the Risks Associated with the Capital Used by the Companies Analyzed

The use or holding of working capital may lead to the risk of the nature of their diminution, loss, or destruction. The risks identified by the economic entities are presented in the notes to the financial statements, a summary of which is presented

Table 9.5 Elements of relational capital in society

Types	A	B	C	D
Expenditure on donations	Yes	Yes	No	No
NGO claims	Yes	Yes	No	No

Source: Authors' processing by annual financial statements

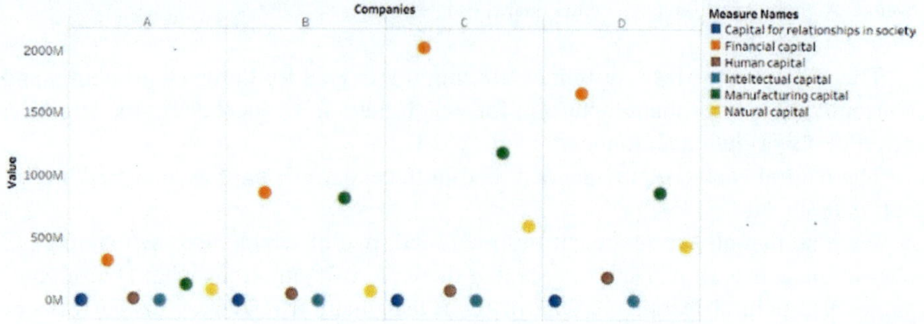

Fig. 9.4 The evolution of the capital used by the economic entities analyzed. (Source: own processing with Tableau 2020.2)

in Table 9.6. As well as others identified by us by professional reasoning, their association, with the capital of the economic entity, is shown in Table 9.7.

We note the presence in the financial statements of the same types of risks by all four economic entities analyzed. On the other hand, we do not find in any of the companies the presentation of risks arising from extraordinary events, such as the pandemic we are all going through.

Looking at the types of risks identified by or suggested by economic entities, we draw attention to the fact that all capital used may be affected by different risks, some even with an indirect impact on them. For example, legislative risk can directly affect the activity of the economic entity by reducing financial capital. Still, it can indirectly affect human capital through any decisions on the reduction of staff employed.

Such a risk may be generated by an increase in the minimum wage in the economy, which may influence decisions to reduce the number of employees since economic entities cannot bear wage increases in operating income.

Another example of a risk that of the pandemic we are all going through has primarily affected this area of activity by deciding to close the activity of hotels and restaurants during the state of emergency or to limit the conduct of some activities during the period of alert. Thus, in addition to the fact that the economic entities were no longer able to make revenues, therefore no profit. This fact led to a decrease in equity, part of the financial capital, but profoundly affected human capital by the transfer of employees to technical unemployment.

The emergence of this pandemic drew our attention to a risk that no one would have thought. We find that companies were closed; for others, it was decided only to reduce the activity, which led to a reduction in capital. Nevertheless, paying off

Table 9.6 Risks presented by economic entities

Types of risks	A	B	C	D
Controllable risks (generated by internal factors)	Yes	Yes	Yes	Yes
Liquidity risk	Yes	Yes	Yes	Yes
Operational risk	Yes	Yes	Yes	Yes
Credit risk	Yes	Yes	Yes	Yes
Uncontrollable risks (generated by external factors)	Yes	Yes	Yes	Yes
Legislative changes	Yes	Yes	Yes	Yes
Market risk	Yes	Yes	Yes	Yes
Pandemic	No	No	No	No

Source: Authors' processing by annual financial statements

Table 9.7 Risks associated with the capital analyzed

Types of risks	Financial capital	Human capital	Manufacturing capital	Intellectual capital	Natural capital	Relationship capital in the company
Liquidity risk	X	X	X	–	–	–
Operational risk	X	X	X	X	X	X
Credit risk	X	–	–	–	–	X
Currency risk	X	–	X	X	X	X
Legislative risk	X	X	X	X	X	X
Market risk	X	X	X	X	X	X
Risk of decapitalization of the company	X	X	–	–	–	X
Reputation risk (negative publicity)	X	X	–	X	X	–
Trade union actions	–	X	–	X	–	X
Pandemic	X	X	–	–	X	X
Natural disasters	X	X	X	–	X	X

Source: Authors' processing by annual financial statements and professional reasoning

debts, without continuing the activity that would have generated revenue, can lead to the company's decapitalization. Many researchers warn that after this medical crisis, an economic-financial crisis is coming.

Thus, we note that the occurrence of a risk cannot be considered a single event and that they can raise more risks, generating each other.

We conclude that the risks to the capital of economic entities are multiple and of very different natures. However, no matter how prudent it is, an event can always occur that generates a risk not taken into account by the management team.

9.7 Identification of Capital Risk Hedging Solutions Used by the Companies Analyzed

Merely identifying the risks that can defend in the business of the economic entity is no big deal. Are there solutions to cover these risks? Can they be reflected in the accounts? These are really significant issues. We know that provisions are the solution used by economic entities to cover any losses associated with certain risks. The types of provisions constituted by the economic entities analyzed are shown in Table 9.8, their graphical evolution being shown in Fig. 9.5

We note that there is no generalization in the formation of the types of provisions, only one type of provision recognized by three of the four companies analyzed: the one for the participation of employees in profit. Thus, we are entitled to say that for these companies, the use of human capital is essential precisely because of this motivation of employees to generate profit, to create added value to the company in which he is an employee.

We note that all economic entities have made provisions, even if some fewer, at the top of Fig. 9.5, showing the evolution of their total value. Analyzing the structure, the majority of the provisions constituted relate to aspects related to human capital: for the awarding prizes, for the payment of rest leave not taken during the financial year, for payments during retirement, or to stimulate executive management.

Thus, in Fig. 9.6, we have presented the evolution of human capital, and provisions reflecting the hedging of the risk hover over it.

We note that the evolution of capital and hedging is mostly the same, which entitles us to say that all economic entities subject to the case study are prudent in terms of human capital.

We have also identified provisions for disputes, but we have not noticed the creation of provisions for the protection of the environment, with economic entities considering that there is no risk of pollution or environmental damage.

For the protection of manufacturing capital, periodic revaluations could be when adjustments for impairment of tangible assets should be recognized in the accounts. We have identified only in the case of single economic entity information on depreciation adjustments, as shown in Fig. 9.7. The other three economic entities did not recognize that the fixed assets lose value and otherwise other than the depreciation.

Table 9.8 Types of provisions recorded by the companies analyzed

Types of provisions	A	B	C	D
For the award of employees	X	–	–	–
For employee participation in profit	X	–	X	X
To boost executive leadership	X	–	–	–
For employee benefits	–	X	–	–
For litigation	–	X	X	–
For employee retirement rights	–	–	X	–
For rest leave not taken	–	–	–	X

Source: Authors' processing by annual financial statements and professional reasoning

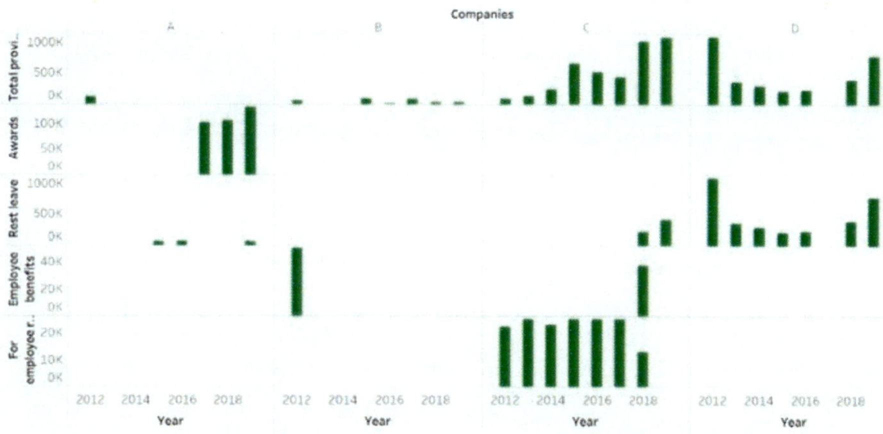

Fig. 9.5 Evolution of established provisions. (Source: own processing with Tableau 2020.2)

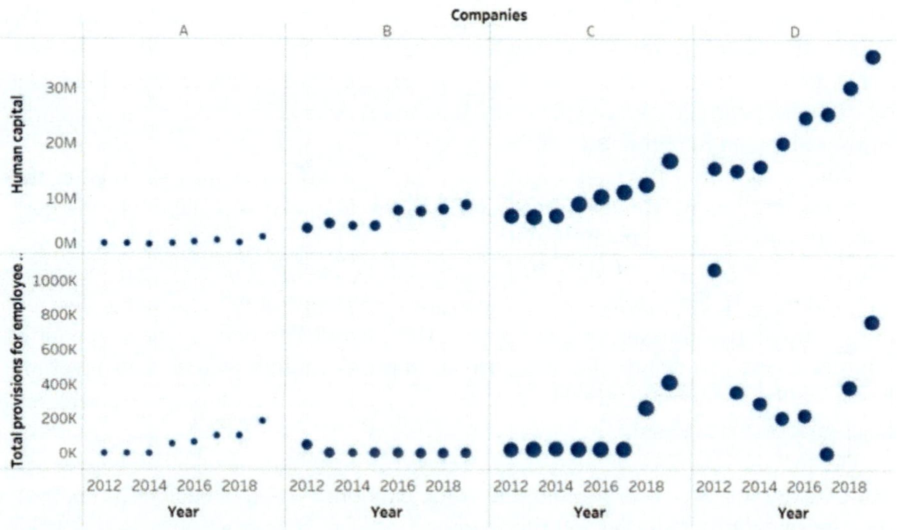

Fig. 9.6 Comparative evolution of human capital and provisions for employee benefits. (Source: own processing with Tableau 2020.2)

We note that for each category of tangible assets, the amount of depreciation adjustments is null, for all economic entities and the entire period under review, except for construction in the case of a single company. The same company also acknowledged that the land owned suffered depreciation.

We conclude that the solutions identified to protect the company from the risks of capital write-downs used are those of the nature of provisions and very little those of the nature of impairment adjustments. Is the cause a fiscal one? Much more laborious research could answer such a question.

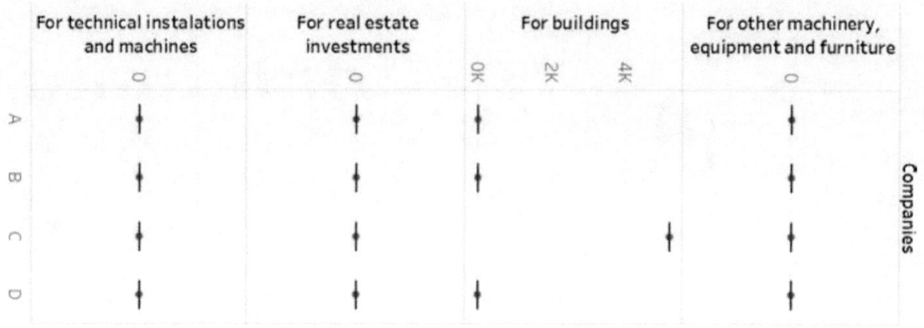

Fig. 9.7 Adjustments for impairment of tangible assets. (Source: own processing with Tableau 2020.2)

9.8 Conclusion

At the end of this research, we can state that the objectives set have been met. The information identified in the financial statements on the capital used by the economic entities subject to the case study may entitle us to conclude the capital used by economic entities. We can also conclude the risks that may affect these capitals and solutions on the limitation of losses.

Thus, concerning *financial capital,* we have identified all the information that economic entities must necessarily submit in the financial statements. In the category of possible voluntary information, we would have liked to identify risks that may directly affect this capital. We believe that the payment of dividends may be a risk of diminishing the financial capital of the economic entity because the distribution of dividends diminishes the equity of the economic entity. The payment of long-term or short-term debts diminishes financial capital. Still, it is a favorable factor for the economic entity because the shareholders' wealth is not affected, and the equity is not reached.

The fact that decision-makers can influence the structure of financial capital also results from this study. We found that some economic entities decided to increase short-term debt by reducing long-term ones.

Thus, they did not put the company at long-term risks. Some economic entities have decided to create independence from various creditors, perhaps for the same reasons of non-exposure to risk.

Human capital has seen upward developments for all economic entities throughout the period under review, which has led to an increase in the degree of risk for companies.

In terms *of manufacturing capital,* we found that economic entities provided very little voluntary information about it, which does not satisfy our need for information. Instead, it leads us to assert that the economic entities have not sufficiently protected their tangible assets from possible risks. We say this because they have not recorded adjustments in the accounts for the impairment of tangible assets. In most cases, depreciation expenses were recorded based on the linear depreciation method. We consider that the linear depreciation method is rather a "commodity" method, which does not fully reflect the economic substance of what depreciation itself represents. A record of the expenditure on the depreciation of hotel buildings, for example, depending on the rooms' occupancy would have resulted in an economic result closer to reality than the accounting one.

As already mentioned, we have not identified the *intellectual capital* of the economic entities analyzed, which makes us wonder whether the presentation of voluntary information is the "guilty" of not revealing such information. Is not there, however, a special recipe in any restaurant that does not want to reveal "how it's made" that something? Is it too complicated to register as a recognized trademark or patent? Here are some questions that invite further research.

Concerning the *natural capital* used by the economic entities analyzed, we have identified information on the type of ownership of the natural resources used and the land on which they operate. We would have liked to have read more information on the costs of protecting these natural resources. We believe that risks may also arise in respect of them, even if they cannot quantify in value. For example, torrential rains can cause landslides, the drought that can reduce water deposits, and winds that can bring clouds that can pollute mountain or sea air.

Good reputation in society, satisfied customers, voluntary activities carried out in the company, means information about *the relational capital in* the company that the economic entity uses in the creation of value. We identified very little voluntary information from the economic entities subject to the case study from the annual reports studied. A single case of a company participated in establishing a non-heritage economic entity, providing complete information, and a commercial company supporting nongovernmental organizations, but does not provide complete information on them. We have not identified information on achieving good repute through adverse publicity events nor on the fact that there have been no such events.

As secondary objectives, *the identification of risks* that may affect capital used by economic entities, as well as solutions for *protection* against these risks, has been divided into two categories: information provided by economic entities and our proposals using professional reasoning. The identified or proposed risks are diverse; for some, there are ways of assessing their value for other damage assessments being very difficult to estimate. As ways of addressing the impact of these risks on the capital used by economic entities, we have identified *provisions* and *adjustments for impairment*.

We believe that another category of risk prevention *solutions* could be *reserves* made up of annual profit. We did not find such information in the financial reports analyzed. Building reserves for extraordinary events, such as that of the current pandemic, could be a solution to avoid the risks generated by such an event. Although, from a tax point of view, only legal reserves are accepted in Romania, we believe that the protection of the economic entity should not be related only to the tax facilities it could benefit.

We conclude that focusing attention on these issues and providing such information may be a determining factor in the value creation of the economic entity as part of *integrated reporting*. In that, the information is real, transparent, and useful to the accounting information user in making its decisions on the economic entity.

Given the relatively recent obligation of integrated reporting for Romanian entities and only some of them, it is premature to conclude a possible link between integrated reporting and the field of activity or performance of the economic entity. We find the same situation as the voluntary or involuntary presentation of information in the annual financial statements.

An investigation of the periodicity of pandemics, earthquakes, catastrophic rains, or droughts, the impact on capital used by economic entities, identifying specific risk assessment criteria of this nature could be the subject of further research. We recognize that there are several limitations to the research, in that such information provided voluntarily, that pandemics of this kind have a very high cyclicality over time. The publication of information on their impact is not mandatory for all types of economic entities, which entitles us to say that finding answers to such questions can be a real challenge.

We also intend to investigate whether there is a particular "reporting discipline" that we can find in Romanian economic entities. Entities that have voluntarily reported multiple financial information report nonfinancial information? These are some of our future research directions.

References

Bobitan, R. I., & Stefea, P. (2017). Integrated reporting for a good corporate governance, "Ovidius" University Annals, Economic Sciences Series, XVII, Issue 1/2017, http://stec.univ-ovidius.ro/html/anale/RO/2017/Section-V/6.pdf. Accessed 23.08.2020.

Buonocore, E., Picone, F., Russo, G. F., Franzese, P. P. (2018). The scientific research on natural capital: A bibliometric network analysis, *Journal of EnvironmentMetallic Accounting and Management,* 6 (4), 381-391, DOI: https://doi.org/10.5890/JEAM.2018.12.010., https://apps-webofknowledge-com.am.e-nformation.ro/full_record.do?product=WOS&search_mode=GeneralSearch&qid=1&SID=D3pvWgOcYozw9aQ2fQw&page=1&doc=14. Accessed 20 Aug 2020.

Chersan, I. C. (2015). Study on practices and tendencies in integrated reporting, Financial Audit, XIII, No. 9(129)/2015, 25–36, ISSN: 1583–5812; ISSN online: 1844–8801.

Dečman, N., & Rep, A. (2018). Do Croatian companies recognize benefits of integrated reporting? *Zagreb International Review of Economics & Business*, *21*, Special Conference Issue, 31–42. https://doi.org/10.2478/zireb-2018-0022

Dumitru, M., Glăvan, M. E., Gorgan, C., & Dumitru, V. F. (2013). International integrated reporting framework: A case study in the software industry, Annales Universitatis Apulensis Series Oeconomica, 15(1), 24-39., http://www.oeconomica.uab.ro/upload/lucrari/1520131/02.pdf. Accessed 20 Aug 2020.

Hurghis, R. (2017). Integrated reporting and Board features. *Financial Audit, XV*(1(145)/2017), 83–92. https://doi.org/10.20869/AUDITF/2017/145/83

IIRC. (2013). *The international integrated reporting framework*. https://integratedreporting.org/wp-content/uploads/2013/12/13-12-08-THE-INTERNATIONAL-IR-FRAMEWORK-2-1.pdf. Accessed 19 Aug 2020.

Khan, E. A., Quadus, M., Weber, P., & Geneste, L. (2020). Micro-start-ups capital and socio-economic performance: In a poor financial resource setting, The Journal of Developing Homes,

54, 2, Spring, https://doi.org/10.1353/jda.2020.0018., https://muse.jhu.edu/article/723898/summary. Accessed 18 Aug 2020.

Männasoo, K., Hein, H., & Ruubel, R. (2018). The contributions of human capital, R&D spending, and convergence to total productivity growth factor. *Regional Studies*. https://doi.org/10.1080/00343404.2018.1445848

Massingham, R., Massingham, P. R., & Dumay, J. (2018). Improving integrated reporting. A new learning and growth perspective for the balanced scorecard. *Journal of Intellectual Capital*, December 2018, https://doi.org/10.1108/JIC-06-2018-0095

Order of the Minister of Public Finance (OMFP) No.3456 of 1 November 2018 on the amendment and completion of accounting regulations published in Official Monitor No 942 of 7 November 2018

Stubbs, W., Higgins, C., Milne, M., & Hems, L. (2014). Financial capital providers' perceptions of integrated reporting. *SSRN Electronic Journal*. https://doi.org/10.2139/ssrn.2473426

Toszewska-Czerniej, W. (2018). Creating value of organization through human capital management, Ekonomia i Prawo. *Ecomomics and Law, 17*(4), 443–457. https://doi.org/10.12775/EiP.2018.032

Úbeda-García, M., Claver-Cortés, E., Marco-Lajara, B., García-Lillo, F., & Zaragoza-Sáez, P.C. (2018). Continuous innovation in the hotel industry: The development of organizational ambidexterity through human capital and organizational culture in Spanish hotels, International Journal of Contemporary Hospitality Management, doi:https://doi.org/10.1108/IJCHM-06-2017-0326. Accessed 21 Aug 2020.

Watson, S. C. L., Grandfield, F. G. C., Herbert, R. J. H., & Newton, A. C. (2018). Ecological detecting thresholds and tipping points in the natural capital assets of a protected coastal ecosystem, Estuarine, Coastal, and Shelf Science, doi:https://doi.org/10.1016/j.ecss.2018.10.006. Accessed 20 Aug 2020.

Weeserik, B. P., & Spruit, M. (2018). Improving operational risk management using business performance management technologies. *Sustainability, 2018*(10), 640. https://doi.org/10.3390/su10030640

Xu, J., & Wang, B. (2018). Intellectual capital, financial performance and companies' sustainable growth: Evidence from the Korean Manufacturing Industry. *Sustainability, 2018*(10), 4651. https://doi.org/10.3390/su10124651. www.bvb.ro

Chapter 10
Highlighting the Driving Forces of the Shadow Economy Among EU Countries: An Empirical Investigation Based on the MIMIC Approach

Adriana AnaMaria Davidescu and Friedrich Schneider

Abstract The chapter aims to reveal the main driving forces of the shadow economy among EU countries using an improved Multiple Indicators Multiple Causes (MIMIC) model grounded in an evidence-based approach putting together the multilevel approach and the dataset of Special Eurobarometer on undeclared work no.402/2013. Therefore, using the multilevel logistic regression model based on the hierarchical nature of the data (individuals within countries), it can be highlighted that in countries with lower levels of economic development, lower qualities of government, a high level of corruption, a lower level of happy planet, a lower level of social progress, smaller levels of ALMP expenditures, lower level of social expenditures and less effective redistribution via social transfers, high unemployment and self-employment levels or low level of tax morale, salary under-reporting is more prevalent. Incorporating all these variables with a crucial role in explaining undeclared work and testing for additional variables from literature, the size of the shadow economy among 28 EU countries has been estimated at the level of 2016 using the MIMIC model. The empirical results revealed as main determinants tax revenues, unemployment rate, active labour market expenditures, social expenditures and the quality of institutions. The empirical evidence highlighted Greece, Cyprus, Bulgaria, Italy, Spain or Romania as the countries with the highest size of the shadow economy, while at opposite side there are United Kingdom, Luxembourg and Austria. After the exercise, it is important to point out that the main causes, the

A. A. Davidescu (✉)
National Scientific Research Institute for Labour and Social Protection, Bucharest University of Economic Studies, Bucharest, Romania
e-mail: adriana.alexandru@csie.ase.ro

F. Schneider
Johannes Kepler University Linz, Linz, Austria

S. L. Fotea et al. (eds.), *Navigating Through the Crisis: Business, Technological and Ethical Considerations*, Springer Proceedings in Business and Economics,
https://doi.org/10.1007/978-3-030-82751-9_10

size and the pattern as well as the consequences of this phenomenon are still subject to debate in the literature and the size of the shadow economy remains an open topic of interest and continuous efforts are necessary to improve the understanding of the shadow economy.

Keywords Shadow economy · MIMIC approach · Driving forces · Official economy · EU countries

10.1 Introduction

The estimation of the shadow economy (SE) has attracted attention in recent decades and efforts have been made in the literature to estimate this phenomenon. Among the main methods used to provide estimates for the SE, the Multiple Indicators Multiple Causes (MIMIC) model offers realistic estimates, having the main advantage of taking into account multiple causes, even if it is not exempt from limitations. On the other hand, the monetary methods, part of the indirect class of methods, has this drawback of being focus only on one cause of the SE (tax).

Currently, we decided to take into account the estimation of the shadow economy for the group of EU countries using an evidence-based approach for the selection of the potential determinants. Thus, instead of using only the relevant studies from the literature, we decided to empirically test three main theoretical perspectives regarding the relationship between the size of undeclared work and various policy measures, trying to identify the key determinants of undeclared work based on the 'modernization' thesis, the 'state under-intervention' thesis and the 'state over-interference' thesis using the multilevel approach. Therefore, in this stage, we will be able to identify the key driving forces of the shadow economy on evidence-based approach. With these results and together with the other relevant determinants from the literature, we will build the MIMIC model in the second stage of the estimation process. In such a way, the result will be a better version of the MIMIC model grounded in an evidence-based approach.

In this context, the main aim of this chapter is to propose an improved process of estimation for the shadow economy phenomenon at EU level grounded on an evidence-based approach incorporating determinants from relevant studies and empirically tested using the Multiple Indicators Multiple Causes (MIMIC) method for the cross-national level at the level of 2016.

The chapter is organized as follows. The second section is dedicated to the presentation of the main estimates of the shadow economy worldwide, pointing out the most relevant studies in the literature. The third section presents the process of modelling the size of the shadow economy among EU countries, highlighting the key hypotheses, the process of selecting the main determinants of the shadow economy, the main data sources, the methodology and the main empirical results. The fourth section presents the size of the shadow economy among EU member states at the level of 2016. The chapter ends with the most important conclusions.

10.2 An Overview of the Main Estimates of the Shadow Economy Worldwide

The size and pattern of the shadow economy have been the subject of many attempts of estimation in the last years. Buehn and Schneider (2012) provided such an example for 162 countries around the world, for the period 1999–2007, revealing that an average size of 16.6% in 2007 for 25 most developed countries, with Luxembourg the main leader(only 9.7% in 2007), while on the opposite side, there were Greece (27.5%) and Italy (27%) with the highest values. For the Eastern European and Central Asian (mostly former transition) countries, the average was 34.2%, with the smallest values registered by Slovakia and Czech Republic (approximately 18%). An alternative estimate has been provided by Schneider (2012) for 21 highly developed countries, with an average of 13.9% in 2007.

Evidence of the main causes of the SE in highly developed OECD countries has been released by the research of Schneider and Buehn (2013a), mentioning as main driving forces tax policies and state regulation, unemployment, self-employment and the tax burden.

Furthermore, Schneider and Buehn (2013b) provided another estimate of the SE for the same countries, revealing as the most important driving forces – indirect taxation, unemployment and self-employment.

In the case of transition countries, they revealed that the most important factors were indirect taxes followed by self-employment unemployment rate, tax morale, business freedom index, personal income tax, and GDP growth (Schneider & Buehn, 2013a, 2013b).

Analyzing the distribution of the main driving forces identifies by countries, it is important to highlight some differences. Thus, the influence of indirect taxation is quite important in countries such as Malta, Bulgaria or Estonia, while self-employment is a particularity for the shadow economy of Romania. On the other hand, unemployment offers some incentives for the decision of going into the unofficial sector for citizens of the Slovak Republic and Poland.

For the particular case of Romanian labour market specificities, self-employment manifested the highest influence of the incidence of SE, followed by indirect taxation and unemployment. The results were in line with the studies of Alexandru and Dobre (2013) and Davidescu (2014, 2016, 2017).

For the case of 21 highly developed countries, the main determinants were found to be indirect taxes, self-employment, personal income tax, unemployment, tax morale, business freedom index and GDP growth. If indirect taxes manifested the highest impact for Iceland, Ireland or Denmark, self-employment was influential in Greece, Portugal and Italy. The unemployment variable had the largest impact in Spain and Germany, while tax morale was fundamental for Luxembourg.

Schneider (2013) examined the size of the shadow economy for the 27 European Union countries during the period 2003–2013, pointing out that an average shadow economy of 18.4% in 2013 with decreasing values for the last years.

Summarizing, the following can be mentioned:

There can be observed a decline in the size of the shadow economy for highly developed OECD countries, and this fact can be put it on the recovery of the official economy.

If the old European Union countries registered a smaller size for the SE, the Eastern and Central countries or the new member are characterized by a high incidence of this phenomenon; therefore, we can mention that there is a wave of increase in this phenomenon manifested from west to east.

Also, a growth in the size of the SE has been registered from north to south, with southern European countries registering higher incidence of the SE.

A recent re-estimation of the size of the shadow economy worldwide, which confirms previous findings of Friedrich Schneider, Andreas Buehn and Claudia Montenegro was provided by Hassan and Friedrich (2016), who estimated the shadow economies of 157 countries between 1999 and 2013 using the MIMIC model revealing that the average size of the shadow economy (as a percentage of official GDP) of the 157 countries averaged over 1999 to 2013 is 33.77%. According to the figures, at the level of 2013, the highest size of shadow economy was registered by Greece (39.4%), Bulgaria (35.6%), Cyprus (33.8%), Italy (32%), Croatia (31.6%) and Romania (30.7%), while on the opposite side, there are Luxembourg (13.5%), United Kingdom (13.3%) and Austria (10.1%). Analyzing the trend of the shadow economy in 2013 compared with 2010, we can mention that a decline trend can be observed during this period in almost all countries with the exception of Greece, Croatia, Italy and Cyprus.

The most recent estimates of the shadow economy around the world were provided by Medina and Schneider (2017) who provides estimates for 158 countries during the period 1991–2015, suggesting that the average size of the shadow economy is 32.5% of official GDP and an average value of 30.66% in 2015. During the period 1991–2015, Cyprus (31.3%), Bulgaria (30.8%), Greece and Croatia (30.3%) and Romania (30.1%) registered the highest values of the shadow economy, while United Kingdom (13.3%), Luxembourg (10.7%) and Austria (10.1%) are situated on the opposite side.

Finally, after many attempts of estimating the shadow economy, the main causes, the size, and the pattern as well as the consequences of this phenomenon are still subject to debate in the literature, and the size of the shadow economy remains an open topic of interest, and continuous efforts are necessary to improve the understanding of the shadow economy. Thus, the research aims to offer an attempt to all these attempts based on an improved specification of the MIMIC model.

10.3 Modelling the Size of the Shadow Economy Among EU Countries

10.3.1 Key Hypotheses

"The MIMIC model presents the statistical relationships between the latent variable and the observed variables divided into causes and indicators, using the covariance matrix of them" (Schneider et al., 2010, pp. 9–10).

"MIMIC model involves the structure of an empirical covariance matrix (the covariance matrix of observed variables), which can be compared with the implied covariance matrix of the model, once the model parameters are estimated and if the two matrices are compatible with each other, then the MIMIC model could be a good approximation of the relationship between the examined variables" (Bollen, 1989, p. 256; Dell'Anno, 2003, p. 6; Long, 1983, pp. 42–45; Schneider & Buehn, 2013a, pp. 21–22).

This model approach will help to examine the multiple causes of the existence and growth of undeclared work, as well as the multiple effects of undeclared work over time. A latent estimator approach using the MIMIC procedure will be applied to estimate the size of undeclared work.

While using the MIMIC model with more than one unobservable variable, to estimate the size and development of undeclared work is problematic, the MIMIC model offers several advantages, including the possibility to take multiple indicator and causal variables into consideration at the same time and the flexibility to allow variation in the choice of causal and indicator variables according to the particular features of undeclared work studied, the period in question, and the availability of data.

"The model has two kinds of equations, the structural model – who revealed the relationships among the latent variable (η) and the causes (X_q) and –the measurement model- who links indicators (Y_p) with the latent variable (non-observed economy)" (Dell'Anno & Solomon, 2007, pp. 6–7).

The mathematical specification of the MIMIC model (Dell'Anno, 2007):

$$Y = \lambda \eta + \varepsilon \tag{10.1}$$

$$\eta = \gamma' X + \xi \tag{10.2}$$

where

η is the latent variable(the size of the shadow economy); $Y' = (Y_1, \ldots .Y_p)$ is the vector of indicators; $X' = (X_1, \ldots X_q)$ is the vector of causes; $\lambda_{(p \times 1)}$ and $\gamma_{(q \times 1)}$ are vectors of parameters and $\varepsilon_{(p \times 1)}$ and $\xi_{(p \times 1)}$ are vectors of errors.

The multilevel[1] logistic regression models based on the hierarchical nature of the data (individuals within countries) have been employed, in order to identify the key determinants of undeclared work grounded in an evidence-based approach having as source the data derived from the 2013 Eurobarometer survey. In the analysis, four proxies for undeclared work have been used: percentage of population participating in undeclared work, percentage of employees receiving envelope wages, share of employment that is undeclared and percentage of employees with no formal contract.

Summing up the main conclusions, the empirical results supported that in countries with lower levels of economic development, lower qualities of government, a high level of corruption, a lower level of the happy planet, a lower level of social progress, smaller levels of ALMP expenditures, lower level of social expenditures and less effective redistribution via social transfers, high unemployment and self-employment levels or low level of tax morale, salary under-reporting is more prevalent.

The phenomenon of working without a formal contract is more widespread in countries with lower levels of economic development and lower level of social expenditures.

It is important to mention that from the four proxies, most of the determinants of undeclared work have been identified in the case of salary under-reporting.

Therefore, starting from these results, we have taken into consideration in the process of estimating the size of the shadow economy the following variables:

- GDP per capita at PPP
- Unemployment rate
- Self-employment (% of total employment)
- Tax morale index
- European Quality of Government Index (EQI)
- Transparency Corruption Perception Index (CPI)
- Happy Planct Indcx (HPI)
- Social progress index(SPI)
- Public expenditure on ALMPs aimed at correcting disequilibria
- Social expenditures
- The impact of social transfers on reducing poverty[2]

The GDP per capita at PPS was used as a proxy for the level of economic development, and the expected sign is a negative one, considering that if the level of economic development of a country is higher the propensity of participating in undeclared activities will decrease.

[1]Which due to space limitations have not been presented here, but which can be made available to the reader.

[2]with poverty defined as the proportion of people with an income below 60% of the national median income

Higher scores for the European Quality of Government Index imply higher quality of government and corresponding a smaller propensity to participate in undeclared work activities, so a negative sign is expected.

The higher the CPI index, the less corrupt the country, and therefore the smaller the propensity to be involved in undeclared work activities.

Happy Planet Index (HPI) is rated on a scale of 0–100, and the index is measured by giving higher scores to countries with lower ecological footprints. The higher the scores of HPI, the smaller the propensity for undeclared work activities.

Social Progress Index (SPI) is rated on a scale of 0–100, with higher scores of SPI revealing a smaller propensity of working in the unofficial sector. Lower values represent higher tax morale and a smaller incidence of the shadow economy.

Increasing expenditure on labour market interventions to protect vulnerable groups, increasing social protection expenditure and increasing social transfers on reducing poverty will lead to a decrease of the undeclared work activity.

Apart from these variables, we have tested also the statistical significance of additional variables from literature:

- *Tax revenues* (% of GDP) supported by the studies of Schneider (1994a, 1994b, 1997, 2002), Johnson et al. (1998a, 1998b), Giles and Tedds (2002), Dell'Anno (2003, 2007) and Christopoulos (2003)
- *Government consumption* (% of GDP): proxy for public sector services (Dell'Anno, 2003)
- *Openness* (% of GDP)
- World Bank Governance indicators: political stability and absence of violence/terrorism, government effectiveness, regulatory quality, rule of law, control of corruption, economic freedom index, business Freedom index, and fiscal freedom index

In order to test the statistical significance of these additional variables, we have used the multilevel models based on the percentage of employees receiving envelope wages, due to the fact that most of the causal variables from the three theories proved their significance for this proxy of undeclared work.

Definitions and data sources for all variables are provided in Table 19.1 from Appendix. All country-level predictors were centred on its sample mean obtained from the weighting scheme (across all individuals regardless of their country). Given the fact that the country-level variables are strongly correlated, sequential models were estimated. We have also tested the impact of additional variables included in the analysis for the proxy of undeclared work with the highest prevalence-envelope wages.

Summarizing, we can mention from the literature body that:

- An increase in tax burden increases the shadow economy.
- The more regulated a country is, the greater the incentives are to work in the shadow economy.
- The lower the quality of state institutions is, the higher the incentives are to work in the shadow economy.

- The lower the tax morale, the higher the incentives to work in the shadow economy.
- The higher the unemployment, the more people engage in shadow economy activities.
- The higher the level of self-employment, the higher the participation in the shadow economy.
- The lower GDP per capita in a country, the higher the incentive to work in the shadow economy.
- The higher the level of freedom, the smaller the size of the shadow economy.

The indicators used in the model to reflect the existence of the shadow economy were:

- Index of real GDP (2010 = 100)

According to Schneider (2005), while unofficial activities boost economic growth for developed economies, they reduce the growth rate of the official GDP for developing countries. This variable has been set to be the reference variable in the model, fix to take the value -1 and hypothesize a negative relationship between the two economies.

Currency Ratio (M1/M2)

As a monetary indicator, we used in the model the currency ratio (M1/M2), under the main hypothesis that part of informal transactions operates with cash, being unnoticeable. All potential determinants included in the analysis were displayed in Fig. 10.1.

10.3.2 Data and Methodology

In order to obtain the optimal model, we will estimate several specifications of the MIMIC model, eliminating the variables that are not statistically significant and taking into account the correlation degree among causal variables. The usual method used to estimate the MIMIC model is the maximum likelihood (ML), but Bollen (1989) drew attention to the detection of multivariate normality of original data using specific tests. For the situation in which this normality is not fulfilled, the recommendation is to use robust maximum likelihood or Satorra-Bentler option for ML estimation having the advantage of keeping the same parameters as ML but improving significantly the goodness of fit.

Due to the fact that the MIMIC model provides only relative estimates of the SE, a calibration procedure is needed to convert these values (Dell'Anno & Solomon, 2007; Schneider et al., 2010; Dell'Anno & Schneider, 2009).

In the estimation process of the shadow economy for 28 European countries, we used data at the level of 2016, the main data sources being Eurostat National Accounts, Employment and Unemployment and Government finance Statistics

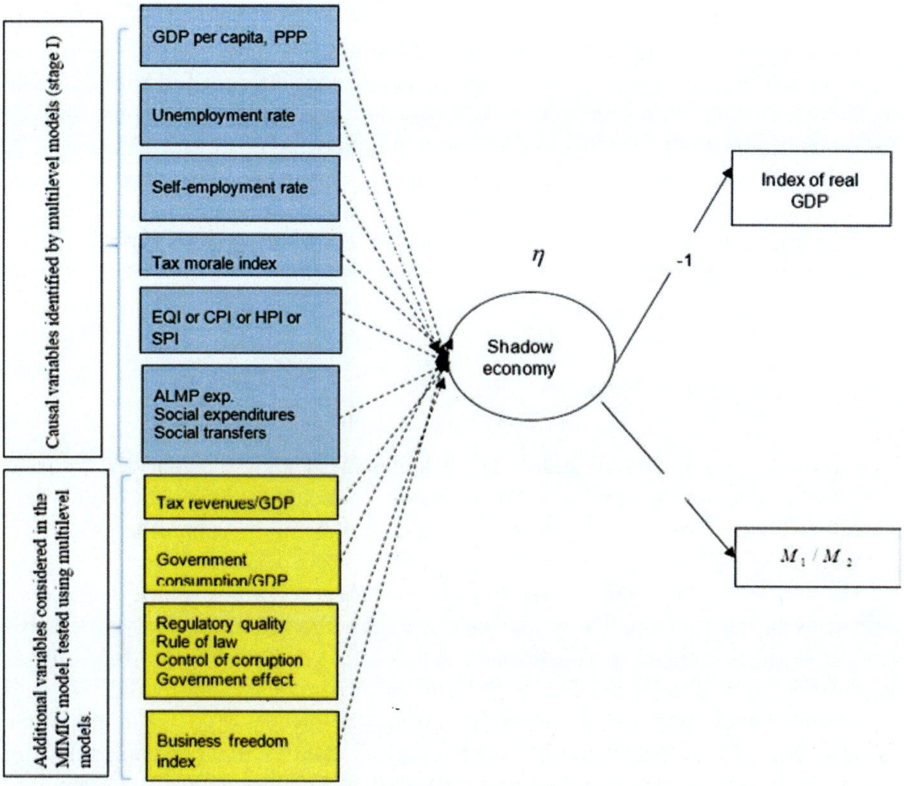

Fig. 10.1 Path diagram of the MIMIC model

databases, World Development Indicators of World Bank, WGI database, Heritage Foundation database and International Financial Statistics (IFS) of International Monetary Fund. Table 10.2 from Appendix offers the details on the dataset. For the estimation of the size of the shadow economy using the maximum likelihood (ML) method, STATA 14 software is used.

The results of Mardia (1970), Doornik–Hansen (2008) and Henze–Zirkler's (1990) rejected the multivariate normality hypothesis. Therefore, several models have been estimated using ML taking into account the Sattora-Bentler option.

10.3.2.1 Multiple Imputation of Missing Values

Multiple imputation based on a system of the chained equation has been applied to the dataset for the series of social progress index for Luxembourg and Malta; public expenditure on ALMPs aimed at correcting disequilibria for Malta and the United Kingdom and the impact of social transfers for Estonia and Ireland. We have used the chained equations (full conditional specification) approach to create multiple imputations of the missing data, based on a regression model of each partially observed variable on the others. For the imputation, we have used the predictive mean matching, involving that for each missing value first to find the predicted mean based on the fitted linear regression model based on the GDP per capita at PPP. The missing value is imputed by randomly choosing one of the observed values (of the variables being imputed) from those two subjects in the dataset who have the two closest predicted values to the predicted value for the subject for whom we are imputing), ten imputations being employed (Schafer & Graham, 2002; Collins et al., 2001; Rubin, 1987).

10.3.3 Empirical Results

In order to test the impact of additional variables included in the analysis, we have used as the dependent variable – the proxy of undeclared work with the highest prevalence – envelope wages, the empirical results being presented in Table 10.3 from Appendix.

The empirical of all models applied to employees receiving envelope wages confirmed as in the previous cases that men are significantly more likely to receive envelope wages compared with women, and this fact is available also for younger employees, as well as those facing difficulties in paying the household bills and those with fewer years of education. Regarding the business types and employee groups' impact on the decision of under-reporting salaries, smaller companies are more likely to underreport wages and unskilled and skilled manual workers, and those who travel for their jobs are more likely to receive envelope wages than those in employed positions at a desk.

Analyzing the potential association between the level of penalties and the participation in the undeclared work, the empirical results infirmed any impact of the detection risk on the decision of under-reporting salaries. Increasing the risk of detection seems not to influence participation.

There is statistically significant and positive impact of tax morality on the decision of under-reporting wages: employees having lower tax morale are more likely to receive envelope wages.

The association between tax morale and participation in undeclared work is strongly significant in all models.

Evaluating the impact of additional variables considered in the analysis, it can be highlighted the statistically significant effect of tax revenues and government consumption on the propensity of receiving envelope wages, while openness does not manifest any statistical impact on the size of salary under-reporting.

Examining the impact of governance indicators on salary under-reporting, the results revealed the statistical significance and a negative expected influence of regulatory quality, rule of law, control of corruption and government effectiveness, while political stability does not exhibit any statistical impact on salary under-reporting.

Analyzing the impact of freedom indices, it can be pointed out the statistical significance of business freedom having an expected negative impact on salary under-reporting, while economic freedom and fiscal freedom does not manifest any statistical significance on envelope wages.

Putting together all these findings, several specifications were estimated in STATA 14 given a high level of correlation between some variables. The empirical results are presented in Table 10.1. Analyzing the empirical results, it can be highlighted that tax revenues, unemployment rate, ALMP expenditures or social expenditures exhibited a significant impact in almost all of the models. The impact of tax revenues is positive and statistically significant, confirming the results of the majority of studies in the field which mentioned tax burden as one of the main causes of the shadow economy worldwide.

The positive sign of the unemployment rate revealed a direct impact on the size of the shadow economy being considered another major cause of the shadow economy. Self-employment does not manifest any impact on the size of the shadow economy among EU countries. The European Quality of Government Index exhibited a negative impact on the size of the shadow economy implying that a higher quality of government will lead to a decrease in the propensity to work in the shadow economy.

Regarding the impact of CPI, the direction of the relationship is that the higher the level of perceived public corruption (corresponding to a smaller CPI) will be, the larger will be the size of the shadow economy. The CPI does not exhibit any statistical impact on the size of the shadow economy. Both Happy Planet Index and Social progress index do not manifest any impact on the size of the shadow economy, even if the social progress index has the expected negative sign highlighting that a higher level of social progress will imply also a smaller level of the shadow economy.

GDP per capita exhibited a negative and statistically significant impact on the size of the shadow economy, confirming in such a way the modernization thesis according to which the likelihood of undeclared work is lower in more modernized developed economies. Starting from the observation of Medina and Schneider (2017) regarding the endogeneity of the use of GDP as cause and indicator, we decided to exclude GDP per capita as causal variables, having in mind that the index of real GDP is set to be the reference variable.

Active labour market expenditures manifested a negative statistically significant impact on the size of the shadow economy, confirming the under-intervention thesis according to which the undeclared work is more prevalent in economies with smaller ALMP expenditures and social transfers (Williams & Horodnic, 2017, p. 87). The social transfers have the expected sign, but the lack of significance in the models do not support the under-intervention thesis.

Instead of this, social expenditures manifested a positive statistical impact on the size of the shadow economy leading to the confirmation of the over-interference thesis, contrary to the results based on the salary under-reporting and percentage of people working without a formal contract according to which the phenomenon of undeclared work is more prevalent in economies with lower levels of social expenditures. The confirmation of over-interference thesis stated that the size of the

Table 10.1 The empirical results of MIMIC models

Models/causes	**MIMIC 8-1-2a**	**MIMIC 8-1-2b**	**MIMIC 7-1-2a**	**MIMIC 7-1-2b**	**MIMIC 7-1-2c**	**MIMIC 6-1-2a**	**MIMIC 6-1-2b**	**MIMIC 6-1-2c**	**MIMIC 5-1-2a**	**MIMIC 5-1-2b**
GDP per capita								−0.00015***		
Unemployment rate	1.32***	1.28***	0.90***	0.994***	0.914***	1.09***	1.198***	1.37***	**1.027*** **	1.33***
Self-employment rate	0.012	0.038						0.146		0.136
Tax morale	−1.24	−1.95	−1.18	−0.446		−2.80	−4.90			
EQI							−3.196*		**−4.85*** **	
CPI			0.062	−0.025		0.212		0.072		
HPI	0.229				0.058					
SPI										−0.375
ALMP exp.	−19.49***	−18.53***	−14.29***		−15.41***	−12.91***	−13.88***	−10.50**	**−12.80*** **	−11.63**
Social exp.	0.405	0.641	1.13***	1.04**	1.18***				**1.188*** **	
Social transfers				−0.01						
Tax revenues	0.989***	0.74	0.71	0.478	0.485	1.21***	1.01***	1.47***	**0.794***	1.52***
Gov. consumption	0.48	0.703			0.707		0.987			
Regulatory quality						−11.07*				
Rule of law			−7.92	−7.69	−7.07***					
Control of corruption										
Government effect.										
Business freed.		−0.066								
Indicators										
Index of real GDP(2010 = 100)	−1	−1	−1	−1	−1	−1	−1	−1	**−1**	−1
Currency(M1/M2)[a]	0.0056**	0.0056*	0.0065*	0.0053*	0.0062	0.0064*	0.0057*	0.0052*	**0.0061***	0.0056*
Global goodness-of-fit statistics										

Chi-square[2] (*p*-value)	856+ (0.28)	12.15+ (0.096)	5.20+ (0.51)	3.91+ (0.68)	5.32+ (0.50)	5.93+ (0.31)	4.63+ (0.462)	54.59 (0.01)	**4.57+ (0.33)**	7.66+ (0.106)
RMSEA[3] (*p*-value)	0.09+ (0.26)	0.162+ (0.12)	0.00+ (0.56)	0.00+ (0.72)	0.00+ (0.54)	0.081+ (0.35)	0.00+ (0.50)		**0.07+ (0.37)**	0.18+ (0.127)
CFI	0.950	0.851	1.00	1.00	1.00	0.971	1.00		**0.985**	0.892
TLI	0.879	0.639	1.05	1.19	1.04	0.925	1.03		**0.958**	0.702
AIC	1197.81	1225.66	954.26	1155.80	1033.28	800.33	778.39	1491.90	**750.47**	868.58
SRMR	0.073	0.085	0.088	0.078	0.090	0.091	0.094	0.09	**0.101**	0.103
CD	0.824	0.810	0.99	0.761	0.973	0.925	0.833	0.766	**0.943**	0.792
Degrees of freed.[4]	58	58	48	48	48	39	39	39	**31**	31

	MIMIC 5-1-2c	**MIMIC 5-1-2d**	**MIMIC 5-1-2e**	**MIMIC 5-1-2f**	**MIMIC 5-1-2g**	**MIMIC 5-1-2h**	**MIMIC 5-1-2i**	**MIMIC 5-1-2j**	**MIMIC 4-1-2a**	**MIMIC 4-1-2b**	**MIMIC 4-1-2c**
GDP per capita											
Unemployment rate	1.32***	1.17***	1.196***	1.035***	1.33***	0.975***	0.916***	1.33***	1.10***	1.36***	**1.229*** **
Self-employment rate											
Tax morale											
EQI			1.028						−6.24***	−2.08	
CPI	−0.139										
HPI		0.276			0.309						
SPI											
ALMP exp.	−12.99***		−11.82**	−14.49***	−18.76***	−13.63***	−13.92***	−17.07***		−11.47**	**−11.42*** **
Social exp.				1.175***	0.393	1.123***	1.19***	0.709	1.11***		
Social transfers		−0.065									
Tax revenues	1.27***	1.09***	1.36***	0.714	1.19*	0.799	0.712	0.973	0.578	1.50***	**1.409*** **
Gov. Consumption	0.67										

(continued)

Table 10.1 (continued)

Regulatory quality		−6.98**	−6.66								**−4.96***
Rule of law							−6.70***				
Control of corruption						−5.01***					
Government effect.				−7.09***							
Business freed.								−0.042			
Indicators											
Index of real GDP (2010 = 100)	−1	−1	−1	−1	−1	−1	−1	−1	−1	−1	**−1**
Currency (M1/M2)	0.0053*	0.0051*	0.0059*	0.0061**	0.0058**	0.0057**	0.0064**	0.0056*	0.0052**	0.0055*	**0.0059***
Global goodness-of-fit statistics											
Chi-square[2] (*p*-value)	4.33+ (0.36)	4.08+ (0.39)	5.45+ (0.24)	4.61+ (0.33)	4.53+ (0.33)	4.15+ (0.38)	4.90+ (0.29)	6.13+ (0.18)	3.28+ (0.35)	4.18+ (0.24)	**4.85+ (0.18)**
RMSEA[3] (*p*-value)	0.05+ (0.29)	0.02+ (0.28)	0.114+ (0.27)	0.074+ (0.366)	0.06+ (0.37)	0.03+ (0.29)	0.09+ (0.33)	0.13+ (0.34)	0.05+ (0.38)	0.11+ (0.27)	**0.148+ (0.209)**
CFI	0.989	0.997	0.955	0.983	0.984	0.996	0.976	0.936	0.992	0.963	**0.945**
TLI	0.970	0.992	0.876	0.954	0.955	0.988	0.935	0.825	0.975	0.889	**0.834**
AIC	889.33	958.78	603.197	725.81	863.94	745.03	733.50	893.35	751.01	609.11	**573.775**
SRMR	0.105	0.078	0.106	0.098	0.087	0.095	0.101	0.106	0.089	0.108	**0.107**
CD	0.749	0.705	0.841	0.930	0.842	0.870	0.975	0.811	0.759	0.771	**0.828**
Degrees of freed.[4]	31	31	31	31	31	31	31	31	24	24	**24**

[a]The negative sign of currency can be explained by drastic changes in the payment habits to non-cash systems

Notes: ***, ** and * represent 1%, 5% and 10%; [+] Means good fitting (*p*-value > 0.05). [2] If the structural equation model is correct and the population parameters are known, then the matrix S (sample covariance matrix) will equal to $\Sigma(\theta)$ (model-implied covariance matrix); therefore, the perfect fitting correspond to *p*-value = 1. This test has a statistical validity if there are large sample and multinormal distributions. [3]*p*-value for test of close fit (RMSEA < 0.05). [4] The degrees of freedom are determined by $0.5(p + q)(p + q + 1) + m - t$, where "p" is the number of indicators, "q" the number of causes, "m" the number of means and intercepts and "t" is the number of free parameters shadow economy is higher in economies with higher levels of social expenditures to protect vulnerable groups.

Tax morale does not manifest any statistical impact on the size of the shadow economy in all models, while government consumption registered the expected positive sign but suffers from a lack of significance.

Regarding the governance alternative measures, the empirical results revealed a significant negative impact on regulatory quality, rule of law, control of corruption and government effectiveness. Business freedom does not exhibit a significant impact on the size of the shadow economy.

Summing up all information provided by the empirical results, it can be revealed that the main determinants of the shadow economy among 28 EU countries for the year 2016 are the unemployment rate, tax revenues, active labour market expenditures, social expenditures and the quality of institutions, which had a strongly statistically significant impact and had also the expected signs.

Following Bollen (1989) and Long (1983), the optimal model has been chosen based on the following criteria: the statistical significance of parameters, the p-value of chi-square, the value of root mean squared error of approximation (RMSEA), standardized root mean square residual (SRMR), the comparative fit index (CFI) and Tucker-Lewis index (TLI), the value of the coefficient of determination and the values of AIC.

Starting from a more general specification of the MIMIC model and trying different specifications taking into account the degree of correlation among variables, the best model identified in terms of statistical properties was MIMIC 5-1-2 with five causal variables (unemployment rate, tax revenues, ALMP expenditures, social expenditures, European quality of government) and two indicators (index of real GDP and currency (M1/M2)).

Tax revenues had a significant influence on the dimension of the shadow economy, while the significant positive sign of the unemployment rate highlighted that SE is considered to be a "buffer" for the official economy.

The negative sign of active labour market expenditures confirmed the under-intervention thesis the undeclared work being more prevalent in economies with smaller ALMP expenditures and social transfers while the positive sign of social expenditures supported the over-interference thesis the incidence of undeclared work being higher in economies higher levels of social expenditures to protect vulnerable groups.

According to Razmi et al. (2013, p. 51), "institutional instability, lack of transparency and rule of law undermine the willingness of frustrated citizens to be active in the formal economy. Citizens will feel cheated if they believe that corruption is widespread, their tax burden is not spent well, their government lacks accountability and they are not protected by the rules of law, increasing the probability to enter the informal sector"(p. 51).

The hypothesis was supported by the negative sign of the European Quality of government index and regulatory quality according to which a smaller quality of government will lead individuals to accept working in the unofficial sector.

Analyzing the empirical results provided by several estimations, we decided to consider for comparison the results of two optimal models: MIMIC 5-1-2 and MIMIC 4-1-2 in order to compare the final results to see potential differences in the size of the shadow economy. Both models have statistically significant coefficients with expected signs and are valid and high a relative high goodness of fit.

Analyzing the standardized coefficients of the first model (5-1-2 MIMIC) in order to quantify the influence of each cause, it was revealed that social expenditures can be considered as the main determinant having the biggest influence on shadow activities (0.65). The second determinant is perceived to be tax revenues with a standardized coefficient of 0.45, followed closely by quality of government index (-0.42), unemployment rate (0.41) and active labour market expenditures (-0.37).

In the case of the second model, a MIMIC model 4-1-2, tax revenues are considered to have the biggest influence on shadow activities (0.78), followed by unemployment rate (0.48), ALMP expenditures (−0.32) and regulatory quality (−0.21).

After we have identified the coefficients of the best MIMIC models, the last step refers to the application of the calibration procedure in order to convert the relative estimates of the MIMIC model to real estimates using an exogenous value of SE of the reference year (2010). For the year 2010, we have taken the exogenous value of the shadow economy for the 28 EU countries from Hassan and Friedrich (2016).

The ordinal time series index of shadow economy based on the structural models is:

MIMIC 5-1-2:

$$\frac{\tilde{\eta}_{2016}}{\mathrm{GDP}_{2010}} = 0.79\mathrm{Taxrevenues} + 1.027\mathrm{UR} + 1.188\mathrm{social\,exp} \\ -4.85\mathrm{EQI} - 12.8\mathrm{ALMP\,exp} \tag{10.3}$$

MIMIC 4-1-2:

$$\frac{\tilde{\eta}_{2016}}{\mathrm{GDP}_{2010}} = 1.41\mathrm{Taxrevenues} + 1.229\mathrm{UR} \\ -4.96\mathrm{Reg\_quality} - 11.42\mathrm{ALMPexp} \tag{10.4}$$

In order to express the SE as the ratio of current GDP, the main steps of the calibration procedure are the following (Hassan & Friedrich, 2016):

$$\eta t = \frac{\tilde{\eta} t}{\tilde{\eta}\ \mathrm{base\ year}} \eta * \mathrm{base\ year} \tag{10.5}$$

where $\tilde{\eta}$ denotes the value of the MIMIC index at time t (2016) according to the structural equation (10.3 or 10.4), $\tilde{\eta}eye$ is the value of the MIMIC index in the base year which in our model is 2010 and $\eta * eye$ is the exogenous (prior) estimation of the size of the shadow economy in the base year (2010) taken from Hassan and Friedrich (2016).

Based on the application of this benchmarking procedure, we are able to calculate the final estimates of the size of the shadow economy as a percentage of GDP for the 28 EU countries at the level of 2016.

10.4 Size of the Shadow Economy of the 28 EU Countries

10.4.1 Difficulties Encountered in the Estimation Process

Although the MIMIC approach increased its popularity in the last years, having this advantage of simultaneity of multiple cases and indicators, it has also its limitations very clearly identified in the literature research among which we can mention the most important: the meaning of the latent variable (Helberger & Knepel, 1988; Giles & Tedds, 2002; Smith, 2002; Dell'Anno, 2003), instability of estimated coefficients with respect to changes the sample size and with respect to alternative model specifications, the benchmark method, the sensitivity of the exogenous value of the shadow economy and the ambiguity in the choice of the variables to be included in the model as causes or indicators. A detailed presentation of the main advantages and disadvantages of this approach was provided by Dell'Anno and Schneider (2009).

Therefore, it is worth mentioning that the final figures of the shadow economy are quite sensitive to the calibration procedure applied and also to starting values or exogenous values of the shadow economy, the results being significantly different having several starting values or choosing different calibration procedures. In order to calibrate the model, we used as starting values the estimates provided by Hassan and Friedrich (2016) as well as Williams et al. (2017).

10.4.2 The Size of the Shadow Economy in the 28 EU Countries

Using the results obtained from the 5-1-2 MIMIC model (Fig. 10.2), the average size of the shadow economy among 28 EU countries is 24.9% of official GDP, with the highest values registered by Greece (46.3%), Cyprus (38.1%), Bulgaria (33.6%), Italy (32.3%) and Romania (31.9%). On the opposite side, there are United Kingdom (14.3%), Luxembourg and Austria (10.9%).

Following the results provided by the estimates of the 4-1-2 MIMIC model (Fig. 10.3), the average size of the shadow economy among the Member States is 25.5%, with the highest values for Greece (51.8%), Cyprus (39%), Bulgaria (38%),

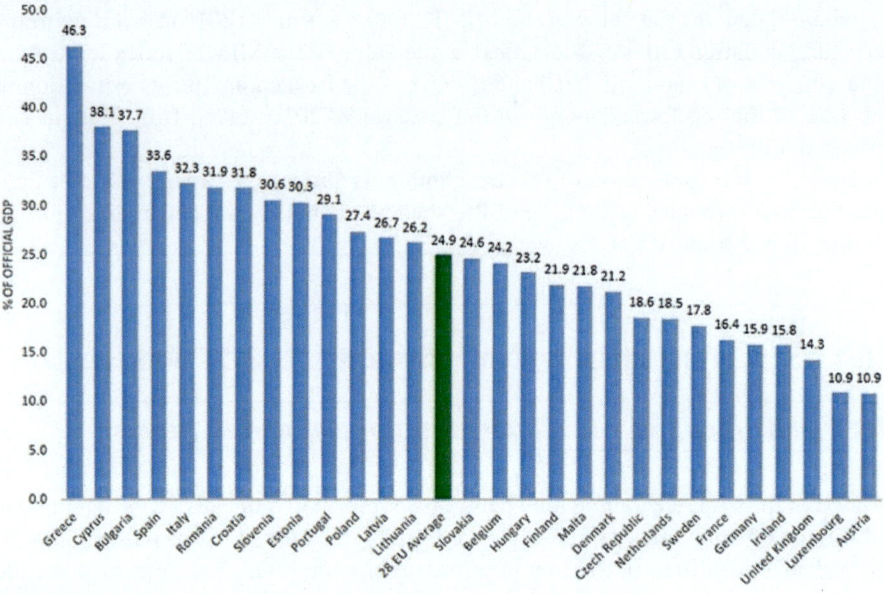

Fig. 10.2 The size of the shadow economy for 2016 among 28 EU countries according to the 5-1-2 MIMIC model

Spain (35.2%) and Romania (33.9%). On the opposite side, we have United Kingdom (12.5%), Luxembourg and Austria (11.4% respectively 11.2%).

Analyzing comparatively the results provided by both models (Fig. 10.4), we can mention that the results are in line with the most empirical studies in the field. Hassan and Friedrich (2016) pointed out in their last estimates an average size of the shadow economy for the 28 EU states of 23.1% of official GDP for the year 2013, with the highest values of shadow economy registered by Greece (39.4%), Bulgaria (35.6%), Cyprus (33.8%), Italy (32%), Croatia (31.6%) and Romania (30.7%). On the opposite side, there were Luxembourg (15.5%), United Kingdom (15.3%) and Austria (10.1%).

Taking into account the estimates of the 4-1-2 MIMIC model and using as starting values for the calibration procedure the estimates of the undeclared work as the percentage of the labour input, we have used as starting values the average between the values of the shadow economy of Hassan and Schneider (2013) and the values of undeclared work as the percentage of labour input taken from Williams et al. (2017). Therefore, we attributed equal weights to both starting values. Based on the application of this benchmarking procedure, we are able to calculate the final estimates of the size of the shadow economy as a percentage of GDP for the 28 EU countries at the level of 2016.

Following the results, the average size of the shadow economy among the Member States was 18.6%, with the highest values for Greece (34.5%), Cyprus (28.6%), Bulgaria (28.1%) and Romania (26.5%). On the opposite side, we have Ireland (9.9%), Luxembourg (8.5%) and United Kingdom (7.4%).

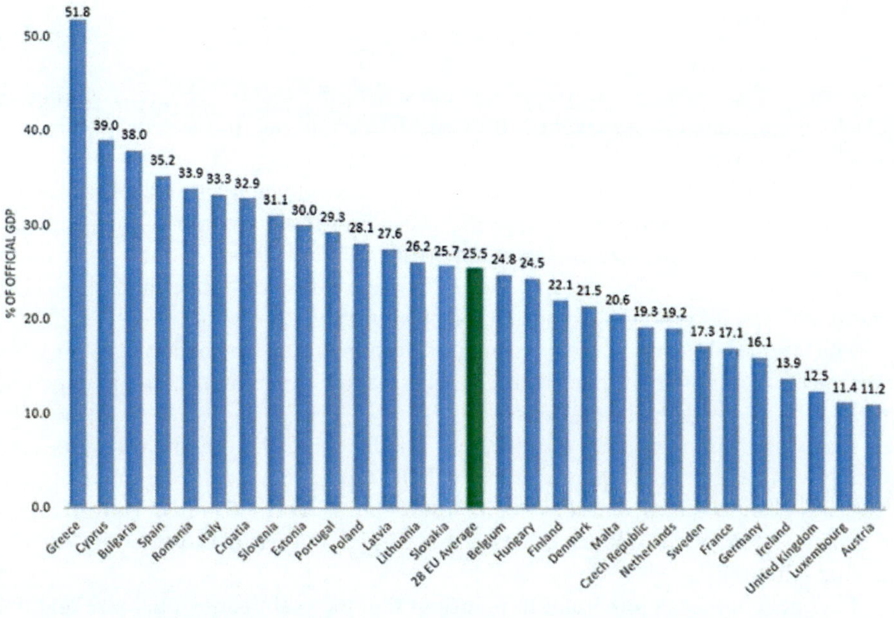

Fig. 10.3 The size of the shadow economy for 2016 among 28 EU countries according to the 4-1-2 MIMIC model

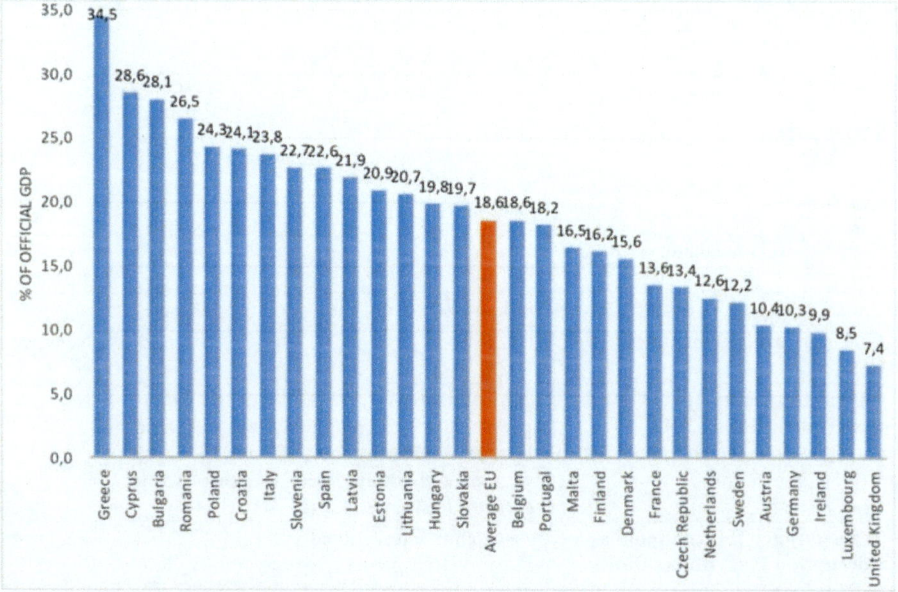

Fig. 10.4 The size of the shadow economy for 2016 among 28 EU countries

10.5 Conclusions

The aim of the research was to estimate the size of the shadow economy among 28 EU Member States at the level of the year 2016 using one of the most commonly used models in the literature – the MIMIC model.

The MIMIC model incorporated the key determinants of undeclared work grounded in an evidence-based approach based on three theoretical perspectives: the 'modernization' thesis, the 'state under-intervention' thesis and the 'state over-interference' thesis using the multilevel logistic regression model and also other additional variables previously tested for meaning.

The empirical results revealed as main determinants of the shadow economy tax revenues, unemployment rate, active labour market expenditures, social expenditures and the quality of institutions.

Analyzing comparatively the different results using the empirical results provided by different specifications of the MIMIC model, the results are quite similar. The informality poles at the level of 2016 are Greece, Cyprus, Bulgaria and Romania, while on the opposite side there are Ireland, Austria, Luxembourg and the United Kingdom.

In conclusion, it is important to point out that the main causes, the size and the pattern as well as the consequences of this phenomenon are still subject to debate in the literature, and the size of the shadow economy remains an open topic of interest, and continuous efforts are necessary to improve the understanding of the shadow economy.

Appendix

Table 10.2 The description of MIMIC variables

Country-level explanatory variables	Data source	Expected sign
Causal variables considered based on the results from multilevel modelling		
GDP per capita (constant 2010 US$)	WDI, 2017	Negative
European Quality of Government Index 2013	Charron, Nicholas, Lewis Dijkstra and Victor Lapuente. 2015. 'Mapping the Regional Divide in Europe: A Measure for Assessing Quality of Government in 206 European Regions'. ***Social Indicators Research***. vol 122 (2): 315–346.	Negative
Transparency International's Corruption Perceptions Index (CPI)	Transparency International http://www.transparency.org/research/cpi/overview	Negative
Happy Planet Index (HPI)	http://happyplanetindex.org/	Negative
Social Progress Index (SPI)	http://www.socialprogressimperative.org/global-index/#data_table/countries/dim3/dim1,dim2,dim3	Negative

(continued)

Table 10.2 (continued)

Country-level explanatory variables	Data source	Expected sign
Public expenditure on ALMPs measures (2–7), % GDP, 2015	LMP expenditure by type of action, Eurostat http://appsso.eurostat.ec.europa.eu/nui/show.do?dataset=lmp_expsumm&lang=en	Negative
Social expenditure as % of GDP, 2014	Expenditures database, Eurostat, http://appsso.eurostat.ec.europa.eu/nui/show.do?dataset=spr_exp_sum&lang=en	Negative
The impact of social transfers on reducing poverty, with poverty defined as the proportion of people with an income below 60% of the national median income, 2014	Employment and Social Developments in Europe 2015 http://ec.europa.eu/social/main.jsp?catId=738&langId=en&pubId=7859&furtherPubs=yes	Negative
Unemployment rate, %	Employment and Unemployment Database, Eurostat	Positive
Self-employment (% of total employment)	Employment and Unemployment Database, Eurostat	Positive
Tax-morality index, 2013	Eurobarometer on Undeclared Work no.402/2013 https://ec.europa.eu/commfrontoffice/publicopinion/archives/ebs/ebs_402_en.pdf	Positive
Additional causal variables taken into consideration		
Government consumption, % of GDP	Government finance statistics database, Eurostat http://appsso.eurostat.ec.europa.eu/nui/show.do?dataset=gov_10a_taxag&lang=en	Positive
Tax revenue, % of GDP, 2015	Government finance statistics database, Eurostat http://appsso.eurostat.ec.europa.eu/nui/show.do?dataset=gov_10a_taxag&lang=en	Positive
Openness, % of GDP	National Accounts Database, Eurostat	Negative
Political stability, 2015	WGI indicators, World Bank	Positive
Government effectiveness, 2015	WGI indicators, World Bank	Negative
Regulatory quality, 2015	WGI indicators, World Bank	Negative
Rule of law, 2015	WGI indicators, World Bank	Negative
Control of corruption, 2015	WGI indicators, World Bank	Negative
Economic freedom index, 2016	Heritage Foundation	Negative
Business freedom index, 2016	Heritage Foundation	Negative
Fiscal freedom index, 2016	Heritage Foundation	Negative
Indicators		
Index of real GDP, chain-linked volumes, 2010=100	National Accounts database, Eurostat	Negative
Currency (M1/M2)	International Financial Statistics (IFS) database, IMF	Positive

Table 10.3 Testing the statistical significance of additional causal variables using multilevel mixed-effects logistic regression of the prevalence of receiving envelope wages

	Model I		Model II		Model III		Model IV	
	β	*exp*(β)	β	*exp*(β)	β	*exp*(β)	β	*exp*(β)
Gender (female)								
Men	0.36***	1.43	0.355***	1.42	0.358***	1.43	0.358***	1.43
Age (mean centred:41)	−0.02***	0.98	−0.021***	0.98	−0.021***	0.98	−0.02***	0.98
Age when stopped education (1–15)								
16–19	0.43*	1.55	0.43*	1.53	0.446*	1.56	0.465*	1.59
20+	0.137	1.14	0.145	1.16	0.137	1.14	0.152	1.16
Occupation (employed position, at desk)								
employed professional	0.407	1.50	0.387	1.47	0.427	1.53	0.421	1.52
General management, director or top management	0.062	1.06	0.056	1.06	0.069	1.07	0.075	1.07
Middle management	0.037	1.03	0.029	1.02	0.038	1.04	0.048	1.05
Employed position, travelling	0.766***	2.15	0.759***	2.13	0.764***	2.14	0.760***	2.13
Employed position, service job	0.311	1.36	0.310	1.36	0.309	1.37	0.312	1.36
Supervisor	0.608	1.83	0.606	1.83	0.620	1.86	0.611	1.84
Skilled manual worker	0.692***	1.99	0.691***	1.99	0.689***	1.99	0.688***	1.99
Unskilled manual worker	0.689***	1.99	0.693***	2.00	0.688***	1.99	0.698***	2.00
Company size (1–4 employees)								
5–9	−0.21	0.81	−0.19	0.82	−0.209	0.81	−0.197	0.82
10–19	−0.28	0.75	−0.26	0.76	−0.276	0.76	−0.256	0.77
20–49	−0.62***	0.53	−0.60***	0.55	−0.611***	0.54	−0.588***	0.55
50–99	−1.08***	0.33	−1.06***	0.34	−1.07***	0.34	−1.05***	0.348
100–499	−1.21***	0.29	−1.18***	0.30	−1.20***	0.29	−1.17***	0.308
500 or more	−1.49***	0.22	−1.46***	0.23	−1.49***	0.22	−1.47***	0/229
Difficulties paying bills(almost never)								
Most of the time	1.18***	3.25	1.14***	3.13	1.18***	3.27	1.14***	3.13

From time to time	0.52***	1.68	0.49***	1.64	0.53***	1.69	0.51***	1.66
Detection risk (small)								
High	−0.07	0.93	−0.068	0.93	−0.062	0.94	−0.060	0.94
Tax_morality (mean centred:2.34)	0.273***	1.31	0.274***	1.31	0.277***	1.32	0.283***	1.32
Constant	−4.16***	0.015	−4.23***	0.014	−4.21***	0.015	−4.14***	0.015
Government consumption (centred)	0.027**	0.972						
Tax revenues, % of GDP (centred)			0.047***	0.953				
Openness (centred)					0.011	1.00		
Political stability (centred)							−0.447	0.639
Observations	8994		8994		8994		8994	
No. of groups	28		28		28		28	
Log likelihood	−1230.00		−1228.05		−1231.60		−1230.61	
Wald chi2	320.70***		328.08***		314.61***		317.54***	
Variance (constant)	0.181		0.134		0.226		0.201	
(Intercept variance) (Standard error)	0.083		0.07		0.095		0.088	
Variance at country level[a] (%)	5.21%		3.91%		6.42%		5.75%	
LR test	19.64 ***		12.19***		28.83***		24.14***	
	Model V		**Model VI**		**Model VII**		**Model VIII**	
	β	***exp*(β)**	**β**	***exp*(β)**	**β**	***exp*(β)**	**β**	***exp*(β)**
Gender (female)								
Men	0.36***	1.43	0.36***	1.44	0.36***	1.43	0.36***	1.439
Age (mean centred:41)	−0.02***	0.98	−0.02***	0.98	−0.02***	0.98	−0.02***	0.979
Age when stopped education (1–15)								

(continued)

Table 10.3 (continued)

16–19	0.49*	1.63	0.45*	1.58	0.45*	1.57	0.44	1.561
20+	0.21	1.23	0.18	1.20	0.18	1.17	0.17	1.185
Occupation (employed position, at desk)								
employed professional	0.436	1.546	0.440	1.55	0.437	1.54	0.428	1.533
General management, director or top management	0.110	1.117	0.130	1.14	0.121	1.13	0.114	1.121
Middle management	0.065	1.067	0.087	1.09	0.075	1.07	0.081	1.085
Employed position, travelling	0.775***	2.172	0.779***	2.18	0.782***	2.18	0.778***	2.177
Employed position, service job	0.341	1.407	0.357	1.43	0.355	1.42	0.360	1.433
Supervisor	0.655*	1.924	0.666*	1.95	0.664*	1.92	0.655*	1.926
Skilled manual worker	0.710***	2.033	0.719***	2.05	0.719***	2.05	0.715***	2.045
Unskilled manual worker	0.740***	2.095	0.752***	2.12	0.749***	2.11	0.742***	2.099
Company size (1–4 employees)								
5–9	−0.195	0.823	−0.204	0.82	−0.21	0.81	−0.204	0.815
10–19	−0.252	0.777	−0.261	0.77	−0.27	0.76	−0.268	0.765
20–49	−0.585***	0.557	−0.599***	0.55	−0.60***	0.55	−0.603***	0.547
50–99	−1.050***	0.350	−1.060***	0.35	−1.06***	0.35	−1.063***	0.345
100–499	−1.159***	0.314	−1.155***	0.32	−1.17***	0.31	−1.166***	0.312
500 OR MORE	−1.432***	0.239	−1.419***	0.24	−1.43***	0.23	−1.431***	0.239
Difficulties paying bills (almost never)								
Most of the time	1.105***	3.020	1.085***	2.96	1.104***	3.01	1.104***	3.016
From time to time	0.482***	1.620	0.465***	1.59	0.476***	1.61	0.473***	1.605
Detection risk (small)								
High	−0.06	0.94	−0.071	0.93	−0.068	0.93	−0.073	0.929
Tax_morality (mean centred:2.34)	0.283***	1.32	0.280***	1.32	0.275***	1.31	0.277***	1.320
Constant	−4.29***	0.014	−4.264***	0.014	−4.25***	0.014	−4.22***	0.015
Reg. Quality (centred)	−0.687***	0.503						
Rule of law (centred)			−0.615***	0.54				

Control of corruption (centred)					−0.388***	0.678		
Government effectiveness (centred)							−0.656***	0.519
Observations	8994		8994		8994		8994	
No. of groups	28		28		28		28	
Log likelihood	−1228.11		−1225.46		−1227.52		−1226.71	
Wald chi2	325.93***		336.07***		327.53***		330.17***	
Variance (constant)	0.139		0.093		0.126		0.119	
(Intercept variance) (Standard error)	0.071		0.056		0.068		0.063	
Variance at country level[a] (%)	4.05%		2.75%		3.68%		3.49%	
LR test	13.95***		8.48***		11.76***		12.54***	
	Model IX	Model X	Model XI	Model IX	Model X	Model XI		
	β	*exp(***β***)*	**β**	**β**	*exp(***β***)*	**β**		
Gender (female)								
Men	0.360***	1.43	0.36***	1.43	0.36***	1.43		
Age (mean centred:41)	−0.021***	0.98	−0.02***	0.98	−0.02***	0.98		
Age when stopped education (1–15)								
16–19	0.470*	1.60	0.45*	1.57	0.40*	1.493		
20+	0.165	1.18	0.18	1.20	0.12	1.127		
Occupation (employed position, at desk)								
employed professional	0.432	1.540	0.436	1.547	0.411	1.508		
General management, director or top management	0.085	1.089	0.099	1.104	0.091	1.095		
Middle management	0.049	1.050	0.055	1.057	0.046	1.047		
Employed position, travelling	0.765***	2.150	0.786***	2.194	0.768***	2.156		
Employed position, service job	0.319	1.376	0.347	1.415	0.318	1.375		
Supervisor	0.632*	1.882	0.667*	1.948	0.635*	1.887		
Skilled manual worker	0.695***	2.004	0.720***	2.053	0.700***	2.014		
Unskilled manual worker	0.709***	2.032	0.746***	2.109	0.711***	2.037		

(continued)

Table 10.3 (continued)

Company size (1–4 employees)								
5–9	−0.203	0.816	−0.206	0.814	−0.209	0.811		
10–19	−0.264	0.768	−0.279	0.757	−0.284	0.753		
20–49	−0.596***	0.551	−0.610***	0.543	−0.619***	0.539		
50–99	−1.061***	0.346	−1.071***	0.343	−1.084***	0.338		
100–499	−1.186***	0.306	−1.193***	0.303	−1.207***	0.299		
500 or more	−1.475***	0.229	−1.463***	0.232	−1.471***	0.230		
Difficulties paying bills (almost never)								
Most of the time	1.152***	3.165	1.15***	3.16	1.134***	3.109		
From time to time	0.514***	1.672	0.50***	1.65	0.496***	1.642		
Detection risk (small)								
High	−0.058	0.94	−0.063	0.938	−0.065	0.937		
Tax_morality (mean centred: 2.34)	0.280***	1.32	0.276***	1.317	0.271***	1.312		
Constant	−4.19***	0.015	−4.29***	0.014	−4.12***	0.016		
Economic freedom (centred)	−0.026	0.974						
Business freedom (centred)			−0.028***	0.972				
Fiscal freedom (centred)					0.020	1.021		
Observations	8994		8994		8994			
No. of groups	28		28		28			
Log likelihood	−1231.05		−1228.95		−1227.76			
Wald chi2	316.25***		324.44***		327.95***			
Variance (constant)	0.212		0.151		0.135			
(Intercept variance) (Standard error)	0.091		0.074		0.070			
Variance at country level[a] (%)	6.05%		4.38%		3.94%			
LR test	25.99***		16.90***		12.77***			

[a]Variance partition coefficient: measures the proportion of the total residual variance that is due to between-group variation

Note: All coefficients are compared to the benchmark category, shown in brackets. All country-level indicators were centred to the mean obtained using weighting scheme (For the sample of 11025 respondents). ***$p < 0.01$, **$p < 0.05$, *$p < 0.10$

References

Alexandru, A. A., & Dobre, I. (2013). The Impact of unemployment rate on the size of Romanian shadow economy. *Public Finance Review, 41*, 608–632. ISSN:1552-7530.

Bollen, K. A. (1989). A new incremental fit index for general structural equation models. *Sociological Methods & Research, 17*(3), 303–316.

Buehn, A., & Schneider, F. (2012). Shadow economies around the world: Novel insights, accepted knowledge, and new estimates. *International Tax and Public Finance, 19*(1), 139–171.

Buehn, A., & Schneider, F. (2013). *Shadow economies in highly developed OECD countries: What are the driving forces?* (No. 2013-17).

Charron, N., Dijkstra, L., & Lapuente, V. (2015). Mapping the regional divide in Europe: A measure for assessing quality of government in 206 European regions. *Social Indicators Research, 122*(2), 315–346.

Christopoulos, D. K. (2003). Does underground economy respond symmetrically to tax changes? Evidence from Greece. *Economic Modelling, 20*(3), 563–570.

Collins, L. M., Schafer, J. L., & Kam, C. M. (2001). A comparison of inclusive and restrictive strategies in modern missing data procedures. *Psychological Methods, 6*(4), 330–351.

Davidescu, A. A. (2014). Estimating the size of Romanian shadow economy. A labour Approach. *Journal of Social and Economic Statistics, 3*(1), summer 2014.

Davidescu, A. A. (2016). Mapping the informal employment in Romania. A comparative analysis based on labour and discrepancy approaches. *Journal of Applied Quantitative Methods, 11*(1), 64–88.

Davidescu, A. A. (2017). What are the main determinants of the Romanian shadow economy? An empirical analysis based on structural equation models. In *Development, growth and finance of organizations from an Eastern European context* (pp. 159–170). Springer.

Dell'Anno, R. (2003). *Estimating the shadow economy in Italy: A structural equation approach* (Working Paper 2003–7). Department of Economics, University of Aarhus.

Dell'Anno, R. (2007). The shadow economy in Portugal: An analysis with the MIMIC approach. *Journal of Applied Economics, 10*(2), 253–277.

Dell'Anno, R., & Solomon, O. H. (2007). Shadow economy and unemployment rate in USA: Is there a structural relationship? An empirical analysis, *Applied Economics*, 1–19.

Dell'Anno, R., & Schneider, F. (2009). A complex approach to estimate shadow economy: The structural equation modelling. In *Coping with the complexity of economics* (pp. 111–130). Springer.

Doornik, J. A., & Hansen, H. (2008). An omnibus test for univariate and multivariate normality. *Oxford Bulletin of Economics and Statistics, 70*, 927–939.

Giles, D. E. A., & Tedds, L. M. (2002). *Taxes and the Canadian underground economy* (Canadian Tax paper n.106). Canadian Tax Foundation.

Hassan, M., & Friedrich, S. (2016). Size and development of the shadow economies of 157 worldwide countries: Updated and new measures from 1999 to 2013. *Journal of Global Economy, 4*(218), 2.

Helberger, C., & Knepel, H. (1988). How big is the shadow economy? A re-analysis of the unobserved-variable approach of BS Frey and H. Weck-Hannemann. *European Economic Review, 32*(4), 965–976.

Henze, N., & Zirkler, B. (1990). A class of invariant consistent tests for multivariate normality. *Communications in Statistics, Theory and Methods, 19*, 3595–3617.

Johnson, S., Kaufmann, D., & Zoido-Lobatón, P. (1998a). Regulatory discretion and the unofficial economy. *The American Economic Review, 88*(2), 387–392.

Johnson, S., Kaufmann, D., & Zoido-Lobatón, P. (1998b). *Corruption, public finances and the unofficial economy*. MIT, The World Bank.

Long, J. S. (1983). *Covariance structure models: An introduction to LISREL*. Sage.

Mardia, K. V. (1970). Measures of multivariate skewness and kurtosis with applications. *Biometrika, 57*, 519–530.

Medina, L., & Schneider, F. (2017). *Shadow Economies around the World: New Results for 158 Countries over 1991–2015* (Cesifo Working Papers). https://papers.ssrn.com/sol3/papers.cfm?abstract_id=2965972

Razmi, M. J., Falahi, M. A., & Montazeri, S. (2013). Institutional quality and underground economy of 51 OIC member countries. *Universal Journal of Management and Social Sciences, 3*(2), 1–14.

Rubin, D. (1987). *Multiple imputation for nonresponse in surveys*. Wiley.

Schafer, J., & Graham, J. (2002). Missing data: our view of the state of the art. *Psychological Methods, 7*(2), 1–47.

Schneider, F. (1994a). *Measuring the size and development of the shadow economy. Can the causes be found and the obstacles be overcome? Essays on economic psychology* (pp. 193–212). Springer.

Schneider, F. (1994b). Can the shadow economy be reduced through major tax reforms? An empirical investigation for Austria. *Supplement to Public Finance, 49*, 137–152.

Schneider, F. (1997). The shadow economies of Western Europe. *Economic Affairs, 17*, 42–48.

Schneider, F. (2002). *The size and development of the shadow economies and shadow economy labor force of 16 Central and South American and 21 OECD countries: First results for the 90's, mimeo*. Johannes Kepler University of Linz.

Schneider, F. (2005). Shadow economies around the world: what do we really know? *European Journal of Political Economy, 21*, 598–642.

Schneider, F. (2012). *Size and development of the shadow economy of 31 European and 5 other OECD countries from 2003 to 2012: Some new facts*. http://www.econ.jku.at/members/Schneider/files/publications/2012/ShadEcEurope31_March 2012.pdf

Schneider, F. (2013). *Size and development of the shadow economy of 31 European and 5 other OECD countries from 2003 to 2013: a further decline* (pp. 5–7). Johannes Kepler Universität. http://www.econ.jku.at/members/schneider/files/publications/2013/shadeceurope31_jan2013.pdf

Schneider, F. (2014). *The shadow economy: An essay*. Department of Economics, Johannes Kepler University of Linz, 23 p.

Schneider, F. (2015). Size and development of the shadow economy of 31 European and 5 other OECD countries from 2003 to 2014: Different developments? *Journal of Self-Governance & Management Economics, 3*(4).

Schneider, F., & Buehn, A. (2013a). *Estimating the size of the shadow economy: Methods, problems and open questions*. http://papers.ssrn.com/sol3/papers.cfm?abstract_id=2353281

Schneider, F., & Buehn, A. (2013b). *Shadow economies in 10 transition and 6 developing OECD countries: What are the driving forces?* Studien/pfuschneu/2013/ShadEcOECD_DrivForces2013.doc

Schneider, F., Buehn, A., & Montenegro, C. E. (2010). New estimates for the shadow economies all over the world. *International Economic Journal, 24*(4), 443–461.

Smith, R. S. (2002). The underground economy: guidance for policy makers. *Canadian Tax Journal, 50*, 1655.

Williams, C. C., & Horodnic, I. A. (2017). Evaluating the illegal employer practice of under-reporting employees' salaries. *British Journal of Industrial Relations, 55*(1), 83–111.

***http://happyplanetindex.org/

***http://www.transparency.org/research/cpi/overview

***http://www.socialprogressimperative.org/globalindex/#data_table/countries/dim3/dim1,dim2,dim3

***Labour Market Policy Database, Eurostat,

http://appsso.eurostat.ec.europa.eu/nui/show.do?dataset=lmp_expsumm&lang=en

***Expenditures database, Eurostat

***Employment and Social Developments in Europe 2015,

***Employment and Unemployment Database, Eurostat

***Eurobarometer on Undeclared Work no.402/2013, https://www.gesis.org/en/eurobarometer-data-service/home
***Government finance statistics database, Eurostat
***National Accounts Database, Eurostat
***WGI indicators, World Bank
***Heritage Foundation, http://www.heritage.org/index/
***International Financial Statistics (IFS) database, IMF.

Chapter 11
To Be Agile or Not to Be: New Business Models for Civil Society Organisations in Times of Crisis

Frank Elbers, Ana-Maria Grigore, and Adela Coman

Abstract There is an increasing realisation of the need for civil society organisations (CSOs) to be agile, given the fast-changing policy, legal and funding environment they operate in. Chatwani (2019) links this agile capacity to the fact that NGOs are norm- and mission-driven and have a strong identity, which facilitates the required knowledge transfer. In this chapter, however, we will identify ideal-type CSO business models and explore how (changing and emerging) business models are the key to agility and innovation. Based on a review of existing academic literature, we will look for examples of innovative thinking in CSOs. Through a survey of CSO leaders, we explore if the ideal-type business models we identified have validity and to what extend they are driven by the business model canvas.

Keywords Civil society · NGOs · Business models · Organisational agility · Innovation

11.1 Introduction

The current COVID-19 pandemic has forced civil society organisations (CSOs)[1] to once again update or change business models in order to be able to realise their mission, the last time being during the 2008 financial crisis. For many years, civil

[1]We define "civil society organisations" (CSOs) as non-state, not-for-profit, voluntary entities formed by people in the social sphere that are separate from the state and the market; they represent a wide range of interests and ties ranging from community-based organisations, service providers to advocacy groups.

F. Elbers (✉)
Research Centre of the University of Bucharest, Bucharest, Romania
e-mail: frank.elbers@icub.unibuc.ro

A.-M. Grigore · A. Coman
University of Bucharest, Bucharest, Romania

S. L. Fotea et al. (eds.), *Navigating Through the Crisis: Business, Technological and Ethical Considerations*, Springer Proceedings in Business and Economics,
https://doi.org/10.1007/978-3-030-82751-9_11

CSOs' main sources of income have been either government subsidies or philanthropy, that is, donations from individual donors—both small and large amounts—and foundations. Only since the beginning of the twenty-first-century non-profit organisations have started to develop alternative models, many of them inspired by the social business model of BRAC in Bangladesh. BRAC was founded in 1974 by Fazle Abed, a Shell executive who sold his London flat to fund the organisation. Currently, BRAC's integrated health, finance and education programmes are active in 70,000 villages in all of the 64 districts of Bangladesh; its microfinance programmes assist more than 7 million borrowers around the world. With almost 100,000 paid staff, BRAC has been the largest CSO in the world for some time (*BRAC*, 2020; NGO Advisor, 2013).

Innovation is the current buzzword in civil society circles—from large institutional grant makers in the development and humanitarian sectors to grassroots advocacy NGOs working in shrinking civil space in transitional democracies. Innovation is often a necessity for CSOs that have limited and restricted funding and resources yet are driven by ambitious missions. Hence, CSOs are constantly forced to think creatively about how to utilise their scarce resources to survive (Funds for NGOs, 2020). As we can see in Fig. 11.1, the gap between required funding and funding received has been increasing in the humanitarian sector every year in the past decade.

Funding, however, is only one, be it important, element of organisational success and survival. Being able to quickly respond to changes in the volatile, changing landscape affected by technological changes, globalisations and migration, among other factors, is just as critical. In the academic and management literature, the notion of continual change is experiencing a revival of sorts under the term "agility"

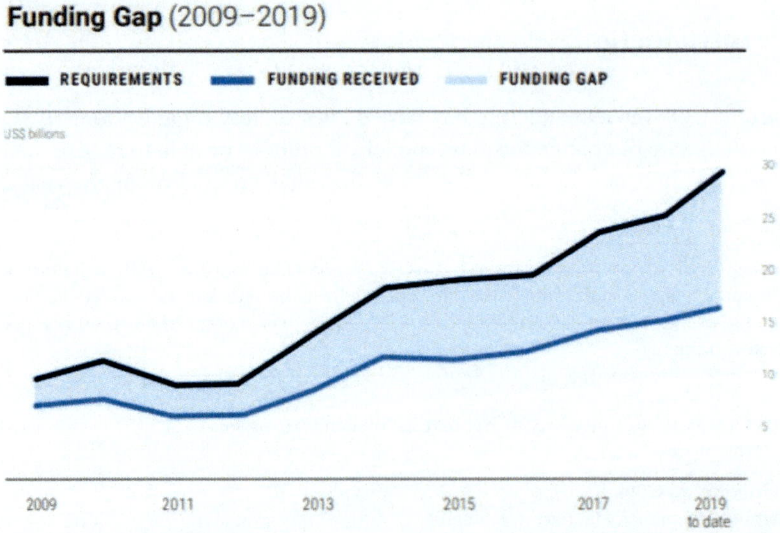

Fig. 11.1 Funding requirements and funding received between 2009 and 2019. (Source: OCHA, 2020: 27)

(Chatwani, 2019). Chatwani defines agile organisations as "organisational systems that thrive in unpredictable or rapidly changing environments" (ibid: 3). For CSOs to aptly respond to crises and change, they will need to be agile. The "business as usual" approach is not just unrealistic but can potentially have severely negative impacts upon beneficiaries and communities (Díaz, 2020).

In this chapter, we will argue that this agility is a function of the business model(s) that CSOs operate under. We will review the existing literature using the following as the main components of business models: revenue streams; key partners and resources; customer (beneficiaries/stakeholders) relationships and channels; and cost structure (Osterwalder, 2013). Based on a systematic literature review, we will determine if and how CSO or innovate or introduce new business models.

The remainder of this chapter is organised as follows. In the second section, we will look at the elements of some existing and emerging business models. In the following section, we explain our research methodology: how we selected the literature based on queries of the Google Scholar and JSTOR databases and conducted a survey among CSO leaders. In Sect. 11.4, we will present if and how CSOs innovate or introduce new business models and to what extent our nine ideal-type business models are represented in the literature and to what extent we need to adjust our model. In the fifth and final Sect. 11.5, we will discuss a possible research agenda on emerging business models of agile CSOs.

11.2 Theoretical Framework

11.2.1 The Specificity of Business Models for NGOs

The application of business models has grown significantly in the past years as they are often associated with securing and expanding competitive advantage (Johnson et al., 2008). Business models can be understood as structured management tools that are indispensable for success (Magretta, 2002). More specifically, a business model is a conceptual tool containing a set of objects, concepts and their relationships with the objective to express the business logic of a specific firm (Osterwalder et al., 2005). A business model defines how an organisation creates value and in the process captures indispensable aspects of how a company conducts its business (Zott et al., 2011).

Innovative business models can result in significant sources of competitive advantage and firm performance. Hence, organisations are motivated to innovate their business model(s) by making fundamental changes in the way they create and capture value (Berends et al., 2016). Yet at the same time, the business model is perceived as a theoretical concept, which is defined and broken down into its components.

In the literature, various labels are used to characterise the various components of business models (Zott et al., 2011). Osterwalder and Pigneur (2010) propose a widely used and detailed framework: a *value proposition* is the core component; *activities*, *resources*, *partnerships*, and *cost structure* are the components needed for value creation; and *customer segments*, *customer relationships*, *distribution channels*, and *revenue streams* define how value gets delivered and how some of that value may be captured. Because components interact, the development of an effective configuration is challenging. Components cannot be considered in isolation; their possible interactions increase the number of effects to consider (Gavetti & Levinthal, 2000), especially in conditions of uncertainty, when those interactions remain unknown (Berends et al., 2016).

The use of the business model canvas is not limited to for-profit organisations. It can be equally used by organisations in the third sector because every organisation ultimately has a business even if they don't call it that. "To survive, every organization that creates and delivers value must generate enough revenue to cover its expenses. Hence, it has a business model. The difference is merely a matter of focus" (Osterwalder & Pigneur, 2010: 264).

How do we use the business model concept if the primary goal is not to earn money, but to fulfil a mission? For many non-profit organisations, the canvas box labelled *revenue streams* doesn't necessarily make sense, because there is not always revenue to measure. Hence, the first step in building a canvas for mission-driven organisations is to change the *revenue stream* box in the canvas and create an alternative that would somehow measure success. Fulfilling a mission can be measured in different ways—ranging from the number of homeless sheltered, the number of children educated, the number of human rights violations reported, the change of legislation protecting women from violence, etc. Other components of the business model canvas should change too: customer segments to beneficiaries; channel to deployment; and customer relationships to buy-in/support (Blank, 2016).

The business model concept is an essential mediator between innovation and the greater good. In other words, without adequate business models, it is not possible to leverage the benefits of innovation. Abdelkafi (2012) offers a promising comprehensive value-focused business model framework, in which business models are defined as the way organisations or individuals communicate, create, deliver, and capture value out of a value proposition; it consists, therefore, of five dimensions.

Based on this framework, open business models are introduced as those business models that exhibit some degree of openness with respect to at least one dimension. Innovations for the greater good are beneficial for society and humanity at large. The value proposition of the business models for the greater good can be socially or common-oriented, and the value capture depends on the fact if the organisation aims to generate profits or not. The combination of both dimensions: value proposition and value capture give rise to four categories of business models for the greater good, for which concrete examples could be found. In this context, it is worth emphasising that profit orientation is not conflicting with the idea of serving the greater good. When individuals or organisations strive for making money, the odds of success are much greater.

The way non-profits operate is generally more complex than for-profits or social businesses, as they do not operate in a linear way. They often have to deal with more stakeholders, sometimes with multiple roles in their dealings with CSOs, such as governments, who can act as donors, programme partners or recipients of NGO funds and services (Sanderse, 2014). As the South African human rights and environmental activist Kumi Naidoo, former CEO of Greenpeace and Secretary General of Amnesty International, once explained:

> *If you want to understand NGOs all you need to be able to do is understand Christopher Columbus. When he set off he didn't know exactly where he was going, and when he came back he didn't know exactly where he had been. But he had a huge impact on the world and he did it all on somebody else's money* (cited in Sanderse, 2014: 19).

11.2.2 From Philanthropy to Online Brokerage: (Emerging) Business Models

Historically, philanthropy has been both the main business model and source of financing for relief programmes for the poor and for CSO services. Religious organisations (e.g. churches, mosques) and rich and prominent citizens—nowadays through foundations that offer tax relief—have traditionally supported voluntary and third sector activities, especially since the 1950s. With the emergence of the modern welfare state in many countries, the state became a financial supporter of human and social development programmes too. Along with the welfare state, advocacy and interest groups sprung up and, with decolonisation, the international aid and relief industry. The voluntary or third sector these days has evolved into a sizeable part of economies both in the so-called global North and South. In Europe alone, the third sector accounted for nearly 13% of the European workforce in 2014, according to the latest Eurostat data (Salamon & Sokolowski, 2018).

How do all these CSOs fund themselves, especially in an environment (global and local) that is marked by a fast-changing policy and legal framework, and funding opportunities; by increased competition for limited resources with other CSOs; by rapidly changing demands and preferences of their beneficiaries; what business models do they apply? Typical revenue streams for CSOs have been project/programme support (subsidies), fees-for-services, child sponsorship, and individual and institutional donations (philanthropy). But it does not suffice to only look at revenue to answer these questions. CSOs, just like SMEs and corporations, operate with a business model in order to realise their mission and serve their stakeholders, beneficiaries or members.

Based both on literature review and experience in the third sector, we will now present the most common models used by CSOs.

The ***project support model*** focuses on identifying and developing projects aligned to a CSO's mission and subsequently seeking funding from donors to fund the project, typically through subsidies or grants (International Civil Society Centre, 2014; Maucuer & Renaud, 2019). This model is used widely by CSOs globally whether they work on human and social development, humanitarian relief (Fowler, 2016) or environmental issues, human rights (Rekosh, 2017) or anti-corruption.

Project funding includes both costs of activities within and (indirect) management costs. The project support model likely accounts for a large part of CSO activities.

The ***advocacy and campaigning model*** is centred around attracting large numbers of individuals to support a special (local or international) campaign or broader campaigning mission (Maine, 2019; VeneKlasen & Miller, 2007). Their work is often built around specific campaigns aligned to its mission, often as part of joint campaigns with partners with close links to affected populations or like-minded international organisations. Those wishing to support the campaign can do so both as supporters or members, making financial contributions to campaigns or regular donations to the CSO. Financial contributions are used to fund research and campaign activities and management costs. Amnesty International, Greenpeace and Oxfam are well-known examples of CSOs that use the advocacy and campaigning model.

Many CSOs operate on a ***membership model***—from the boys and girls scouts to professional associations. Members are both the main beneficiaries/customers and the main sources of funding for this type of CSO (Srinivas, 2015). This model is often based on *volunteerism*.

A unique model in the third sector is the ***child sponsorship model***. Sponsoring a child and communities in need in developing countries to pay for school fees, clothing and other needs has been a powerful model since the 1960s, directly connecting individual donors (often in the global North) with beneficiaries (International Civil Society Centre, 2014). CSOs like World Vision (with 40,000 staff worldwide the second-largest CSO in the world) and Plan International have built their operations around this model for seventy years (King, 2019).

Fees for services, ***including public service contracting***, is a model often used by CSOs that provide highly specialised training or other services at cost for which customers pay or which are paid for by government subsidies. The specialised character of services allows for a steady stream of revenue from fees or public contracts (CSOs sometimes have a quasi-monopoly on the training or service), close relationships with customers (so that services can be tweaked/customised on an ongoing basis), and costs are predictable and directly linked to activities.

Professional (pro bono) voluntarism is a business model that is becoming more and more widely used (Rekosh, 2017). Originally used to bring young professionals to the developing world (e.g. the U.S. Peace Corps), international aid departments of North European states have been recently using this model to provide assistance by retired senior managers. Human rights and legal CSOs are applying this model to run rule of law programmes in different parts of the world as it significantly improves their cost structure.

The ***social enterprise model*** is becoming a growing business model. Social enterprises typically apply business solutions to social problems. By selling goods and services in the open market, social enterprises reinvest the money they make back into their business or the local community, typically tackling social and environmental problems. As in a non-for-profit CSO, there are no shareholders, the profits of a social enterprise are reinvested in the work of the CSO itself (Lane, 2011; Bielefeld, 2009). Some academics and advocates even speak about an emerging fourth sector, which combines market-based approaches of the private sector with the social and environmental aims of the public and non-profit (third) sector to address pressing problems. Endeavours in this sector, also known as for-benefit enterprises, come in a wide variety of models, from mission-driven businesses, social enterprises and sustainable businesses to cooperatives, benefit corporations and faith-based enterprises, among many others (Sabeti, 2009). In this chapter, we will limit ourselves to business models in the third, voluntary sector.

Online brokerage models link people online who are concerned about a global issue with people, projects or campaigns that are seeking to address the issue (International Civil Society Centre, 2014). Changes in ICTs and the desire of donors to seek a more direct relationship with a specific local or national activity or campaign have made this model possible. CSOs can connect people in new ways and fund their services by charging a small fee or commission. The costs of intermediation are rather low, whereas the relationship with "customers" is direct and impact relatively high. An example is the globalgiving.com platform (Thorpe, 2018). Millennials, for example, expect information to be decentralised, and they want to integrate their personal, professional and financial objectives into more meaningful lives. As a result, generational change can drive this business model forward.

11.3 Methodology

11.3.1 Literature Selection

To determine if CSOs innovate and which new business models or combinations thereof CSOs are applying, we conducted a review of academic articles using search parameters related to the third sector (Table 11.1, column 1) and the business models terms we identified (column 2).

We searched journal articles in the JSTOR and Google Scholar databases. We assessed the full text of articles with a relevant title and abstract (N= 40) in order to determine if they were eligible for our study. Eventually, we selected 19 articles for our analysis (see Fig. 11.2).

All selected articles were published between 2010 and 2020 and hence are relatively recent. There is a good balance in research methodology too: 10 articles

Table 11.1 Topic-related search terms

Sector-related search term (full text	Business model related search terms (full text)
"Civil society" OR "nonprofit" OR "non-profit" OR "third sector" OR "voluntary" OR "not-for-profit" OR "not for profit"	Business model
	Agility
	Innovation

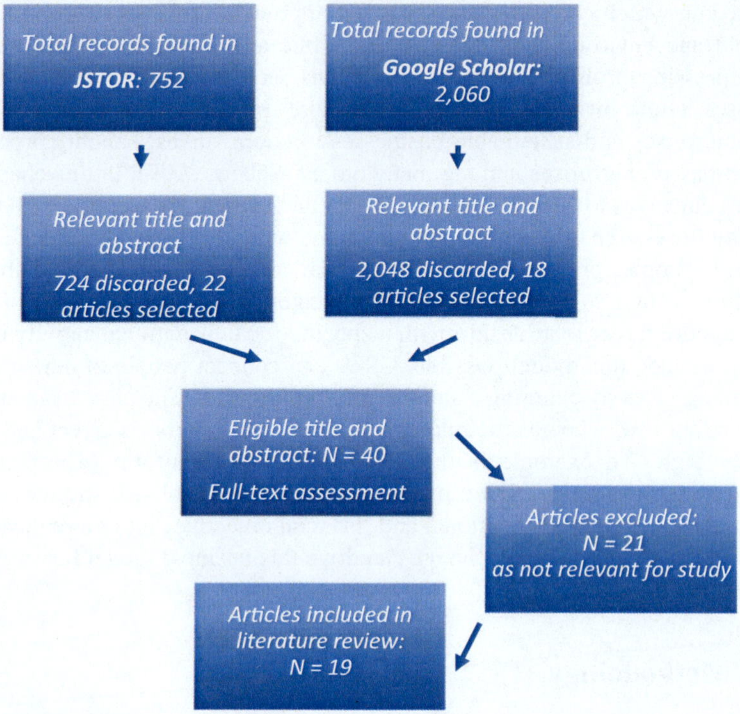

Fig. 11.2 Search strategy

applied qualitative methods and nine articles on quantitative methods. The articles appeared in a variety of journals with *Voluntas* (5), being the main one. The reviewed articles represented a good mix of sectors, ranging from studies of human rights and environmental advocacy NGOs to international humanitarian and disaster relief organisations to CSOs providing human welfare/social services. Geographically, there is also a large spread: from various countries on the African continent (Kenya, Tanzania) to Asia (Cambodia, Philippines), Eastern Europe (Czechia and Slovakia), North America and Europe (Germany, the Netherlands).

11.3.2 Survey of CSO Leaders

To validate the results of the literature review, we also conducted an online survey among CSO leaders. A questionnaire was sent to the professional network of one of the authors of this article who has worked in the civil society sector for 25 years. A total of 252 selected contacts (with titles of CEO, director or chairperson) received the questionnaire in the first week of August 2020. Fifty-one of the surveyed CSO leaders completed the questionnaire (N=51); the response rate was 20.2%.

They represented CSOs in Austria, Bangladesh, Belgium, Cameroon, Congo DRC, Denmark, Ethiopia, Germany, Indonesia, Italy, Kenya, Latvia, Lebanon, Mali, Netherlands, Nigeria, Norway, Romania, Sierra Leone, Spain, Sweden, Switzerland, Ukraine, United Kingdom and the United States. About 72.5% were international NGOs and 27.5% national NGOs. Many of them were very well-established organisations, some of them even founded in 1921, the 1940s and 1950s. About 13.7% of the surveyed CSOs had more than 5,000 paid employees, while 21.6% of them had less than five paid employees; 50% of them had 6–50 employees. Of the sampled CSOs, 35.3% had an annual turnover between 1 and 5 million euros; 19.6% reported an annual turnover above €5,000,000 (of which 3.5% above €15,000,000).

11.4 Findings

Given the fact that the sampled literature is very diverse in terms of research questions, concepts (few focus on business models *per se*), context (different sectors), methodology and geographic focus, we cautiously formulate two main findings based on the overview presented in Table 11.2 (Annex A).

First, there is little evidence in the literature that CSOs are explicitly using business model canvasses as a framework to respond to rapid changes in their environment and purposely innovate and be agile. That doesn't mean that CSOs don't intentionally try to innovate and become more agile, but they are not using the business model framework for that.

The second conclusion from our literature review is that there are few explicit references to the eight business models that we identified. This should not come as a surprise given our first conclusion that CSOs referenced in our literature sample are not explicitly using the business model framework and canvass. There is one notable exception, however. The social entrepreneurship model is very frequently mentioned and, in some cases, applied. This is probably mainly due to the fact that in the literature on non-profits and NGOs, the concept of social entrepreneurship, social businesses and corporate social responsibility is pervasive, albeit it mostly from a business perspective, not that often from the perspective of not-for-profit ventures, with a few exceptions. As one researcher (Duldulao, 2012: 62) on NGOs in the Philippines put it:

> Social entrepreneurship as an engine to these NGOs has created innovations that build the capacity, agility, and competencies.

Our survey results validate our findings from the literature review: CSOs themselves report that they are rarely using the business model canvas. As shown in Fig. 11.3, only 7.8% of the surveyed CSOs indicated that they are using the business model canvas. About 70.6% of the respondents specified they were not using the business model canvas or did not know. About 21.6% of the surveyed answered that they do not currently use the business model canvas but are considering it; we

Table 11.2 Introduction of innovative and agile business models in CSOs

Applied business model	Revenue streams	Key partners and resources	Customer (beneficiaries, stakeholders) relationships and channels	Cost structure
Preliminary data provide support for the importance of board attribute and process variables for an organisation's capacity for continuous innovation and suggest that considering cultural contexts when assessing the usefulness of established models might be paramount (Jaskyte, 2015). Open innovation activities in non-profit sports clubs (permeability of the club's boundary; application and implementation of open innovation practices; managerial competencies; and the environmental and organisational surroundings in which the club operates) determine how and why sports clubs are successful at implementing innovations and how their nonprofit status (e.g. *volunteer* work) contributes to (or is in conflict with) innovation (Wemmer & Koenigstorfer, 2016). A case study illustrates how tensions within a network with a dual (social and economic) mission focus present themselves at three key stages of business model innovation (initiation, exploration and exploitation); network tensions are managed through dynamic capabilities (sensing, seizing and transformational). While engaging in BMI can improve the competitiveness of SPOs, the tensions emerging from a dual mission focus in a multi-stakeholder network are complex, which need to be addressed by careful and nuanced planning in practice (Best et al., 2020).	Social enterprises have struggled to generate sufficient revenue through their business activities and often resort to soft money or grant sources to offset the deficits. Social enterprises must therefore either find highly profitable commercial niches with significant social impact or be satisfied with diversified revenue-generating portfolios, including grants and donations. (Galvin & Iannotti, 2015). NGOs are trying to reduce dependency on foreign aid that has mixed effects on the organisations such as the unpredictability of funding, goal displacement, reduced organisational autonomy and top-down accountability. Funding from commercial activities is more predictable and potentially promotes bottom-up accountability and increases organisational autonomy but may conflict with the mission-drift of NGOs (Khieng & Dahles, 2015).	Some resources and capabilities are more important than others in adapting the business model components (customer value proposition, key resources) in response to external and internal turmoil (Poisson-de Haro & David Montpetit, 2012). Disruptive innovations by firms offering public services like health care and education in developing countries require careful nurturing. The development of path-breaking business models, for instance, requires access to critical financial, social, and human capital along with stakeholder support to help legitimise the enterprise (Valente & Crane, 2010). Due to their small size, lack of competitive capital and inability to acquire complex opportunities, the majority of SMEs and non-profits find it difficult to cope with the required speed of change. This study in Tanzania shows that dynamic time/ cost-effective and fluid creation of temporary collaborative networks wrought by ICTs is an enabler for enhancing competitiveness. Such collaborative networks are hampered in Tanzania particularly related to the availability of required technologies and systems and lack of proper customised business models (Msanjila & Kamuzora, 2012).	Social entrepreneurs have a hard time meeting potential clients and partners (Witkamp et al., 2011). Social enterprises are adept at working with their stakeholders in the ideation stage of social innovation. In contrast, they often fail to harness knowledge and expertise from their partners during the social innovation implementation phase (Phillips et al., 2019).	*Volunteer* work allows for experimenting with innovation without affecting the bottom line (Wemmer & Koenigstorfer, 2016). Probono legal advice by legal professionals is a major cost-saving for human rights NGOs that provide legal assistance or do litigation (Rekosh, 2017).

Applied business model	Revenue streams	Key partners and resources	Customer (beneficiaries, stakeholders) relationships and channels	Cost structure
-A study of 328 non-profits in Kenya established that innovation (process innovation, product innovation and organisation innovation) strongly enhances organisational performance but not references to business models (Odhiambo, 2019). Online brokerage is a new business model that links people who are concerned about an issue with people, projects or campaigns that are seeking to address the issue (International Civil Society Centre, 2014).				

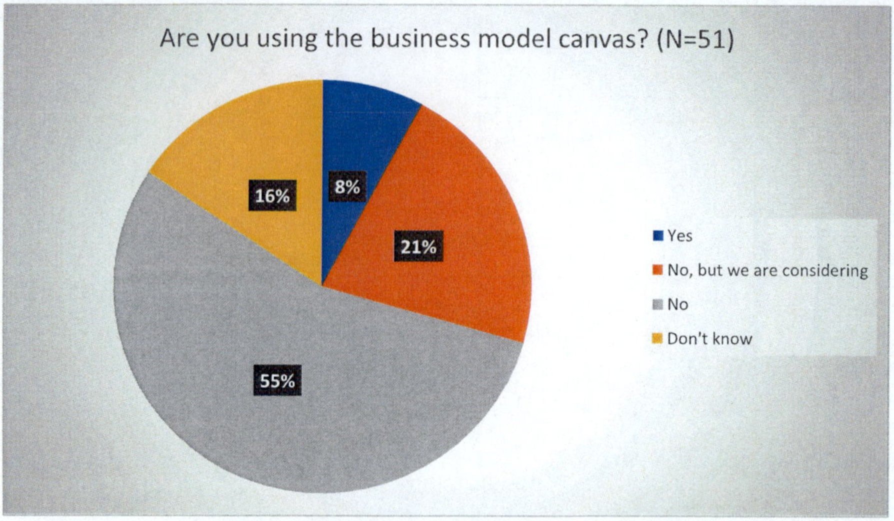

Fig. 11.3 CSOs and the business model canvas

suspect that for a substantial number of respondents, this is a socially desirable answer as they would like to be perceived as innovative although they are not using the business model canvas. Those CSOs that are using the business model canvas have very little in common as they differ substantially in staff size and annual turnover and geographic base (although they are all headquartered in the European Union). They do have one thing in common: these CSOs were all established in 2000 or after.

The online survey among CSO leaders did also validate the eight business models that we identified in Sect. 11.2.2 of this chapter (Fig. 11.4). The data show that the project support model through grant support is still by far the most dominant business model that CSOs apply, although it must be emphasised that some CSOs also use more innovative and new online brokerage and social entrepreneurship models.

Business models are undeniably required in order to serve the greater good, but business models are not enough in order to put a business into action (Abdelkafi, 2012). From a management perspective, business models may be thought of as a layer between strategy and operations. Models represent, of course, an abstraction, and consequently, a business model necessarily includes less detail than operations, which refer to day-to-day business. Hence, a sophisticated business model is still no guarantee for success; poor implementation of a good business model does not bring us far. Devising good business models is not sufficient; devising methods that translate business models into concrete operational activities are also required.

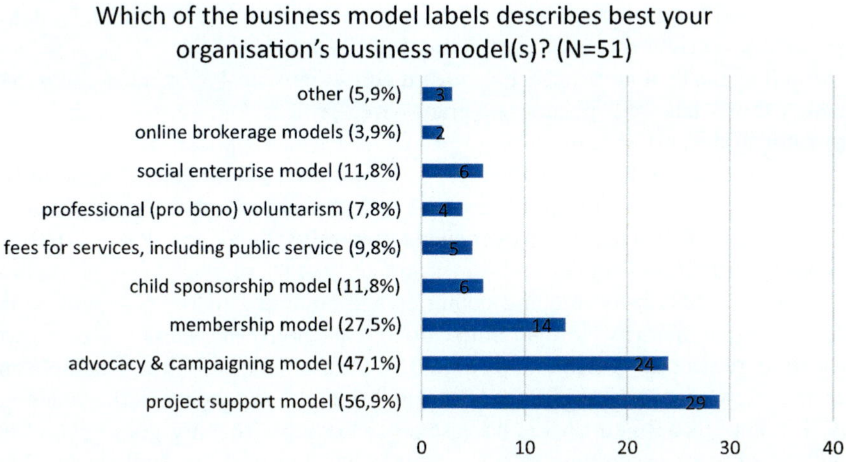

Fig. 11.4 The business models used by CSOs

11.5 Discussion and Conclusion

Resourceful, agile and resilient as they are, CSOs have always risen to the challenges. To successfully respond to a dramatically changing landscape, such as the COVID-19 pandemic, it may be especially helpful for CSOs to examine the assumptions in their business models. Probing the relationships between value propositions, revenue streams, cost structures, assets, activities, strategic partnerships and other elements of a business model can result in insights that could potentially transform the way they operate.

The new coronavirus pandemic makes us realise that everything that we used to consider as "normal" is upended. This includes the logic and *modus operandi* under which institutions and other organisations, including CSOs, have been operating. "Perhaps this is an opportunity for NGOs to escape the temptation of 'business as usual' and emerge with new alternatives in a scenario that is still unfolding before our eyes" (Díaz, 2020).

Such unknown situations need specific solutions, that is, a process of continuously observing and assessing and providing feedback (Díaz, 2020). Nicolescu (2020) suggests that organisational management needs to remodelled and inherent opportunities that the pandemic offers seized. Along three dimensions: entrepreneurial—in the sense that the decision process must be flexible, bold and fast; innovative—new methods and techniques to tackle decisions and actions of management at all levels; collaborative—to bring together all the identifiable stakeholders that may contribute to the proper functioning, survival and sustainability of the organisation. Such a collaborative approach is intrinsic to many NGOs.

The belief that management with an entrepreneurial mentality would alter the mission of a non-profit organisation is obsolete. Things are different now. NGOs that want to survive and have the desire to take their fate into their own hands have to change and become more business-oriented (de Jong, 2018). Ultimately, entrepreneurship is primarily a matter of acting (Ferris, 2007).

Simultaneously, innovation is considered almost inescapable by most CSOs, particularly those that are dependent on grant-based project funding. Most funders, be they foundations, private donors or governments, require applicant CSOs to demonstrate the innovative nature of their proposed projects—no matter if they deliver services, advocacy for change or respond to a disaster or other emergencies. To secure funding, CSOs the world over need to innovate (Funds for NGOs, 2020).

Perhaps *frugal innovation*—a business model that is common to some, particularly smaller CSOs in developing countries and emerging markets—could be the solution for the majority. "Frugal innovation means delivering more value at lower costs to more people" (Mahmood et al., 2014: 2). The DNA of CSOs is simple and extremely low cost without sacrificing the quality of the experience of the beneficiaries. Scholars like Bhatti (2012) have stressed that this frugality goes beyond the reduction of costs. According to Bhatti, this is because of three challenges, which are related to the environment in which frugal innovations are meant to be designed, produced and marketed: (1) resource constraints related to not only available materials and financial means but also knowledge and human resources; (2) institutional voids, such as lack of services, formal rules, laws and constitutions; and (3) specific needs of the population at the bottom of the pyramid (Mahmood et al., 2014).

In our view, research on the application of the business model canvas framework is critical in order for CSOs to have a better understanding of how to combine business models and to be innovative and agile. At the moment, very little such research exists, which may partially explain why CSOs are not applying the business model framework despite the success of the social entrepreneurship model. It would be particularly important to get a better understanding of how CSOs' leadership (boards, executive management) thinks about business models and to what extent they are thinking in terms of business model canvasses to stay agile and innovate their advocacy or services.

References

Abdelkafi, N. (2012). Open business models for the greater good – A case study from the higher education context. *Die Unternehmung, 66*(3), 299–317.

Berends, H., Smits, A., Reymen, I., & Podoynitsyna, K. (2016). Learning while (re)configuring: Business model innovation processes in established firms. *Strategic Organization, 14*(3), 181–219.

Best, B., Miller, K., McAdam, R., Moffett, S. (2020). Mission or margin? Using dynamic capabilities to manage tensions in social purpose organisations' business model innovation. *Journal of Business Research.* Available online 19 February 2020. https://doi.org/10.1016/j.jbusres.2020.01.068.

Bhatti, Y. A. (2012). What is frugal, what is innovation? Towards a theory of frugal innovation. Imperial College London. Available at SSRN: https://ssrn.com/abstract=2005910 or. https://doi.org/10.2139/ssrn.2005910

Bielefeld, W. (2009). Issues in social enterprise and social entrepreneurship. *Journal of Public Affairs, 15*(1), 69–86. https://doi.org/10.1080/15236803.2009.12001544

BRAC. (2020). *BRAC annual report 2019*. BRAC. http://www.brac.net/downloads/BRAC-AR-2019.pdf

Blank, S. (2016). The Mission Model Canvas – An adapted Business Model Canvas for Mission-Driven Organizations. February 23, 2016.

Chatwani, N. (2019). *Organizational agility: Exploring the impact of identity on knowledge management*. Palgrave Macmillan.

de Jong, H. (2018). Sustainability and entrepreneurship for Local Civil Society Organisation and CSO Networks in Cambodia. https://www.academia.edu/37943727/SUSTAINABILITY_AND_ENTREPRENEURSHIP_FOR_LOCAL_CIVIL_SOCIETY_ORGANISATIONS_AND_CSO_NETWORKS_IN_CAMBODIA?email_work_card=minimal-title

Díaz, D. A. (2020). NGOs on coronavirus mode: The risks of 'Business as Usual'. *E-International Relations*. https://www.e-ir.info/2020/04/27/ngos-on-coronavirus-mode-the-risks-of-business-as-usual/

*Duldulao, G. A. (2012). Social entrepreneurship and sustainability in three non-governmental organizations in the Philippines: A case study. MA thesis, University of Hawai'i.

Ferris, T. (2007). *The 4-hour workweek: Escape 9–5, live anywhere, and join the new rich*. Crown Publishing Group.

Fowler, A. (2016). Non-governmental development organisations' sustainability, partnership, and resourcing: Futuristic reflections on a problematic trialogue. *Development in Practice, 26*(5), 569–579. https://doi.org/10.1080/09614524.2016.1188883

Funds for NGOs. (2020). *Ten of the most innovative NGOs in the world*. Retrieved on 14 August 2020 from: https://www.fundsforngos.org/free-resources-for-ngos/ten-innovative-ngos-world/

*Galvin, M. D., & Iannotti, L. (2015). Social enterprise and development: The KickStart Model. *VOLUNTAS: International Journal of Voluntary and Nonprofit Organizations, 26*(2), 421-441.

Gavetti, G., & Levinthal, D. A. (2000). Looking forward and looking backward: Cognitive and experiential search. *Administrative Science Quarterly, 45*(1), 113–137.

*International Civil Society Centre. (2014). Diversify, adapt and innovate. Changing ICSO Business Models. : International Civil Society Centre.

*Jaskyte, K. (2015). Board of directors and innovation in nonprofit organizations model: Preliminary evidence from nonprofit organizations in developing countries. *VOLUNTAS: International Journal of Voluntary and Nonprofit Organizations, 26*(5), 1920-1943.

Johnson, M. W., Christensen, C. M., & Kagermann, H. (2008). Reinventing your business model. *Harvard Business Review, 86*(12), 57–68.

*Khieng, S., & Dahles, H. (2015). Resource dependence and effects of funding diversification strategies among NGOs in Cambodia. *VOLUNTAS: International Journal of Voluntary and Nonprofit Organizations, 26*(4), 1412-1437.

King, D. (2019). World Vision tinkers with its 70-year-old child sponsorship model, *The Conversation*, November 4, 2019. https://theconversation.com/world-vision-tinkers-with-its-70-year-old-child-sponsorship-model-124383.

Lane, M. J. (2011). *Social Enterprise: Empowering Mission-driven Entrepreneurs* (1st ed.). American Bar Association.

Magretta, J. (2002). Why Business Models Matter. *Harvard Business Review, 80*(5), 86–92.

Mahmood, P., Kondis, A., & Stehli, S. (2014). Frugal innovation: Creating and capturing value in emerging markets. International Institute for Management Development. Insights No. 31., https://www.imd.org/research-knowledge/articles/frugal-innovation-creating-and-capturing-value-in-emerging-markets/

Maine, R. (2019). Are INGO advocacy and campaigning up to today's challenges? *From Poverty to Power Blog (Oxfam)*, April 16, 2019. https://oxfamblogs.org/fp2p/are-ingo-advocacy-and-campaigning-up-to-todays-challenges/

Maucuer, R., & Renaud, A. (2019). Company's Business Models and NGOs: Inputs from the Partnerships Portfolio. *Management international = International management = Gestión internacional*, HEC Montréal et Université Paris Dauphine, *23*(3), 172–185.

*Msanjila, S. S., & Kamuzora, F. R. (2012). Collaborative networks as a mechanism for strengthening competitiveness: Small and medium enterprises and non-state actors in Tanzania as Cases. *Journal of Language, Technology & Entrepreneurship in Africa, 3*(2), 68-81.

NGO Advisor. (2013). Website: https://www.ngoadvisor.net/top100ngos

Nicolescu, O. (2020). Newsletter #133, SAMRO – Societatea Academica de Management din Romania Academica de Management din Romania, https://sites.google.com/site/samronewsletter/2018/nl133#TOC-Oportunit-ile-manageriale-asociate-crizei-coronavirus

*Odhiambo, A. (2019). Innovation and Performance of Nonprofit Organisations in Kenya. MA thesis, University of Nairobi.

Osterwalder, A. (2013). A Better Way to Think About Your Business Model. *Harvard Business Review*, May 6, 2013.

Osterwalder, A., & Pigneur, Y. (2010). *Business model generation*. Self-published.

Osterwalder, A., Pigneur, Y., & Tucci, C. L. (2005). Clarifying business models: Origins, present, and future of the concept. *Communications of the Association for Information Systems, 16*(1). https://doi.org/10.17705/1CAIS.01601

*Phillips, W., Alexander, E. A. & Lee, H. (2019). Going it alone won't work! The relational imperative for social innovation in social enterprises. *Journal of Business Ethics, 156*, 315–331. doi:https://doi.org/10.1007/s10551-017-3608-1.

*Poisson-de Haro, S., & Montpetit, D. (2012). Surviving in Times or Turmoil: Adaptation of the Théâtre Les Deux Mondes Business Model. *International Journal of Arts Management, 14*(3), 16-31.

*Rekosh, E. (2017). Rethinking the Human Rights Business Model. New and Innovative Strategies for Local Impact. : Center for Strategic & International Studies.

Sabeti, H. (2009). The Emerging Fourth Sector. In *A new sector of organisations in the intersection of the public, private and social sectors*. Fourth Sector Network.

Salamon, L. M., & Sokolowski, W. (2018). The size and composition of the European third sector. In *The third sector as a renewable resource for Europe*. Palgrave Macmillan. https://doi.org/10.1007/978-3-319-71473-8_3

*Sanderse, J. (2014). The business model canvas of NGOs. MA thesis, Open Universiteit, Faculteit Managementwetenschappen.

Srinivas, H. (2015). The NGO funding mix: A Continuum of Sources. GDRC Research Output E-112. Kobe, Japan: Global Development Research Center. Retrieved from https://www.gdrc.org/ngo/funding/funding-mix.html and https://www.gdrc.org/ngo/ngo-models.html on Wednesday, 12 August 2020.

Thorpe,D.(2018).Thiscouplemayhaveinventedmoderncrowdfunding,*Forbes*,July17,2018.,https://www.forbes.com/sites/devinthorpe/2018/07/17/this-couple-may-have-invented-modern-crowdfunding/#3e8df0561efd

United Nations Office for the Coordination of Humanitarian Affairs (OCHA). (2020). *Global humanitarian overview 2020*. OCHA. https://www.unocha.org/sites/unocha/files/GHO-2020_v9.1.pdf

*Valente, M., & Crane, A. (2010). Public responsibility and private enterprise in developing countries. *California Management Review, 52*(3), 52-78.

VeneKlasen, L., & Miller, V. (2007). *A new weave of power, people and politics: The action guide for advocacy and citizen participation*. Practical Action Publishing.

*Wemmer, F., & Koenigstorfer, J. (2016). Open innovation in nonprofit sports clubs. *VOLUNTAS: International Journal of Voluntary and Nonprofit Organizations, 27*(4), 1923-1949.

*Witkamp, M. J., Royakkers, L. M. M., & Raven, R. P. J. M. (2011). From cowboys to diplomats: Challenges for social entrepreneurship in The Netherlands. *VOLUNTAS: International Journal of Voluntary and Nonprofit Organizations, 22*(2), 283-310.

Zott, C., Amit, R., & Massa, L. (2011). The business model: Recent developments and future research. *Journal of Management, 37*(4), 1019–1042.

Chapter 12
Towards a Romanian Entrepreneurial and Ecological University: Learning Talent Management from “Big-Tech”

Sebastian Văduva, Daniel Burtic, Lois Văduva, and Robert Hisrich

Abstract Sustainability is an increasingly important subject matter for universities, which are faced with the dilemma to either help shape the current debate or risk becoming obsolete in the future. This research presents an overview of the main factors, shaping the future of universities, from climate changes and "going green" trends to entrepreneurship initiatives that can provide real economic growth and development. In this fourth industrial revolution, technological advances profoundly impact higher education initiatives; traditional universities must find creative solutions to thrive and develop in this era. The solution to sustainability that the authors of this chapter propose is to borrow key strategies from tech companies, which could be replicated at a university level. Among the most critical factors in the quest for sustainability is the continuous investment in faculty development, which can result in a culture of entrepreneurship and ecology.

Keywords Sustainability · Entrepreneurial university · Green university · Romanian education system · Faculty development

12.1 Introduction

In the past half-century, many changes in society started within universities, as they have been considered a beacon of light and innovation (Brennan et al., 2020). One of the most controversial and thought-provoking issues of our time is the subject of

S. Văduva · D. Burtic (✉) · L. Văduva
Emanuel University of Oradea, Oradea, Romania
e-mail: daniel.burtic@emanuel.ro

R. Hisrich
Kent State University, Kent, OH, USA

S. L. Fotea et al. (eds.), *Navigating Through the Crisis: Business, Technological and Ethical Considerations*, Springer Proceedings in Business and Economics,
https://doi.org/10.1007/978-3-030-82751-9_12

sustainability, as the world is witnessing significant shifts, both in terms of the environment and constant technological innovations. In this modern era, universities are facing numerous challenges, as traditional campuses with full-time professors and staff are under significant financial shortages. At the same time, educational entrepreneurs initiate online teaching courses with little fixed costs accessing and millions of students across the world, which can bring in significant revenue. Some researchers feel that universities need to identify and replicate what other knowledge producers are offering, remaining relevant in the current competitive environment (Czarniawska & Genell, 2002) or else face extinction. Other researchers believe that the future of universities is linked to the entrepreneurial paradigm, as this is a global phenomenon (Etzkowitz et al., 2000). These perspectives indicate that there is little future for traditional universities. The authors of the book *The Innovative University: Changing the DNA of Higher Education from the Inside Out* argue that is it vital for universities to find ways to thrive through what they call "disruptive innovation." From their perspective, to survive, universities must become more affordable and offer the necessary competencies to fulfill the needs of the current generation while also maintaining their capabilities. One of the critical roles of a relevant university is to help students with the necessary tools and knowledge to decipher and sort through the millions of research results that Google offers. One estimate showed that 90% of data had been created in the past two years (Kourtis & Arvanitakis, 2016). As we demonstrate, this endeavor can only be achieved by developing a competent and passionate faculty, which can contribute to the quality of higher education.

This chapter analyses and explains the phenomenon of disruptive change in higher education concerning sustainability, by synthesizing previous work on this topic, and presenting an original concept, which can positively impact the Romanian higher education context. The chapter first focuses on the external and internal challenges that Romanian universities face. From an external perspective, Romanian universities are facing the fourth industrial revolution, which is changing the very nature and structure of education. From an internal viewpoint, Romania is influenced by its sociopolitical past, which can be detrimental to future initiatives. In this context, we present the opportunity for future development, through which a university can remain successful and sustainable by implementing an entrepreneurial and ecological framework. The key to this initiative is investing more in faculty development and adopting some of the practices of successful technology companies, which can be replicated at a university level.

12.2 Internal Challenges Facing Romanian Universities

Thus far, we have outlined the realities of the fourth industrial revolution along with the global challenges it poses to traditional education systems. There are many expectations of universities, which need to focus on civic-minded, entrepreneurial, and ecological in teaching and practice. These same global realities are affecting the educational system of Romania. Romanian society, similar to its global counterparts, is looking to its universities for leadership and guidance in the area of entrepreneurship and ecology. Before developing a few recommendations for the Romanian universities, it is essential to understand the history and the context.

European universities were established about ten centuries ago, such as the University of Bologna in 1088, Oxford University in 1096, Salamanca University in 1134, Paris University in 1170, and Cambridge in 1209. In contrast, the first Romanian modern universities were established towards the end of the nineteenth century under the leadership of Alexandru Ioan Cuza. Before then, king Vasile Lupu established Academia Vasiliană (1634) in Iasi, and king Constantin Brincoveanu established Academia Princiară (1694) in Bucharest, at the request of the Orthodox Church (Anghelache et al., 2018). One of the main issues during this time was the language of teaching, as Romania was still divided and under the heavy influences of neighboring powers. According to Murgescu (Murgescu, 1999), the first law establishing a national education system similar to Western Europe was issued in 1864, with the primary purpose being to unite the country and build the Romanian identity. It took into account the Romanian realities but was influenced by modern European thinking and practices. The universities were established in Iasi and Bucharest, but according to Bădiliță (Bădiliță & Stanciu, 2019), many Romanian intellectuals continued to study outside Romania in the main European capitals. Since Romanian society was mainly agrarian and deeply divided, most of the entrepreneurial activities were directed towards statecraft and culminated with the grand unification of 1918. Some international collaborations and private entrepreneurial activities existed under the guidance of the German royal household, mainly in infrastructure, banking, and the energy sector.

The end of WWI resulted in Romanian double in its territory with the integration of Transylvania, a region more advanced economically and culturally, but lacked Romanian tradition; substantial efforts were needed to integrate Transylvania into Romania. Since new territory needed administration, causing the central government in Bucharest to allocate significant resources towards the training and hiring of public administrators to the detriment of the private sector. Culturally, there was a substantial shift among the Romanian elites who saw a government job as the ultimate goal for their professional career, given its stability and high compensation. Ironically, this unintended consequence prepared the Romanian society and its elites for the communist period, where the government employed the entire nation and private, entrepreneurial activities became criminal activities.

From 1947, under heavy Soviet influence, the Romanian society embarked upon forced industrialization with significant investments into heavy industry without any regard for the environment (Oldson, 1996). Farmland was nationalized while the peasants were forced to relocate to the cities and work in heavy industries. Efforts to eliminate entrepreneurial thinking and private initiative were systematically undertaken, especially in institutions of higher education, which were viewed as essential for the dissemination of communist ideology. In the late 1970s, there were benefits in the area of mass technical education. According to Petrescu et al. (Anghelache et al., 2018), between the years 1899 and 1914, Romania had an average of 10 students per 10.000 inhabitants; in the period 1919–1938, it had an average of 15 students per 10.000 inhabitants. As indicated in Fig. 12.1, in the 1980/81 academic year, Romania reached 87 students per 10.000 inhabitants.

It is worth mentioning that during this period and especially since 1975, when Elena Ceausescu, the wife of the Romanian dictator, assumed direct control over the education system, a double standard of living evolved. Many of the activities undertaken in the education system were "for show only," and the corruption and hypocrisy, which engulfed society, affected education as well (Sadlak, 1994). Nevertheless, technical and engineering education benefited since this education was in line with the goal of the Communist Party to develop the Romanian manufacturing base and heavy industry. Unfortunately, there was a complete disregard for the environment, and some economic activities, illegal in the West due to their high pollution, were transferred to Romania who did not have stringent environmental legislation (Irimie, 2014).

After the fall of the communist regime, the Romanian education system, along with the entire Romanian society, entered a period of transition and transformation. First, several private, for-profit universities entered the market competing for students. Culturally speaking, one of the legacies of the Communists period was that

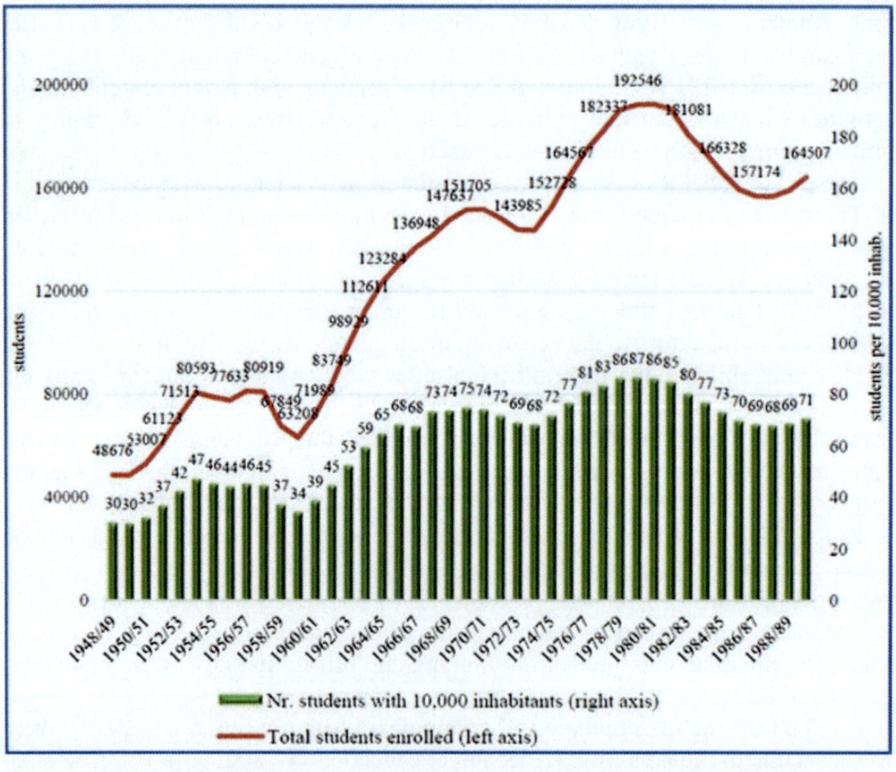

Fig. 12.1 Evolution of number of students in Romania. (Source: Petrescu et al., 2018)

students of higher education had an almost guaranteed higher quality of life (Andrei et al., 2010; Serban et al., 2013). Many private universities in the early 1990s speculated on this cultural tendency and enrolled a record number of students without particular emphasis on the quality of the education process. Some of them positioned themselves to be similar to elite private schools in the west, claiming to be entrepreneurial in their behavior and philosophy. Unfortunately, the quality of their graduates and their academic output was not good, and to a certain degree, the term "entrepreneurial education" received a negative, sometimes illegal connotation (Cristian, 2014; Ţigu et al., 2015). Second, the Romanian education system underwent a series of reforms influenced by chaotic internationalization and ad hoc financing opportunities. In response to the heavily centralized nature of academic management during communism, after its fall, Romania moved to the opposite extreme and resisted coordination and collaboration. A chaotic and competitive academic culture emerged characterized by speculation and influence, secrecy, and inefficiency. This situation was exacerbated by waves of international collaboration and financing opportunities, leading to the overall academic culture to become noncommittal and opportunistic. In this context, Romania had close to 30 ministers of education in the last 30 years, has adopted the Bologna process, and is in the process of being integrated into the European Union. Given this reality, Romanian universities have a problematic heritage to overcome, but this situation should not prevent universities from seeking to develop and prepare themselves for a sustainable future.

12.3 The Challenges and Opportunitie for Sustainable Romanian Universities

Etzkowitz et al. (2000) provide an outline for the structure of an ideal future entrepreneurial university, equipped to respond to the challenges of the twenty-first century. According to them, the entrepreneurial university both embodies entrepreneurial behavior internally and at the same time disseminates this entrepreneurial knowledge externally through its teaching, research, and social engagement. An entrepreneurial university assumes a third, civic mission not only to research and teach but also to actively attempt to solve societal problems (Frye, 1997). Besides accomplishing its stated goal of research and pedagogy, the entrepreneurial university has the unintended consequence of providing for itself and its faculty members financial sustainability. As the US "Ivy League" universities have provided through large endowments and substantial honorariums for star professors (Paunescu, 2007). Some academics perceive entrepreneurship as a threat to academic integrity. In many cultures, entrepreneurial activities are associated with illegal or questionable behavior, where the entrepreneurial strategy is based on "rent-seeking" and speculation of various "conflicts of interest." Those acts of corruption are regrettable, but they do not neutralize the need for universities and their faculty members to become more entrepreneurial. As we later recommend for the

Romanian universities, those tendencies have to be acknowledged transparently, and constructive solutions must be discovered since:

> The momentum towards the emergence of an 'entrepreneurial university' is powerful, even if its development poses important institutional and governance questions for those involved. The concept of the entrepreneurial university envisions an academic structure and function that is revised through the alignment of economic development with research and teaching as academic missions (Etzkowitz et al., 2000).

Initially, universities were entrepreneurial and socially engaged and were not designed disjointedly by society and their departments (Geuna, 1998). Since most universities can trace their roots to a religious community with shared beliefs, joint undertakings, and multiple stakeholders, entrepreneurial and civic activities are part of the university's foundations. It was not until the nationalization of higher education and its public financing that entrepreneurial and social engagement were greatly reduced, and universities became another government bureaucracy. In the twenty-first century, as governments are faced with unsustainable educational costs and the perception of inefficient academic management, they are nudging universities towards entrepreneurship (Miroiu & Aligica, 2004; Herbst, 2007). According to Guerrero and Urbano (2012), the entrepreneurial university has formal and informal partnerships, networks, and business activities with public and private companies, national and international governmental agencies, and various civic organizations. The entrepreneurial university aims to improve education and research activities and to provide technological, social, and economical solutions to their community. The ideal entrepreneurial university has the following four features:

Formal factors: entrepreneurial organizational and governance structure, support measures for entrepreneurship, and entrepreneurship education
Informal factors: the attitudes of the university community towards entrepreneurship, entrepreneurial teaching methodologies, role models, and reward system
Resources: human capital, financial, physical, and commercial
Capabilities: status and prestige, networks and alliances, and localization

Fernández-Nogueira et al. (2018) list the following eight characteristics of an entrepreneurial university: (1) innovation, (2) transferability, (3) transversality, (4) sustainability, (5) usefulness, (6) efficiency, (7) impact, and (8) evaluation.

The European Union encourages its universities to become entrepreneurial. Through the "Strategies for Smart Specialization" and the approach of the "quadruple helix," the European Union aims to stimulate research, technology, and innovation and for the university to become a hub within an entrepreneurial ecosystem (European University Association, 2014; Park, 2014; Committee, 2016). The "Entrepreneurial Discovery Process" is perhaps the most critical instrument and the force behind the "Strategies for Smart Specialization," as it encourages various stakeholders to interact with each other and identify areas of potential collaboration. It is built on the realization that the government alone should not set the socioeconomic agenda of a region and that universities, as paramount knowledge institutions, should actively contribute to the entrepreneurial discovery process.

The European Commission and OECD have jointly developed "HEInnovate," which is an assessment of how entrepreneurial a university is. Their framework evaluates the following: (1) leadership and governance; (2) organizational capacity, funding, people, and incentives; (3) entrepreneurial teaching and learning; (4) preparing and supporting entrepreneurs; (5) digital transformation and capability; (6) knowledge exchange and collaboration; (7) The internationalized institution; and (8) measuring impact.

Ierapetritis (2019) gives the following examples of European entrepreneurial universities: EM Lyon Business School (France), which is structured in such a way to support entrepreneurial learning and provide "the skills and attitudes to become an entrepreneur"; the University of Wismar (Germany), which has the goal of spreading an entrepreneurial spirit via integrating a set of skills into study programs; the University of Applied Sciences Jena (Germany), which, via the Center for Innovation and Entrepreneurship, supports entrepreneurial behavior from the creation of awareness and stimulation of ideas to development and implementation; The Aalborg University (Denmark), which operates the Supporting Entrepreneurship program that supports, facilitates, and motivates knowledge-based entrepreneurship and prepares students for a career after their studies as entrepreneurs, through the provision of training, mentoring, coaching, and the provision of infrastructural support; and a group of Finnish Universities such as the University of Tampere (Finland) which integrates innovation projects with Demola, (a Finnish open innovation platform that provides support from professors and industry professionals to multidisciplinary student teams).

According to Spigel (2017), universities are supposed to generate and manage entrepreneurial ecosystems and have social, political, cultural, and economic initiatives to support the creation and growth of start-ups. Individuals are further encouraged to assume social and economic risks as they attempt to create wealth through business initiatives and solve social problems through civic activity. Thriving entrepreneurial ecosystems are composed and actively manage the following three characteristics:

Social: talented human resources, active local entrepreneurs mentoring the next generation, access to investment capital, serendipitous networking opportunities, knowledgeable consultants and attorneys, and other social opportunities that encourage collaboration and knowledge diffusion

Cultural: supportive culture that encourages risk-taking and does not punish failure

Material: adequate living conditions, professional governments, local firms, and nonprofits, as well as proper education and research activity

The entrepreneurial ecosystem has a geographical but an even more specific communicative and collaborative dimension. As China is exemplifying, infrastructure and artificial institutions are insufficient to generate entrepreneurial activity without proper combination. The entrepreneurship ecosystem is similar to other economic development instruments such as industrial parks, business clusters, learning regions, or free trade zones, but with the significant difference that it focuses on the individual entrepreneur more than institutions (Malecki, 2018).

Individual entrepreneurs are the soul of the entrepreneurial ecosystems. They are either an initiator of new start-ups or investors, mentors, or consultants to new start-ups. Frequently, they contribute to local or international collaboration through various social networking initiatives. Governments must maintain the legal framework and ensure sufficient physical infrastructure, but individual entrepreneurs must initiate and manage the ecosystem through voluntary firms and associations. According to the World Economic Forum (2016), the secret ingredient of an entrepreneurial ecosystem is human talent, shaped by a university that promotes entrepreneurship and establishes a healthy business culture.

Among the many problems, the world is experiencing, perhaps none is more complex and controversial than the global ecological challenge. The world is experiencing substantial climate modifications; some argue, due to carbon emissions and greenhouse gases, that the current economic development model is built upon "dirty fuel" (i.e., wood, coal, gas, and petrol) consumption. The world is further experiencing a demographical explosion, with its population forecasted to reach 10 billion people by 2050. This reality will create significant pressures upon water resources and necessitate substantial agricultural land, invariably leading to deforestation and an increase in farm animal production, further depleting the earth's natural resources. If the additional population also adopts a western lifestyle, as China has in the past three decades, we can expect further consumption along with significant waste, pollution, and environmental damage. Most environmental damage is taking place in the developing world under the justification that it "is our turn to develop" similar to how the West developed in the nineteenth and twentieth centuries. Most ecologically conscious activities begin in the West, who is telling the rest of the world, "Please do not repeat our mistakes." It seems that the economic development model of the first and the second industrial revolutions may be unsustainable in the fourth industrial revolution, and entrepreneurial efforts should concentrate on identifying alternative models of economic development.

The European Union is interested in creating a sustainable Energy Union to accomplish its long-term climate and energy objectives (E. European Commission, 2015). Developing an entrepreneurial, ecology sector would enable the European Union not only to lower its dependence on fossil fuel and diversify its energy supply but also to create startups and new jobs ready to service the global market, thus creating an export-led economic growth (European Environmental Agency, 2012). After the ratification of the Kyoto Protocol, member nations have been active in legislating and implementing restrictive environmental policies. Some of the legislation adopted early on was the 1997 White Paper on Renewable Sources and the 2005 EU emissions trading system design to reduce carbon emissions. Several other initiatives were deployed to stimulate the "green" (ecological) industry, such as loans, grants, and subsidies for research and development and green start-ups, feed-in tariffs, quotas, green certificates, and others (Peters et al., 2012; Costantini et al., 2015). The adoption of this restrictive ecological legislation has been a sore point for the newly integrated nations of Eastern Europe, which were obligated to comply with EU environmental policies. Fortunately, at the European level, these efforts have paid off, and the European Union is leading the world in the green sector:

> Our analysis thus provides suggestive evidence that the commitment of the EU to renewable energy development and deployment supported and promoted a more robust integration of the innovation space. As such, climate mitigation comes as an opportunity to strengthen the EU position in the strategic field of RES, eventually resulting in sustainable growth (Conti et al., 2018).

Considering the global ecological challenge and the European response, it was natural that European universities would play a decisive role in transforming the challenge into an opportunity. Historically, European universities played an essential role in the development of the modern world and the supremacy of the West (Simons, 2006). Universities continued to play a vital role in the socioeconomic development of many nations, as they are considered to be institutions primarily charged with the acquisition and dissemination of knowledge. They produce knowledge within their laboratories while equipping students with the skills and attitudes necessary for the labor market. Over the past century, the world has experienced a proliferation of universities competing for an international student pool. This situation has prompted several global ranking systems such as the World University Ranking, Shanghai Ranking, QS World Ranking, and SCImago Institutional Ranking to emerge. Naturally, this ranking system and the competition it has prompted have been beneficial for all stakeholders. It has increased and will continue to increase the entrepreneurial tendencies of most universities as they are evaluated mainly by research outputs and student employability. Unfortunately, most traditional ranking systems omit issues of ecology and sustainability, perhaps since the economic paradigm of wealth creation through resource consumption has not yet been upgraded (Botezat et al., 2018; Andronie et al., 2019). Considering the ecological challenges of the world and the opportunities it could produce, most European universities should focus their entrepreneurial and social engagement effort towards solving this global challenge.

Naturally, ecological sustainability is a complex issue with economic, social, and political implications. It is unrealistic to expect an overnight solution, yet the quest to ask the right questions and experimenting with possible mini solutions fits best within the scope of academic activity. The World Commission on Environment and Development in their 1987 publication "*Our Common Future*" (Development, 1987) was among the first to suggest that universities may have a role in solving the environmental challenges of our times. Initially, it was a call to raise awareness of the inverse relationship between economic development and the conservation of nature. However, considering the demographic explosion along with the integration of billions of people within a western-style, modern economy over the last three decades, the ecological challenge has been considerably elevated. Initially, the quest for sustainability was primarily about maintaining the quality of the environment, but later, it was expanded to include the social, economic, and environmental dimensions (Bell & Morse, 2012; Kuhlman & Farrington, 2010; Farley & Smith, 2013). Unfortunately, sustainability is not a uniform concept, and there is no uniformity of laws to allow for its implementation globally. Instead, it is shaped by national and institutional contexts with a different emphasis on the three dimensions. There are significant international efforts to both define and legislate sustainability and ecological challenges the world faces through networks such as the International Sustainable Campus Network, the United Nations Sustainable Development Solutions Network, and the Association for the Advancement of Sustainability in Higher Education.

Starting in the late 1990s, several universities have adopted the mission of becoming sustainable and ecological themselves while promoting the concepts in society at large. Several studies were published outlining the significance of sustainable development and providing a blueprint for universities wanting to become ecological and sustainable (Weenen, 2000). Sharp (2002) saw ecological transformation as a moral crusade and the apostolic responsibility of the educational sector as a whole. Recent studies have combined ecology with entrepreneurship and community engagement to provide the university with a sustainable, all-inclusive strategy (Alshuwaikhat & Abubakar, 2008; Lukman et al., 2010; Baboulet & Lenzen, 2010; Ribalaygua Batalla & García Sánchez, 2016). The consensus is that before universities have the moral high ground to promote sustainability, green living, and ecological, economic development, they must first model it themselves. This idea would have the added benefit of instilling ecological values within their students, who would presumably behave ecologically after graduation and positively influence their environment. Given the high profile and substantial impact of most universities, along with their high level of campus activity, many ecological assessment tools have been developed over the years. The Green League was developed in 2007 and the Environmental and Social Responsibility Indexed in 2009, and most notably, GreenMetric was developed by the University of Indonesia in 2010 (Grindsted, 2011).

Initially, only 95 universities participated in the UI GreenMetric World University Ranking, but by 2018, the number had increased to 719. The ranking primarily evaluates the three major components of sustainability: (1) the environment, which includes the use of natural resources, pollution prevention, and the management of the environment; (2) the economic, which measures cost savings and economic benefits; and (3) the social, which focuses on education, community and social participation. The GreenMetric ranking system has the flexibility accountant for varying situations and understandings of sustainability, including the budget a certain university can allocate towards ecological initiatives. It operates under a points system what maximum of 10,000 points comprised of the following six indicators with their respective proportion (Table 12.1):

Next to technology, the ecological challenges stemming from the global demographic explosion are perhaps the most significant issues society has to solve. What seems to be a problem throughout the world could become an opportunity for the European entrepreneurial landscape. However, European universities need to find ways to implement the policy directions set forth by the European Union of becoming both entrepreneurial and ecological. This mandate is a tall order for traditional universities with an adequate budget and an honorable tradition, less alone for Romanian universities who neither have the tradition nor the budget of their older counterparts. Nevertheless, in the following section, we shall attempt to offer a few implementation practices "borrowing" from the techniques of consecrated

Table 12.1 University of Indonesia's GreenMetric framework

Settings and infrastructure (15%)	**Waste (18%)**
• Outdoor surface/total surface (3%) • Outdoor surface/campus population (3%) • Campus area covered with forest vegetation (2%) • Campus area covered with cultivated veg. (2%) • Campus surface with water-absorbing capacity (3%) • University budget allocated to sustainability (2%)	• Program to reduce the consumption of paper and plastic on campus (3%) • University waste recycling program (3%) • Toxic waste management (3%) • Treatment of organic waste (3%) • Inorganic waste treatment (3%) • Wastewater disposal (3%)
Energy and climate change (21%)	**Transportation (18%)**
• Intelligent buildings (3%) • Energy-efficient appliances (2%) • On-campus renewable energy production (3%) • Total energy consumption/Campus Population (3%) • Renewable energy prod. /energy consumption (2%) • Green building implementation element (3%) • Programs for reducing greenhouse gas emissions. (2%) • Total carbon footprint/campus population (3%)	• Vehicles/campus population (2%) • Transfer services/campus population (2%) • Bicycles/campus population (2%) • Types of parking areas (2%) • Transportation initiatives to reduce vehicles on campus (2%) • Reduction of parking areas for private vehicles in the last three years (2%) • Relocation services (3%) • Pedestrian and bicycle policy on campus (3%)
Water (10%)	**Education & Research (18%)**
• Water conservation program (3%) • Water recycling program (3%) • Use of water-efficient appliances (2%) • Consumption of piped water (2%)	• Subjects on sustainability/total subjects (3%) • Investment in sustainability research/total investment in research (3%) • Sustainability publications (3%) • Sustainability events (3%) • Student organizations related to sustainability (3%) • Sustainability websites (3%)

technology firms such as Google, Microsoft, and Facebook in making a Romanian university more entrepreneurial and ecological. We believe that Romanian universities have an opportunity to "leapfrog" their western European counterparts if they would concentrate their energy and effort upon individual staff development.

In addition to the past research outlined in the literature review, many of the following recommendations are based upon our past 20 years of consulting experience in the Romanian and the US technology sector. We have worked in the area of "technology talent development" directly with the talent development departments (the old HR departments in traditional firms) within approximately 50 companies, training over 5.000 knowledge IT workers, and coaching and mentoring close to 200 high-level executives and CEOs. Many of the firms we worked with experienced annual growth rates of 100%, with their staff doubling every 3–4 years. Endava, one of our anchor clients, was successfully listed on the New York Stock exchange in 2018 for $127 mill, and Softvision acquired a US firm and then merged with Cognizant, an Indian IT giant in 2018, forming a $450 mill. IT firm.

12.4 An Innovative Solution to a Prevailing Challenge

For the Romanian society, with the fall of Communism, free-market capitalism and the accompanying entrepreneurial behavior became acceptable or, as some would argue, even encouraged. In most entrepreneurial comparative socioeconomic studies, the Romanian public ranks higher than their European counterparts in their desire to start their own companies. Similar statements are true about most Romanian universities. Since integrating into the European Union, there is a consensus that Romanian universities must be more entrepreneurial and also teach the community around them to behave more entrepreneurially. Substantial funding and other efforts have been implemented to stimulate universities, and significant declarations have been made, starting with the Ministers of Educations on to university presidents and college deans. However, the 2019 assessment entitled "Supporting Entrepreneurship and Innovation in Higher Education in Romania" undertaken by OECD concludes:

> The assessment of the performance of the Romanian higher education system in delivering knowledge exchange using the HEInnovate model demonstrates that overall volumes and values remain low. Performance is limited by cultural and institutional issues both within the system and individual universities. Some demand for traditional forms of technology transfer is evident in places but low overall, with a focus currently only on large-scale incoming inward investors, often in the sectors of engineering, manufacturing, and information and communications technology (ICT). The challenging economic geography of Romania, with widening disparities of performance at the regional level and differential but critical levels of depopulation, coupled with the growing dominance of an agglomerating capital-city region, all remain structural issues of fundamental importance (Marin et al., 2018).

Ecological education is most likely going to be the next trend. As mentioned above, the European Union has the most advanced and innovative ecological sector in the world and is leading the world in self-imposed ecological policies. Upon integrating Romania within the European block, there is a high level of expectation that Romania will at least adopt these policies in earnest and perhaps play a role in its ecological sector. This same is true of its universities: they need to become ecological and to disseminate ecological knowledge within society.

Unfortunately, Romania has a long anti-modernization tradition dating back to the late nineteenth century when the first wave of Europeanization attempted to change the patterns and behaviors. Often people and institutions verbally and sometimes legally agreed to a particular thing without having the slightest intention of implementing it. They will then look for an opportunity to break their commitment while offering little explanation, or more often not even acknowledge their commitment in the first place (Mungiu-Pippidi, 2005). If Romanian universities genuinely want to become entrepreneurial and ecological, we recommend for them not only to target cultural transformation but also to follow the examples and best practices of successful technology companies such as Google and Apple. They should not focus on bureaucratic reform alone but instead concentrate on making the behavior of their faculty members more ecological and entrepreneurial.

Fortunately, entrepreneurial behavior exists in most universities and most faculty members. Dating back to the communist times, but even more recently given reduced compensation structures, people in all sectors, including education, learn to operate in the gray market or "to take care of themselves." This reality may entail trading favors, charging for extra services, speculating a public position for personal gain, selling their influence, or using public resources for personal gain. Naturally, this is unethical and sometimes illegal behavior, but it is a reality upon which an entrepreneurial culture can be developed with the proper acknowledgment, transparency, communication, and instruction. Unfortunately, some faculty members behave as small bazaar merchants and do not know that they can become shareholders in the next unicorn to be listed on the New York Stock Exchange. It is the responsibility of the universities to have people development offices and to make talent development their number one priority, similar to big technology companies (Smith et al., 2005).

Peter Drucker was the first to observe that the knowledge economy was going to be built on individuals, not institutions (Drucker, 1999). Unfortunately, most universities operate on the assumption that their faculty members, since they teach others (students) for a living, do not need any personal development at all. This initiative would be further complicated by the possible unwillingness of faculty members to be developed, considering that they are doing an adequate job already (Bouwma-Gearhart, 2012).

Nevertheless, the following is a list of practices used by most tech companies. We realize that every university would have to contextualize this list of recommendations; a substantial improvement in the implementation and the creation of an entrepreneurial and ecological culture would result.

- *Recruitment Is Key*

Technology companies have numerous corporate recruiters who travel to college campuses and meet with potential recruits from competing firms to ensure an adequate supply of candidates. If a quality individual becomes available, but the firm does not have a job opening, the candidate would be hired and "put on the bench" until a position is available. The typical recruitment process takes months and is being done by the human resources department, not by the direct manager.

- *Onboarding Is Essential*

Technology companies have learned the importance of the first 100 days, and little is left to chance in that early period. Extra effort is devoted to "onboarding" new candidates and ensuring proper integration within their team and the overall company culture. During this time, mentors are assigned both for the technical and the political environment. Regardless of previous experience, all the candidates are trained in the company culture and evaluated to ensure that their performance is according to company standards.

- Separation of Power

Even if every employee has a direct technical supervisor, the human resources department will remain active in the life of every employee to ensure a lack of managerial bias and objective evaluations. A culture of transparency is promoted, with individuals continuously receiving feedback. This initiative eliminates favoritisms and collegial coverups.

- *Professional Development* Plan and Periodic Evaluations

Every person within a technology company has a precise job description that may be updated monthly; it is written with clearly communicated expectations. Next, every individual has a professional development plan, which is supervised by both the human resources department and technical supervisors. This plan has specific and measurable key performance indicators (KPIs) and is evaluated at least once every six months. Evaluations are done constructively with "brutal honesty" as a paramount value.

- Performance Measurement

"Only what is measured can be managed" is a saying of Bill Gates; large technology companies are experts on measuring and reporting everything in real time. Every person has their performance and behavior measured and reported in real time, with improvement feedbacks provided almost instantly. Another beneficial practice is "benchmarking," which is comparing the performance with colleagues from the same department or other competing firms.

- *Performance-Based* Remuneration

Even though many technology firms have social objectives to change the world, they also have realism, realizing that people work mainly for income. Technology firms are some of the most transparent organizations concerning their income and expenses. The average IT compensation is based on performance (not seniority) and is comprised of a fixed, market-based salary, individual and team bonuses, plus company stock options and dividends.

- *Putting the User First*

One of the greatest achievements of successful technology companies is their ability to fulfill needs that the consumers did not even realize they have. Innovation has always stemmed from the ability to foresee potential and future needs and find solutions for them. As Henry Ford said, his goal was not to search for faster horses. In the higher education world, this translates to professors that are trained to be aware of future trends and dynamics and teach their students how to deal with these new disruptions.

- *Leading, Not Following*

Technological companies that have an impact in the world use competition to their advantage to become better and create something new. The sustainable universities of the future will always find creative ways to outperform other educational trends. In this global context, universities that will focus on entrepreneurship and the "green" trend in a creative way will have a competitive advantage.

- *Not Afraid of Disruption*

Since continuous change is the trademark of the future, another important lesson that we can learn from the technology industry is not to run away from creative disruption but embrace it. Universities that understand the current challenges and embrace them will have a better chance at sustainability, mainly if they invest in the quality and abilities of their faculty. Small steps, such as ensuring that all professors have adequate computer skills and understand the basics of artificial intelligence, could go a long way towards developing a university that is ready for the future.

12.5 Conclusions

The present research explained and analyzed the current challenges that the higher education system faces with an emphasis on the Romanian context. In the first part of this chapter, we presented the external and internal conditions that Romanian universities have to understand and deal with this new era of constant change and disruption. We showed how the world is facing the fourth industrial revolution, with numerous changes and rapidly growing technologies. We also presented the Romanian historical context of higher education. In this global and local context, which is impacted by entrepreneurship and ecological difficulties, Romanian universities must find creative ways to sustain themselves in the future.

We also identified some characteristics of sustainable universities and different initiatives that are being undertaken in other parts of the world. Given that one of the most rapidly growing and innovative sectors in the world is the technological one, we propose that Romanian universities look at some of the critical concepts which make this sector successful and begin a process of innovation through the most crucial asset in higher education—the faculty. Naturally, all of these practices would have to be properly contextualized for the Romanian education system and each university, college, and department. The adoption of such practices would not happen overnight, and significant opposition may ensue given the historical tradition, context, and institutional inertia. However, if Romanian University would adopt such practices, the benefits would not only be that they would become more entrepreneurial and more environmentally friendly in this particular context. The main benefit would be that they would position themselves with the necessary institutional culture to face the future challenges of the twenty-first century. The fourth Industrial Revolution is only starting. Many experts forecast that transformation and disruptions will most likely come from China, which is vying to dominate the twenty-first century and its technological innovations. After embracing democracy and free-market capitalism in the 1990s, Europeanization in the 2000s, Romanian institutions of higher education, and the Romanian society also needs to embrace Asian ideology and practice. Without the proper cultural management and individual faculty development, Romanian universities may struggle to survive and have little impact on the global economy.

References

Alshuwaikhat, H. M., & Abubakar, I. (2008). An integrated approach to achieving campus sustainability: Assessment of the current campus environmental management practices. *Journal of Cleaner Production, 16*, 1777–1785. https://doi.org/10.1016/j.jclepro.2007.12.002

Andrei, T., Teodorescu, D., & Oancea, B. (2010). Characteristics of higher education in Romania during transition. *Procedia - Social and Behavioral Sciences, 2*, 3417–3421. https://doi.org/10.1016/j.sbspro.2010.03.526

Andronie, M., Gurgu, E., Spiru Haret University, Bucharest, Romania, Dijmğrescu, A., University of Medicin and Pharmacy Carol Davila Bucharest, Romania, Dijmğrescu, I., Emergency Clinical Hospital for Children Grigore Alexandrescu Bucharest, Romania, & Simion, V.-E. (2019). Social responsibility of firms and the impact of bio-economy in intelligent use of renewable energy source. *AE, 21*, 520. https://doi.org/10.24818/EA/2019/52/520

Anghelache, C., Anghel, M. G., Iordan, P., & Emil, G. (2018). *Geneza Şi Evoluţia Învăţământului Superior Din România – În Date Statistice –*; Editura Economica. ISBN Emilia Gogu, Mădălina Gabri.

Baboulet, O., & Lenzen, M. (2010). Evaluating the environmental performance of a university. *Journal of Cleaner Production, 18*, 1134–1141. https://doi.org/10.1016/j.jclepro.2010.04.006

Bădiliţă, C., & Stanciu. (2019). *Geniul Greco-Catolic*. Bucureşti: Vremea.: Bucureşti.

Bell, S., & Morse, S. (2012). *Sustainability indicators: Measuring the immeasurable?* Routledge. ISBN 978-1-136-55602-9.

Botezat, E. A., Dodescu, A. O., Văduva, S., & Fotea, S. L. (2018). An exploration of circular economy practices and performance among Romanian producers. *Sustainability, 10*, 3191. https://doi.org/10.3390/su10093191

Bouwma-Gearhart, J. (2012). Research university STEM faculty members' motivation to engage in teaching professional development: Building the choir through an appeal to extrinsic motivation and ego. *Journal of Science Education and Technology, 21*, 558–570. https://doi.org/10.1007/s10956-011-9346-8

Brennan, J., King, R., & Lebeau, Y. *The role of universities in the transformation of societies: An international research project*. Available online: http://www.open.ac.uk/personalpages/y.lebeau/Transfo.pdf. Accessed 16 Sept 2020.

Committee, C. of the R. (2016). *Using the quadruple helix approach to accelerate the transfer of research and innovation results to regional growth*. Available online: http://op.europa.eu/en/publication-detail/-/publication/6e54c161-36a9-11e6-a825-01aa75ed71a1/language-en. Accessed 16 Sept 2020.

Conti, C., Mancusi, M. L., Sanna-Randaccio, F., Sestini, R., & Verdolini, E. (2018). Transition towards a green economy in Europe: Innovation and knowledge integration in the renewable energy sector. *Research Policy, 47*, 1996–2009.

Costantini, V., Crespi, F., Martini, C., & Pennacchio, L. (2015). Demand-pull and technology-push public support for eco-innovation: The case of the biofuels sector. *Research Policy, 44*, 577–595.

Cristian, T. (2014). Educaţia Antreprenorială: O Soluţie Pentru Provocările Globale Ale Liderilor? *Amfiteatru Economic, 16*, 720–737.

Czarniawska, B., & Genell, K. (2002). Gone shopping? Universities on their way to the market. *Scandinavian Journal of Management, 18*, 455–474. https://doi.org/10.1016/S0956-5221(01)00029-X

Development, W.C. on E. (1987). *Our common future*. Oxford University Press. ISBN 978-0-19-282080-8.

Drucker, P. F. (1999). Knowledge-worker productivity:..., *41*, 17.

Etzkowitz, H., Webster, A., Gebhardt, C., & Terra, B. R. C. (2000). The future of the university and the university of the future: Evolution of ivory tower to entrepreneurial paradigm. *Research Policy, 29*, 313–330. https://doi.org/10.1016/S0048-7333(99)00069-4

European Commission, E. (2015). *A framework strategy for a resilient energy union with a forward-looking climate change policy – European Environment Agency*. Available online: https://www.eea.europa.eu/policy-documents/com-2015-80-final. Accessed 16 Sept 2020.

European Environmental Agency, E. (2012). *Greenhouse gas emission trends and projections in Europe 2012 – Tracking progress towards Kyoto and 2020 targets – European Environment Agency*. Available online: https://www.eea.europa.eu/publications/ghg-trends-and-projections-2012. Accessed 16 Sept 2020.

European University Association. (2014). The Role of Universities in Smart Specialization Strategies. Report on Joint EUA-REGIO/JRC RC Smart Specialisation Platform expert workshop. Available online: https://eua.eu/downloads/publications/report%20on%20joint%20eua-regio%20the%20role%20of%20universities%20in%20smart%20specialisation%20strategies.pdf

Farley, H. M., & Smith, Z. A. (2013). *Sustainability: If it's everything, is it nothing?* Routledge. ISBN 978-1-136-00936-5.

Fernández-Nogueira, D., Arruti, A., Markuerkiaga, L., & Saenz, N. (2018). The entrepreneurial university: A selection of good practices. *Journal of Entrepreneurship Education, 21*, 1–17.

Frye, J. H. (1997). Bill readings. The University in Ruins. Cambridge, Mass.: Harvard University Press, 1996. Pp. x, 238. $29.95. *History of Education Quarterly, 37*, 208–209. https://doi.org/10.2307/369361

Geuna, A. (1998). The internationalisation of European universities: A return to medieval roots. *Minerva, 36*, 253–270. https://doi.org/10.1023/A:1004391922122

Grindsted, T. S. (2011). Sustainable Universities: From declarations on sustainability in higher education to national law. *Environmental Economics, 2*, 29–36.

Guerrero, M., & Urbano, D. (2012). The development of an entrepreneurial university. *The Journal of Technology Transfer, 37*, 43–74. https://doi.org/10.1007/s10961-010-9171-x

Herbst, M. (2007). *Financing public universities* (Higher education dynamics) (Vol. 18). Springer. ISBN 978-1-4020-5559-1.

Ierapetritis, D. G. (2019). Discussing the role of universities in fostering regional entrepreneurial ecosystems. *Economies, 7*, 119. https://doi.org/10.3390/economies7040119

Irimie, R. C. (2014). Daily life under communism. The case of Romania. *SEA - Practical Application of Science*, 266–283.

Kourtis, A., & Arvanitakis, J. (2016). The citizen scholar: The Academy at the University of Western Sydney. In J. Arvanitakis & D. J. Hornsby (Eds.), *Universities, the citizen scholar and the future of higher education* (pp. 54–68). Palgrave Macmillan. ISBN 978-1-349-71155-0.

Kuhlman, T., & Farrington, J. (2010). What is sustainability? *Sustainability, 2*, 3436–3448. https://doi.org/10.3390/su2113436

Lukman, R., Krajnc, D., & Glavič, P. (2010). University ranking using research, educational and environmental indicators. *Journal of Cleaner Production, 18*, 619–628. https://doi.org/10.1016/j.jclepro.2009.09.015

Malecki, E. J. (2018). Entrepreneurship and entrepreneurial ecosystems. *Geography Compass, 12*, e12359. https://doi.org/10.1111/gec3.12359

Marin, A., Boanţă, L. F., Ţelinoiu, A., Darie, G., & Din, M. A. (2018). *Supporting entrepreneurship and innovation in higher education in Romania* (pp. 9938–9947). OECD, European Union.

Miroiu, A.; Aligica, P.D. *Public financing, fees and institutional structure and change in the Romanian higher education system*; 2004;

Mungiu-Pippidi, A. (2005). Deconstructing Balkan particularism: The ambiguous social capital of Southeastern Europe. *Southeast European and Black Sea Studies, 5*, 49–68. https://doi.org/10.1080/1468385042000328367

Murgescu, M.L. *Între "bunul creştin" şi "bravul român": Rolul şcolii primare în construirea identităţii naţionale româneşti (1831–1878)*; Editura A '92: Iaşi, 1999;

Oldson, W. O. (1996). Background to catastrophe: Romanian modernization policies and the environment. *East European Quarterly, 30*, 517.

Park, H. W. (2014). Transition from the Triple Helix to N-Tuple Helices? An interview with Elias G. Carayannis and David F.J. Campbell. *Scientometrics, 99*, 203–207. https://doi.org/10.1007/s11192-013-1124-3

Paunescu, C. (2007). Developing and strengthening model of entrepreneurial university in Romania. *The Amfiteatru Economic Journal, 9*, 54–62.

Peters, M., Schneider, M., Griesshaber, T., & Hoffmann, V. H. (2012). The impact of technology-push and demand-pull policies on technical change – Does the locus of policies matter? *Research Policy, 41*, 1296–1308.

Ribalaygua Batalla, C., & García Sánchez, F. (2016). Creating a sustainable learning district by integrating different stakeholders' needs. Methodology and results from the University of Cantabria Campus Master Plan. In W. Leal Filho & L. Brandli (Eds.), *Engaging stakeholders in education for sustainable development at university level* (World Sustainability Series) (pp. 3–20). Springer. ISBN 978-3-319-26734-0.

Sadlak, J. (1994). The emergence of a diversified system: The state/private predicament in transforming higher education in Romania. *European Journal of Education, 29*, 13–23. https://doi.org/10.2307/1503415

Serban, D., Gruiescu, M., & Mitrut, C. (2013). Quantitative study on students satisfaction concerning private economics universities in Romania. *Procedia - Social and Behavioral Sciences, 83*, 723–728. https://doi.org/10.1016/j.sbspro.2013.06.136

Sharp, L. (2002). Green campuses: The road from little victories to systemic transformation. *International Journal of Sustainability in Higher Education, 3*, 128–145. https://doi.org/10.1108/14676370210422357

Simons, M. (2006). 'Education through research' at European universities: Notes on the orientation of academic research. *Journal of Philosophy of Education, 40*, 31–50. https://doi.org/10.1111/j.1467-9752.2006.00493.x

Smith, K. G., Collins, C. J., & Clark, K. D. (2005). Existing knowledge, knowledge creation capability, and the rate of new product introduction in high-technology firms. *AMJ, 48*, 346–357. https://doi.org/10.5465/amj.2005.16928421

Spigel, B. (2017). The relational organization of entrepreneurial ecosystems. *Entrepreneurship Theory and Practice*. https://doi.org/10.1111/etap.12167

Ţigu, G., Iorgulescu, M. C., Răvar, A. S., & Lile, R. (2015). A pilot profile of the social entrepreneur in the constantly changing Romanian economy. *Amfiteatru Economic Journal, 17*, 25–43.

Weenen, H. V. (2000). Towards a vision of a sustainable university. *International Journal of Sustainability in Higher Education, 1*, 20–34. https://doi.org/10.1108/1467630010307075

World Economic Forum The Future of Jobs: Employment, Skills and Workforce Strategy for the Fourth Industrial Revolution 2016.

Index

S. L. Fotea et al. (eds.), *Navigating Through the Crisis: Business, Technological and Ethical Considerations*, Springer Proceedings in Business and Economics,
https://doi.org/10.1007/978-3-030-82751-9